GLORIOUS WITNESSES FOR AFRICA

By

Lowell A. Gess, B.D., M.D.

First Edition
First Printing: 2011

ISBN # 978-0-615-44119-1

Graphic/layout design and prepress production:
Spectrum Marketing Services, Alexandria, MN

Books ($10, plus $5 S/H) may be ordered from:
Alexandria United Methodist Church
2210 6th Avenue East
Alexandria, MN 56308
320-763-4624
Email: info@alexumc.org

Dedication

To those whose names are
found in this book as "WITNESSES"
for the Lord Jesus Christ and who
shared the Gospel that
brought Glory to Africa.

*"You will be my witnesses
to the ends of the earth."
— Acts 1:8*

Foreword

Dr. Lowell A. Gess gives us a personal "behind the scenes" story of the astounding growth of Christianity in Sub-Saharan Africa. From his unique perspective as a lifelong medical missionary, he identifies faithful witnesses who have been ambassadors of Jesus Christ in transforming Africa. This story reveals how God uses dedicated individuals to forge a better world, one witness at a time.

Bishop John L. Hopkins
Ohio East Area

Bishop John L. Hopkins and Lowell Gess

Acknowledgements

I thank Bishop John Hopkins for writing a "Forward" to *Glorious Witnesses for Africa*. My high esteem for him as a bishop and leader in the United Methodist Church makes my gratitude all the more. I pray that the message and content of this book, with Bishop Hopkins' encouragement, will cheer United Methodists everywhere that Christ's truth goes marching on throughout the whole wide world.

Heartfelt thanks are given to Amy Krammes who accepted the manuscripts, corrected them, arranged them and edited them with thoughtful, expert and spiritual modifications. All hope had been abandoned for the publishing of this book before she was willing to share her expertise.

Amy Krammes and her daughter, Lillie

Appreciation is given to Malika Ouferoukh, secretary in the office of the General Board of Global Ministries, for the provision of email addresses for bishops in Africa.

I am grateful to Melanie and Roger Reiners for the generous supply of pictures of co-workers taken at the reunion of the Servants of Sierra Leone meeting in Cedar Rapids, Iowa, in July 2010.

I am especially grateful to those who were willing to submit information about their life and work and how it became a part of the glorious growth of the church in Sub-Saharan Africa.

Even in this awesome age of technology, some computer glitches occurred with loss of material. I am deeply sorry for that. I am hoping that enough material was saved to present a dramatic picture of the astounding growth of the Church during the past ninety years.

I acknowledge the leadership of the Holy Spirit in putting together this book during times of personal hardship for Ruth and me, and her ultimate "home going" on October 25, 2010. To be in the 90th year of one's life is a challenge all of its own.

"Bless the Lord, O my soul, and all that is within me, bless His holy name!"
– Psalm 103:1

Please Note

Glorious Witnesses for Africa looks into some aspects of early African Christianity and spans to the present day.

In 1900, there were 9 million Christians in Africa.[1] Today there are 500 million, which is half the population of modern day Africa.

From 1921 to 2011, the dates that encompass my lifetime, the United Methodist Church in Nigeria has grown from 0 to 600,000 members. (The first mission station of the United Methodist Church was established at Bambur in December 1923.)

The background for this historic and dramatic growth of the United Methodist Church is touched upon in the accounts and witness-stories of:

- Twelve bishops who lead United Methodist churches in Sub-Saharan Africa.
- A score of indigenous Christian leaders and commissioned expatriate missionaries who had two or more terms of missionary service in Africa.

Most are still living and all are or were personally known to me. Those who responded with contributions have "stories to tell."

Yale University historian Lamin Sanneh stated, "African Christianity was not just an exotic, curious phenomenon in an obscure part of the world, but that African Christianity might be the shape of things to come."[2]

Statistics from the World Christian Encyclopedia illustrate the emerging trend of dramatic Christian growth on the continent and supposes that in 2025 there will be 633 million Christians in Africa.[3]

"Upon this rock (witnesses – originally Peter) *I will build my Church."*
– Matthew 16:18*

*All scripture references are from the New International Version (NIV) unless otherwise noted.

Table of Contents

Section III: Co-Workers in Christ
United Methodist Indigenous and Expatriate (as received)

Other Co-workers *(as received)*

Section IV: My Participation

- C. V. Rettew / Rotifunk Martyrs
- List of Personally Known Missionaries
- Dr. Lowell Gess' Curriculum Vitae
- Populations of the Continents

Preface

Glorious Witnesses for Africa was born during an inspirational moment experienced January 13, 2010. My wife, Ruth, and I had just finished our daily devotions. We were sitting silently in our easy chairs, deep in our own thoughts. Eventually, we began to reminisce memorable experiences: our simple beginnings, our conversions and calls to missionary service, our training years, our marriage, the births of our children, the missionary commissioning service and our service in Nigeria, Africa, from 1952 to 1955. It was exhilarating.

When I was born in 1921, there was no United Methodist Church in Nigeria. The initial work began two years later in December 1923, when Rev. C. W. Guinter and Rev. Ira McBride established a mission at Bambur. After our tour of service in Nigeria at Bambur's Guinter Memorial Hospital was completed in 1955, there were reportedly 900 baptized members. On a return trip to Zing, Nigeria, to do eye surgery and participate in the dedication of the Zing Eye Centre fifty years later, I learned that the membership in the Nigerian church was in the hundreds of thousands. Mr. Peter Jusu, recently reporting annual conference statistics, noted that the present membership now is over 600,000! How remarkable! In my lifetime of ninety years, the United Methodist Church in Nigeria has grown from 0 to more than 600,000 members, and the Christian Church in Africa has grown from 17 million to more than 500 million – half the population of the entire continent![4]

Marvelous! Miraculous! Glorious! A happening like this should be heralded. Christians should know of this outpouring of the Holy Spirit in Africa and the consequences of their many prayers and generous giving to missions. A book should be written on this "glory for Africa."

With the help of God, I decided to do just that – to write a *personalized* account of happenings during my lifetime. Yet, I struggled with how to present the main theme and thrust for such a project. Then, on February 13, 2010, our devotional scripture reading was from Acts, chapter 5, on how the apostles were miraculously freed from prison and then preached to the council. Four verses leapt out – 29 through 32:

> *But Peter and the apostles answered and said, "We must obey God rather than men. The God of our fathers raised up Jesus whom you had put to death by hanging Him on a cross. He is the one whom God exalted to His right hand as a Prince and a Savior, to grant repentance to Israel, and forgiveness of sins. And we are* **WITNESSES** *(emphasis mine) of these things; and so is the Holy Spirit, whom God has given to those who obey Him." (NASB)*

A few days later, Ruth and I read in Acts 10:39-43:

*We are **witnesses** of everything he did in the country of the Jews and in Jerusalem. They killed him by hanging him on a tree, but God raised him from the dead on the third day and caused him to be seen. He was not seen by all the people but by **witnesses** whom God had already chosen – by us who ate and drank with him after he rose from the dead. He commanded us to preach to the people and to testify that he is the one whom God appointed as judge of the living and the dead. All the prophets testify about him that everyone who believes in him receives forgiveness of sins through his name.*

The answer was now obvious – the theme and structure for the book would be on witnessing told by the witnesses themselves. "You shall be my witnesses… to the ends of the earth." (Acts 1:8) The glorious growth of the Christian Church in Sub-Saharan Africa resulted from witnesses and witnessing. Victories were celebrated – exultant successes – because of witnesses.

In the 1940s, the *World Evangel* quoted Mrs. Aletha Faust serving in Pero, Nigeria, as saying: "If we would not have witnessed, we would have failed Jesus." This boldness of witnessing came to the Christians in Sub-Saharan Africa following the seed planting of early missionaries. With the inspiration and direction of the Holy Spirit, there was added to the Church tens upon tens of thousands.

Today, the growth of the Christian Church in Africa is under the leadership of its own people. Histories of early beginnings and development of the United Methodist Church are presented in this book by African bishops, or their appointed representatives, of the Sub-Saharan countries who write about things they know, real and true. These stories are followed by the testimonies of indigenous pastors, missionaries, teachers, church workers and lay workers – and are ordered not alphabetically, but in the order they were sent to me. With the exception of several bishops, nearly all of the contributors to this book are still alive and were personally known to me while I performed eye surgery in Sierra Leone, Nigeria, Ghana, Kenya, Zambia, Zimbabwe, Malawi and Mozambique.

Each witness has a story to tell of following in the footsteps of Christ. Jesus witnessed to the glory of God – and it meant the cross for Him. Eleven of the twelve apostles witnessed to their last breath, dying as martyrs. Down through the ages, converts have witnessed to one another, obeying the command of Jesus. Many graves in foreign lands – Africa included – give testimony to the seriousness of witnessing.

Feeling surrounded by such a cloud of witnesses, *Glorious Witnesses for Africa* is a story that needs to be told and be in print. The world needs to know of the glory for Africa, of Africa's transformation into a truth-seeking continent.

It is my sincere hope and prayer that *Glorious Witnesses for Africa* will be:

- Of historical value,
- Interesting and entertaining reading of real life experiences,
- A challenge to the lay Church for appropriate giving and service,
- A revelation of individual witnesses, participating in the glorious growth of the Christian Church in Sub-Saharan Africa.

In His service,
Lowell A. Gess, B.D., M.D.
January 4, 2011

Section I: Introduction

"Now an angel of the Lord said to Philip, 'Go south to the road — the desert road — that goes down from Jerusalem to Gaza.' So he started out, and on his way he met an Ethiopian eunuch, an important official in charge of all the treasury of the Kandake (which means 'queen of the Ethiopians'). This man had gone to Jerusalem to worship, and on his way home was sitting in his chariot reading the Book of Isaiah the prophet. The Spirit told Philip, 'Go to that chariot and stay near it.'

"Then Philip ran up to the chariot and heard the man reading Isaiah the prophet. 'Do you understand what you are reading?' Philip asked.

"'How can I,' he said, 'unless someone explains it to me?' So he invited Philip to come up and sit with him.

"This is the passage of Scripture the eunuch was reading:
'He was led like a sheep to the slaughter,
and as a lamb before its shearer is silent,
so he did not open his mouth.
In his humiliation he was deprived of justice.
Who can speak of his descendants?
For his life was taken from the earth.'

"The eunuch asked Philip, 'Tell me, please, who is the prophet talking about, himself or someone else?' Then Philip began with that very passage of Scripture and told him the good news about Jesus.

"As they traveled along the road, they came to some water and the eunuch said, 'Look, here is water. What can stand in the way of my being baptized?' And he gave orders to stop the chariot. Then both Philip and the eunuch went down into the water and Philip baptized him. When they came up out of the water, the Spirit of the Lord suddenly took Philip away, and the eunuch did not see him again, but went on his way rejoicing."

— Acts 8:26-39

Chapter One

We've A Story to Tell

We've a story to tell to the nations
That shall turn their hearts to the right,
A story of truth and mercy,
A story of peace and light . . .

We've a song to be sung to the nations
That shall lift their hearts to the Lord,
A song that shall conquer evil
And shatter the spear and sword . . .

We've a message to give to the nations,
That the Lord who reigneth above
Hath sent us His Son to save us,
And show us that God is love . . .

We've a Savior to show to the nations
Who the path of sorrow hath trod,
That all of the world's great peoples
Might come to the truth of God . . . .

– H. Ernest Nichol, 1896

A story to tell. A song to be sung. A message to give. A Savior to show.
Witnessing – evangelism – is at the heart of the Gospel, and is demonstrated
as well as proclaimed in the church, in the classroom, in social action, in the
agricultural field and in the medical clinic.

From the days of Calvary and the resurrection, the Gospel story has been
unfolding through witnesses.

The Early Church

The early Christians were fearless. Jesus himself faced and accepted death at Calvary. Eleven of the apostles died as martyrs, even though immediately after the crucifixion, they cowered in the upper room, afraid to go out.

Yet, their strength and courage prevailed once the Holy Spirit descended upon them. Many disciples and followers of Jesus in the first century encountered tremendous persecution – and many times, tortuous death:

- Matthew suffered martyrdom by being slain in the city of Ethiopia
- Mark died at Alexandria, after being dragged through the streets of that city
- Luke was hung on an olive tree in Greece
- John was put into a vat of boiling oil in Rome before being exiled to Patmos
- Peter died crucified in Rome with his head downward
- James the Lesser was thrown from a pinnacle of the temple, then beaten to death
- Bartholomew was flayed alive
- Andrew was bound to a cross, where he preached to his persecutors until he died
- Jude was shot to death with arrows
- Matthias was first stoned and then beheaded
- Barnabas was stoned to death at Salonica
- Paul, after various tortures and persecutions, was beheaded in Rome by Emperor Nero[5]

With all their hearts, these followers of Jesus knew and believed that "God was in Christ, reconciling the world to Himself." II Corinthians 5:19

By 380 A.D., Christianity was recognized throughout the Roman Empire. Then for a thousand years, during which there was little to no recorded persecution, support lagged for a Church that had become institutionalized. Renewal came with witnesses in the persons of Luther, Zwingle and Tyndale. Their sixteenth century Protestant Reformation, with its evangelical fervor for witnessing, stirred Christendom. The eighteenth century finally realized the birth of an organized missionary outreach, following revivals that began to sweep across Europe and North America. This continued into the nineteenth century.

Early Methodist Church History

The Wesleys. John (1703-1791) and Charles (1707-1788) Wesley cofounded the English Methodist movement. John Wesley was an Anglican clergyman and a persuasive evangelist. He graduated from Oxford where his methodical lifestyle and fervent piety were noted. On May 24, 1738, at a meetinghouse on Aldersgate Street in London, Wesley was listening to Martin Luther's "Preface to Romans" when his heart was strangely warmed with what he called his "conversion." This prompted his evangelistic worldwide ministry. His brother, Charles, with his musical genius, was eloquent. While today John's sermons must be retrieved from printed texts or online archives, his brother's lilting songs and inspired saving verses can be heard sung on any given day around the world.

Albright. Jacob Albright (1759-1808), founder of the Evangelical Association (later to be called the Evangelical Church), was born to immigrant German parents near Pottstown, Pennsylvania, and later baptized into the Lutheran church. After having participated in the American Revolution, he became a farmer and manufacturer of tiles and bricks. Around 1790, following the death of several of his children, he converted to Methodism in which he felt he received more comfort. He felt the call to take the message of Methodism to German-speaking people. He considered himself unfit to preach but records reveal that he was a powerful and moving speaker, using German, the Pennsylvania Dutch dialect, and enough self-taught English for presentations. However, the insistence that he forego his preaching in German, led him to establish classes among the German settlements.

In 1807, these classes formed a conference at which Albright was elected bishop. Within a year, overwhelmed with exhaustion and tuberculosis, he died. However, "Albright's People" (Die Albrechtsleute) flourished and ultimately merged with the United Brethren in Christ Church in 1946 to become the Evangelical United Brethren Church (EUB), and then with the Methodist Church in 1968 to become the United Methodist Church (UMC).

Otterbein and Boehm. Philip Otterbein (1726-1813) founder of the United Brethren in Christ Church, born in Germany, came as a missionary to the German Reformed immigrants in Pennsylvania in 1752. In 1765, he attended a revival in the Isaac Long barn near Lancaster. The preaching of Mennonite Martin Boehm inspired Otterbein. They became friends, "brothers in Christ." Martin Boehm was expelled by the Mennonites for being too evangelical. In 1789, Otterbein and Boehm, with others, held a conference that resulted in the founding of what would be called the United Brethren in Christ Church. In 1800, Philip Otterbein and Martin Boehm were elected bishops of this new indigenous, American born, denomination.

Chapter Two

The First African Witnesses

*"I had frequent opportunities of hearing these expressions at Sierra Leone;
and though I was assured that they had not heard them from Christians, ...
they possessed correct ideas of a future state of reward and punishment. Truly
God has not left Himself without witnesses!" – Samuel Crowther*

Samuel Crowther

Africa has played an integral role in the world's civilization, with Egypt being specifically significant in Biblical history. Joseph, sold by his brothers into slavery in Egypt, became Pharaoh's confidant and second in command. Moses, an adopted prince of Egypt, ultimately responded to the Lord's directive to lead the Israelites out of Egypt to the Promised Land. The Queen of Sheba, who visited Solomon, and Simon, the Cyrenian, who helped carry Jesus' cross, were African. And it was in Egypt that Joseph and Mary sought refuge following the birth of Jesus.

Introduction of Christianity

The Coptic Church, now over nineteen centuries old, founded by Saint Mark during the reign of Roman emperor Nero, is still present in a hostile environment. Saint Augustine, the Bishop of Hippo, born in 354 in what is now present day

Algeria, is noted for composing a spiritual autobiography containing one of the most celebrated conversion accounts in all of Christian literature *(Confessions III. iv.8).*

Christianity was introduced below the Sahara Desert in the mid-fifteenth century by Portuguese Catholic missionaries. A significant resurgence took place in the 1840s with the coming of the White Fathers – and the Holy Ghost Fathers.

This was also the time when the Protestant missionary movement came to a dramatic rise. Former slaves who had embraced the Christian faith were returned to Africa. An especially large group was from Nova Scotia, Canada, who had supported the British side in the American war of Independence, settled in what was to become Freetown, Sierra Leone.

The Nineteenth Century Missionary Movement

Famous events and personalities involved during the nineteenth century were key to introducing the African continent to the Savior.

Crowther. It was in Freetown that Samuel Ajayi Crowther (1809-1891) was put ashore. Born in Yorubaland (modern western Nigeria), he was captured by African slavers, sold to Portuguese traders, rescued by a British naval squadron and released in Freetown where he was converted. Crowther was educated in England and in 1843 was ordained as an Anglican minister for service with Henry Venn's Church Missionary Society. He returned to his native Yorubaland and was a successful evangelical missionary. It is reported that Crowther was the first Christian to step on the land of Bambur, Nigeria, in 1854, and that it would be nearly seventy years before Christian missionaries C. W. Guinter and Ira E. McBride would select Bambur as the site to begin work of the Evangelical Church which later was to unite with the United Brethren in Christ Church as the Evangelical United Brethren Church.

Crowther was ordained in 1864 as an Anglican bishop. The Church Missionary Society directed him to an impossible mission along the Niger River. He was careful in his relationship with Muslims, and while often mentioning items from the Koran, his apologetic was grounded almost entirely on quotations from the Holy Bible. He received little African help and the western missionaries who wanted to help would die a short time after arrival. The lack of response toward the Africanization of the Christian faith prompted a new and inexperienced British leadership to strip Bishop Crowther of his ecclesiastical authority in 1890, an infamous occurrence in the growth of the Christian Church in Sub-Saharan Africa.

Harris. Mr. William Wade Harris (1860-1929) was another outstanding African missionary who especially impacted the growth of the Christian Church in Cote d'Ivoire as well as in Ghana. While a political prisoner in Liberia, he felt the call to preach. He had been raised under Methodist teaching and also did some teaching in an Episcopal church. Mark A. Noll in *Turning Points*, delineates decisive moments in the history of Christianity, and includes Bishop Crowther and William Harris as indigenous leaders with the latter presenting an indigenous Christianity in mid-nineteenth and early twentieth centuries.

This Christianity emphasized one God, one theocentric law (the Ten Commandments), one day (Sunday), one book (the Bible), one symbol (the cross), one (early) baptism (break with "fetishes"), one place of worship, one institution (church leadership by "twelve apostles"); prayer as a replacement for sacrifice; use of traditional music and dance; use of cross, Bible, calabash and baptismal bowl; liturgical vestments following the model of Harris (long, white gown), and self-supporting preachers chosen from within the local congregation.[6]

Harris' messages were Christ-centered, but he exhibited a disappointing tolerance for polygamy. However, his urging of converts to connect with churches directed by European missionaries brought rejoicing for the harvest that Harris and his colleagues reaped so fully in areas where western missionaries had been unsuccessful.

The English Church Missionary Society. European and American missionaries came in great numbers but with the harsh tropical conditions and diseases, many died. In the case of Sierra Leone, the English Church Missionary Society began sending out missionaries as early as 1802. Within the scope of two or three decades, 53 missionaries died. Writing in *The Religions Telescope*, the Rev. Walcott B. Williams on March 1, 1905, recorded a series of missionary deaths. A few of these entries include:

> *About the year 1843, Miss Harnden went out, but was permitted to labor but a few months, when she died; Mr. Garnick reached the mission February 4, 1847, and died July 10, 1847; Rev. William Raymond reached the mission in February, 1842, and died November 26, 1847; Anson J. Carter reached it in July, 1848, and died eight days later. The first Mrs. Brooks died of African fever, in 1849, before reaching the station; Miss Joanna Alden died at the mission-house in Freetown, May 3, 1851; Mrs. Minerva Dayton Arnold died June 9, 1851, the same year that she arrived, and the next day Mrs. Elizabeth Tesfft died….*

Those who survived spent their active lives sharing the Gospel.

The Amistad and The United Brethren in Christ. The *Amistad* was the ship on which 53 West African slaves mutinied landing on Long Island in 1839. Freed by action of the United States Supreme Court, they were resettled in Sierra

Leone in 1841, accompanied by two missionaries, one of whom soon died. The remaining missionary, the Rev. William Raymond with his wife and baby, leased land from the Tucker family the following year near Kaw Mendi, on a tributary of the Jong River near the coast.

> *In the United States, Lewis Tappan's committee of anti-slavery people, formed to defend the Amistad Mende, could not afford to support a mission. In 1846 it joined with various missionary bodies to form the American Missionary Association, a nondenominational, evangelical organization based on anti-slavery principles.... In 1883, these missions, known collectively as the Mendi Mission, were transferred to another group already in the field, The United Brethren in Christ (UBC) (ultimately becoming The Evangelical United Brethren in 1946 and in 1968 the United Methodist Church), which continued the work.[7]*

The UBC, through the Home, Frontier, and Foreign Missionary Society, had organized a Shenge Mission in 1855 with land secured from Chief Thomas Stephen Caulker, even though he was not friendly to its presence apart from the schools and service projects that it provided. However, in 1871, with the coming of the Rev. Joseph Gomer, a black missionary, the intractable Chief Caulker was converted to the lordship of Jesus Christ. The name "Caulker" remains famous to this very day with living persons such as the Rev. David H. Caulker and Rev. Paramount Chief Doris Lenga Gbabiyor Caulker II.

Livingston. David Livingston (March 19, 1813 – May 1, 1873) was a Scottish Congregationalist pioneer medical missionary who also qualified as an explorer in his search for the headwaters of the Nile River. He was encountered in Ujiji, Tanzania, November 10, 1871, by Henry Stanley, a Welsh man, African explorer and field journalist for the *New York Times*, who approached Dr. Livingston with the famous greeting: "Dr. Livingston, I presume." Livingston stayed in Africa until his death, witnessing to God's saving grace.

Chapter Three

Taiama Martyrs

*"...The law of sacrifice is the first law of the kingdom of God....The
mother gives her life for her child, the patriot dies for his country, and the
missionary dies for his King."– Bishop J. S. Mills*

Rev. Lowery and Clara McGrew

The loss of life among missionaries was staggering in the mid-1800s, due
mostly to the harsh tropical conditions and diseases – especially malaria and
yellow fever. Perils also existed from indigenous people who felt they were being
wronged and abused and whose ways of life and culture were being threatened.

Published accounts of the Mende uprising at Shenge and of the five
missionaries martyred on May 3, 1898, at Rotifunk, Sierra Leone, are descriptive
and complete. Not so for the Rev. and Mrs. L. A. McGrew, missionaries to
Taiama, who were martyred five days later. Only brief statements can be found
that how, on May 8, 1898, the McGrews were taken to a small stony island in the
Tai River where they were beheaded and their bodies thrown into the river never
to be recovered.

In 1967, while Ruth and I were conducting the general clinic and Taiama
Eye Clinic, a visitor, Mr. Richard Andrew Corby, arrived from the United States.
He visited primarily with the Rev. B. A. Carew who was pastoring the United

Methodist Church referred to as "The Cathedral in the Bush." Mr. Corby was doing research on the events at Taiama that led to the martyrdom of the McGrews. Once he left the area, we never heard from Mr. Corby again.

Thirty-seven years later, I happened upon "parts" of a thesis written by Mr. Corby that contains a remarkable account of the McGrews' race for freedom and safety:

Taiama, in the heart of Mendeland, felt the full brunt of the Mende uprising. Here the U.B.C. mission was new and the buildings were still unfinished in May 1898. The familiar rumors of war reached Taiama by the end of April and on Sunday, May 1, Chief Foray Vong told the Rev. and Mrs. Lowry A. McGrew, the only two American missionaries in his chiefdom, that there was war in the Imperi country. The chief suggested that the McGrews report this to Kwelu, the headquarters of the Ronietta District in which Taiama was located. The two Americans had no way of so doing. Immanuel Inskrip, a Christian Mende trained at Rotifunk, told the chief he would take the message to Kwelu, twenty miles distant, after church was over, not forgetting his Christian duty to invite the non-Christian chief to divine worship.

Some of the "war-boys" were even then, early on Sunday morning, in Taiama. A corporal in the Frontier Police, passing through town on the way to Mongheri, recognized one of the Mende rebels and arrested him. When the news spread through Taiama that a policeman was in town, the head warrior and his followers, lurking in the bush outside town, fled. Inskrip informed the American missionaries of this and they decided to leave also. Inskrip got twelve hammockmen, but since one had recently been sick, they postponed their departure until the next day. On such small matters does the fate of mortals depend.

By the morrow, Monday, May 2, all the hammockmen had been sufficiently intimidated to refuse to carry the McGrews. They decided to walk to Kwelu. The helpful Inskrip secured the services of a "government man" he knew to accompany the couple and himself. After the four had crossed the Tai River, one of Chief Vong's sons overtook them, and said the chief wanted them to return to Taiama. He promised the missionaries enough men on Tuesday to carry them to Kwelu. While the McGrews considered the proposal, a man arrived and told them that Mende insurgents had burned Kwelu and killed all the police. This completely untrue report (probably planted by the chief himself) so confused the missionaries that they agreed to the chief's offer. The McGrews returned to town and Inskrip proceeded to Kwelu, verified the falsity of the report and returned to Taiama that evening to tell the McGrews. Another opportunity to escape was lost.

11

The next morning, the third of May, the American couple crossed the Tai again, but Chief Vong sent men after them, who seized the two and returned them to Taiama. Inskrip, however, escaped and made his way through the bush to Kwelu. Meanwhile at Kwelu, the Frontier Police, under Capt. E. D. d'H. Fairtlough, repulsed the Mende, the attackers believing that so long as the McGrews remained alive, Kwelu could not be taken. Chief Vong promised to protect the two in Taiama, and from the third to the eighth (or ninth) of May he kept them prisoners. Then, perhaps yielding to pressures from the insurgents, the mission buildings were burned and the McGrews were taken to the bank of the Tai, over which two times they had attempted to escape. The two UBC missionaries were beheaded as they prayed for their murderers (according to one account), and their bodies were washed down by the swift current of the river and never found.[8]

At the memorial service for the martyrs in Dayton, Ohio, later that year, Bishop J. S. Mills stated: "… The law of sacrifice is the first law of the kingdom of God. The life of the Master illustrated this fact, for even 'the Son of man came not to be ministered unto, but to minister, and to give his life a ransom for many.' From the beginning obedience to this law has been the condition of human progress. The mother gives her life for her child, the patriot dies for his country, and the missionary dies for his King."[9]

Chapter Four

Forces At Work

"The problem now was not primarily an ecclesiastical one, rather, it had become an issue of personalities, secular opinion and was heavily conditioned by ethnic prejudice." – Dr. Dean Gilliland

Sierra Leone child soldier

Missionaries brave dangers because of their response to the call of Jesus Christ to "go into all the world and preach the good news to all creation." (Mark 16:15) They have a redeeming message to share, a story to tell to the nations. Yet, the number of missionaries who have died in service pales in the face of the thousands upon thousands of indigenous African Christians who, through trials and persecutions, gave up their lives for the sake of the Gospel.

Yet, persecution has not been the only force at work to quell the spreading Gospel message. Satan has also used wars and pestilence of various forms to impede the growth of Christianity in Africa.

Wars and Rumors of Wars

During the past ninety years, wars have raged throughout the world and on the African continent. Almost every Sub-Saharan nation has had a major conflict touch its country in the past sixty years.

- **Angola:** 1975-2002 civil war
- **Burundi:** 1993-2005 conflict due to ethnic divisions between Hutu and Tutsi
- **Congo (formerly Zaire):** 1998-2003 Second Congo War, Africa's "World War" and the deadliest conflict throughout the world since World War II. This war involved eight African nations (Angola, Chad, Congo, Libya, Namibia, Rwanda, Sudan and Zimbabwe) and killed 5.4 million people due mostly to disease and starvation. Hostilities continue to this day.
- **Kenya:** 1952-1960 Mau Mau war and 2007-2008 post election war
- **Liberia:** 1989-2003 civil war
- **Mozambique:** 1975 anti-colonial war ended; 1977-1992 civil war in which an estimated 900,000 died
- **Nigeria:** 1967-1970 civil war (Nigerian-Biafran War)
- **Rwanda:** 1994 April-July genocide with over 800,000 people massacred
- **Sierra Leone:** 1991-2002 civil war
- **Uganda:** 1987 to today of government forces fighting against the Lord's Resistance Army

Disease

In Africa, the Ebola virus that produces Ebola Hemorrhagic Fever rears its ugly head from time to time. But of all the diseases, HIV/AIDS has been the most devastating to the continent. In 2008, an estimated 1.9 million people in Sub-Saharan Africa became newly infected with HIV, bringing the total number of people living with HIV to 22.4 million. Sub-Saharan Africa accounted for 67% of HIV infections worldwide.

Tribalism

Tribalism continues to be a mighty force in the upheaval of churches. In the case of the United Methodist Church in Nigeria, Dean Gilliland writes in Esther Megill's *Return to Africa* of its impact during the schism and reconstruction between 1973 and 1990. "The problem now was not primarily an ecclesiastical one, rather, it had become an issue of personalities, secular opinion and was heavily conditioned by ethnic prejudice."[10]

Chapter Five

The World's Religions

That the Christian Church could survive – and even GROW – during the last century in Africa has proven the power of the Holy Spirit and the strength of the Church. And so this growth begs the question: Where does the world as a whole stand today with its religions?

World Population and Major Religions

World population as of 2/23/10	6,803,231,490

Major Religions (2007)[11]
• Christian	2,199,817,400
o Roman Catholic	1,121,516,000
o Independents	433,096,000
o Protestants	381,811,000
o Orthodox	233,146,000
o Anglicans	82,586,000
• Muslims	1,387,454,500
• Hindus	897,726,000
• Chinese universalists	385,621,500
• Buddhists	385,609,000
• Sikhs	22,927,500
• Jews	14,956,000

Population vs. Christians in Africa
Population of Africa	934,499,752
Christians in Africa	500,000,000
Population of Nigeria	140,000,000
Christians in Nigeria	56,000,000 to 75,000,000

Almost one third of the world – at least in name – are followers of Jesus Christ. It is estimated that another 40% have been confronted with the Christian Gospel but have not responded.

Unfortunately, there remains 30% of the world's unreached population who have never heard of Jesus or seen a Bible. These people groups are largely among the Hindus, Buddhists and Muslims. As was with Africa, the Lord is calling for laborers to "look on the fields, that they are white for harvest" John 4:35 (NASB) – for witnesses who have a story to tell to the nations.

Section II: Sub-Saharan African Bishops

"We are witnesses of these things, and so is the Holy Spirit, whom God has given to those who obey him."

– Acts 5:32

Chapter Six

Angola

"...There before me was a great multitude that no one could count, from every nation, tribe, people and language, standing before the throne and in front of the Lamb. They were wearing white robes and were holding palm branches in their hands.

And they cried out in a loud voice: 'Salvation belongs to our God, who sits on the throne, and to the Lamb.'" – Revelation 7:9-10

Bishop Gaspar Joao Domingos, West Angolan Conference

Bishop Jose Quipungo, East Angolan Conference

The Methodist mission started in Angola with the self-supporting projects of the Rev. William Taylor, who was elected missionary bishop of Africa in 1884. The Rev. Emilio de Carvalho, an Angolan national, was elected bishop in 1972. Membership in the Angolan United Methodist Church has risen dramatically with more than 200,000 current members.

A second annual conference was formed in 1988 with Bishop Moises D. Fernandez occupying the Episcopal role in East Angola, headquartered at Malange, and Bishop de Carvalho remaining the bishop of West Angola headquartered in Luanda.

With a spirit of self-reliance, the church intends for all missionaries to work under Angolan leaders, requesting that key personnel – such as medical doctors or agriculturalists – serve only for limited periods of time. However, the church finds itself in need of financial help to meet the salaries of its missionary nationals, sustain its aggressive evangelistic program and create scholarship for leadership training. Churches are needed for newly opened districts, but despite good stewardship, insufficient funds are available to meet the rising cost of building chapels and parsonages.

The Cost of War

The protracted civil war in Angola destabilized the country's economy and physical infrastructure, including roads, buildings and churches. From 1975 to 2000, The World Council of Churches estimates that the conflict between the MPLA (supported by the former Soviet Union), and UNITA (supported by the U.S. and South Africa), led to hundreds of thousands of displaced people, millions of refugees and 1.5 million deaths. In 1992, MPLA won an election but UNITA refused to accept the results and resumed the armed struggle. The conflict lasted until a truce was signed in 2002. This time UNITA conceded at the polls.

Rebuilding and Restoration

Following the war for liberation and Angolan independence from Portugal in 1975, the women of the Angolan church began to reorganize and function as an autonomous group – and now are significantly represented in all the major decision-making church boards. They have initiated missions programs, helped pay salaries of pastors, supported newly organized congregations, funded scholarships for potential church leaders and assisted in the development of new churches. And to further expand their knowledge and outreach, they are building new relationships through exchange programs with other women in Africa, Europe and the U.S.

Due to twenty-seven years of civil war and the fighting following the 1992 elections, much of the Quessua Training Center, eight miles from Melange, was destroyed. Yet the dream is alive to restore and agriculturally expand the 8,000 acres along the Lombe River, the William Taylor Bible School and the Educational and Medical Center even though landmine clearance has been a serious obstacle.

In 2007, Tim and Carol Crawford reported the rebuilding of the church and school. (Carol taught as part of the theological school while Tim worked to establish a food production program for the secondary school, seminary and clinic participants.) In May 2010, John Michael De Marco reported on further progress of Guessua restoration by several Florida Conference short-term missionary teams. Helping for a year is Rev. Dr. Armando Rodriquez, Jr., a Florida Conference pastor, his wife, Icel, on staff with the conference's global mission ministry, and their twenty-one year old daughter, Amanda, through United Methodist Volunteers in Mission. Armando teaches at the School of Theology in Quessua, Icel is conference director of global mission, and Amanda mentors orphans and teaches English to secondary school students.

In March 2010, the Northern Kwanza Norte province's deputy governor for Economic and Social Affairs, Manel Abreu, recognized the contribution made by the United Methodist Church to Angola's struggle for national independence. Speaking at the celebration of the 125th anniversary of the United Methodist Church in Angola, he highlighted the participation of the congregations in the struggle to construct an independent, free and democratic nation. He noted the necessity of the presence of the church to preserve moral and civic values, and commended the United Methodist Church for clarifying the religious sect's phenomenon that is spreading over the country.

Angolan Episcopal Oversight

Episcopal oversight falls to Bishop Jose Quipungo, present bishop of the United Methodist Church in East Angola. His wife, Dr. Laurinda Quipungo, serves as the health coordinator for the conference, runs a clinic at the conference headquarters, works part-time in the Malanje Provincial Hospital and serves as public health coordinator for the province. She personally cares for more than 20 orphans living in the orphanage.

Bishop Gaspar Domingos oversees the United Methodist West Angolan Conference. He received his training in Brazil and Switzerland, and prior to his election to the episcopacy in 2000, he worked for the Angola Council of Christian Churches as Director of the Department of Justice, Peace and Reconciliation and then as General Secretary. As recently as June 2010, Bishop Domingos visited the New England Conference of the United Methodist Church, challenging Americans on how Angolans worship God in the midst of pain and poverty. This conference covenant relationship (as well as the relationship with the Detroit and Rocky Mountain Conferences) is meant to bring support to brothers and sisters in distant continents – the U.S. and Africa – and specifically in this case, West Angola.

Chapter Seven

Democratic Republic of Congo (Formerly Zaire)

"The North Katanga Annual Conference seeks to create disciples for Christ through outreach, evangelism, and through seeking holiness through the process of sanctification with a focus on triune worship; it seeks to bring honor to God by following the model of Jesus Christ, which is made possible by the power of the Holy Spirit." – Mbayu Ilunga Watete

Bishop Katembo Kainda, South Congo (Zambia) Conference	Bishop Ntambo N'kulu Ntanda, North Katanga (Tanganyika-Tanzania) Conference	Bishop David Kakeumba Yemba, Central Congo Conference

Early in the twentieth century, Kalwashi, a freed slave from Angola, was sent by his friends to the Democratic Republic of Congo (D.R.C.) to do evangelism. He met Bishop John McKendree Springer, a U.S. citizen. Together, they planted the first Methodist Mission in Kabongo around 1917 in what was then known as the Belgium Congo. Rev. Springer was elected bishop in 1936. The first Congolese elected bishop for the entire Congo was John Wesley Shungu (1964-1972) whose temporal episcopal residence was in Kamina (currently Kamina Center). As the church grew, the Congo Episcopal Area was divided into two annual conferences: Central Congo with Bishop Onema succeeding Bishop Shungu, and the South Congo with Bishop Njoy Kimba Mwenze Wakadilo.

In 1962, the provisional North Katanga Annual Conference was officially established with Bishop Ngoy Kimba M. Wakadilo becoming the first bishop of the North Katanga Annual Conference in 1976. After Wakadilo's death, Bishop Ntambo N'kulu Ntanda was elected in 1996. His subsequent re-election conferred on him the entitlement of "Bishop for Life." He and other leaders envision church-related communities that care for the mind, body and soul through new churches and pastors, employment enterprises, agriculture, health care, education, orphanages and other ministries. In some instances, the churches are the only providers of education and health care in the D.R.C.

In Bishop N'kulu's second role as senator, he has been instrumental in overseeing major development projects. In April 2010, he welcomed the UN ambassador and delegation at Kamina where the United Methodist Church had dug a canal ditch to help prevent Kamina City from perpetual floods to which it was being subjugated year in and year out. This, along with mosquito nets, medicines and pharmaceuticals made available by the UN and UMC, would prove of help to prevent the ravages of malaria. The UMC endeavors to be socially responsible as well as being the center of hope and salvation for the people.

The impressive growth of the Church in Sub-Saharan Africa is illustrated by the example of the North Katanga Conference, along with campus ministry and camp meetings, working in the following areas:

- **Evangelism.** In 2008, the Tanganyika-Tanzania Annual Conference was divided into two conferences: The Tanganyika Annual Conference and the Tanzania Provisional Annual Conference. Consequently, North Katanga consists of three conferences with a total of thirty-six districts with an average of fifteen to twenty-seven local churches per district. The 980 clergy average twenty-seven pastors per district. There are 1.4 million members and participants.
- **Education.** North Katanga has 209 primary schools, 162 secondary schools, eight colleges and two universities.
- **Health.** There are seventy-seven health centers, one hospital in Kabongo, and two clinics (Nyembo Umpungu and Shungu Memorial), the latter providing free testing and counseling for HIV/AIDS in Kamina where a new hospital is being constructed. There is eye screening and provision for eyeglasses. Thirty-two wells for clean water have been drilled.
- **Agriculture.** There are eight farms that have cows, pigs, chickens, geese, turkeys, bees, fish pond with the cultivation of corn, groundnuts, sunflowers, beans, maringa and fruit trees.
- **Construction.** The manufacturing of bricks is one of the ongoing construction projects.

- **Social welfare.** Programs include providing for orphans, widows, retired pastors, the teaching of sign language for the deaf, woodworking, sewing and library services.
- **Income-generating projects.** To help boost the local economy, carpentry and wood maizer hammer mill projects have been established.
- **Church and state relations.** The bishop played a major role in the "Peace and Reconciliation" process during the civil war (2003-2007). The church, through the World Food Program and UMCOR/NGO, sheltered the internally displaced people, and fed and clothed them. The UMC was engaged in many public projects.
- **Transport and communication.** Through this avenue, ham radios were distributed as well as bicycles, motorbikes and vehicles.
- **"Wings of the Morning."** This medical ministry has four operating aircraft that fly VIM teams to needed destinations, transport patients needing skilled care and deliver medical supplies to remote areas.

Bishop David Kekumba Yemba oversees the Central Congo Area, one of the church's largest episcopal areas with four annual conferences and two provisional annual conferences covering ten out of eleven provinces in the Democratic Republic of Congo. The membership exceeds 850,000. His re-election entitles him to be a bishop for life. Bishop Yemba feels challenged to serve in such a large area: "The Congo has just gotten out of repeated wars and we need people trained to deliver what is needed. We need district superintendents, lay people . . . all pledging to work together with the bishop." He wants to deal with people and accompany them in their spiritual journey. For this he intends to draw on his theological education and ecumenical experience to analyze the spiritual, moral and material needs of a country coming out of war.

Before succeeding Bishop Fama Onema who had served the area for more than thirty years, Bishop Yemba was a professor and founding dean of the theology faculty at the United Methodist-related Africa University in Zimbabwe. He had previously been a senior lecturer and associate professor at Zaire Protestant Seminary. He supports the priorities set forth by the 2008 United Methodist General Conference held in Forth Worth that focused on leadership, strengthening congregations, global health and fighting poverty.

Bishop Katembo Kainda is the bishop of South Congo. The South Congo Annual Conference has four different conferences with 600 churches, 400 pastors, 300,000 members, a theological seminary, fifty secondary schools, many primary schools, a number of institutions similar to colleges, hospitals and clinics.

24

Bishop Katembo was not born into a Christian home. In a mission school, he was encouraged to attend church where he was converted to Christianity. His mother followed in subsequent years. His experience mirrored countless others who attended United Methodist schools, which contributed to the dramatic growth of the Christian Church in the last seventy to ninety years in Sub-Saharan Africa.

Bishop Katembo concurs with the United Methodist Church's position in caring for both the social and spiritual needs of the people. They have especially been mindful of the many war orphans. Spiritually, the conference has dynamic men and women involved in evangelism and prayer meetings. The people are interested in revivals and love worshipping.[12]

Wikipedia[13] estimates there are 75 million people worldwide who belong to the Methodist community. There has been a steady decline in North America where an increasing number of people are becoming more inclined to join theologically conservative denominations. In Sub-Saharan Africa, there has been a phenomenal growth of the United Methodist Church in the last ninety years. Representative of the theological position of the UMC in Africa may be found in Rev. Mbayu Ilunga Watete's article on "The Historical Growth, Teaching and Impact of the United Methodist Church in North Katanga"[14]:

> *The North Katanga Annual Conference seeks to create disciples for Christ through outreach, evangelism, and through seeking holiness through the process of sanctification with a focus on triune worship; it seeks to bring honor to God by following the model of Jesus Christ, which is made possible by the power of the Holy Spirit. It is given that "the United Methodist Church is a Methodist Christian denomination which traces its roots back to the evangelical, holiness, revival movement of John and Charles Wesley within the Anglican Church. As such, the church's theological orientation is decidedly Wesleyan."*

The United Methodist Church of North Katanga bases its teaching on "salvation by faith." This implies three things that are foundational to Christian faith:

1. That people are all, by nature, "dead in sin," and consequently "children of wrath."
2. That they are "justified by faith alone."
3. That faith produces inward and outward holiness.

In North Katanga, evangelism is the principal work. The church strives to help people and make them disciples of Jesus. Also, it serves not only to extend God's Kingdom by preaching but also in various services to the communities around the church for helping them and church members with sustenance. In harmony with John Wesley who noticed four evils which were affecting people – "poverty, war, ignorance, and diseases"[15] – the United Methodist Church of North Katanga is primarily interested in meeting people's practical needs. Regarding the impact of the United Methodist Church of North Katanga, the Methodists have proven to be Christians engaged in ministry to the world:

- They established institutions for higher learning.
- They started hospitals and dispensaries for medical care, and shelters for children and the elderly.
- They adopted a social creed and social principles to guide them as they related to God's world and God's people.
- They participated with other religious groups in ecumenical efforts to be in mission.

In the North Katanga United Methodist Church, every member is to be in servant ministry with and to others. All of God's people – children, youth and adults – are called to be ministers. In other ways, all United Methodists are involved in the ministry of all Christians. Most of these people are laity, baptized Christians of all ages who minister in formal or informal ways within the church and beyond it. Though their gifts vary widely, they are all called to be engaged in the one ministry of Jesus Christ.

In more or less than seventy-five years, the church of North Katanga area grew first at lower speed, and later at a very high speed to the extent of reaching even beyond its geographical borders. Through its various ministries, the church encourages Christians to give themselves to Christ, to ground their lives in the living God, and to carry out the mission of the Church by everyone who is called to discipleship.

At the time of independence from Belgium, the United Methodist Church had 60,000 members. Now over a half-century later, the number is in the hundreds of thousands. The Katanga Methodist University and the Women's School, among others, are strong factors for its growth

Chapter Eight

Ghana

"I have a sense of calling to help feed the world – and especially – to support less-privileged communities." – Mozart Adevu

Bishop Robert Aboagye-Mensah oversees the autonomous 800,000-member Methodist Church of Ghana, which has fifteen dioceses, 3,814 societies, 1,066 pastors, 15,920 local preachers, 24,100 lay leaders, many schools, an orphanage, hospitals and clinics.[16] The church came into existence as a result of the missionary activities of the Wesleyan Methodist Church, inaugurated with the arrival of Joseph Rhodes Dunwell to the Gold Coast (Ghana) in 1835. In the first eight years of the church's life, eleven out of twenty missionaries who worked in the Gold Coast died.

Paul Adu

Methodist evangelization of northern Ghana began in 1910 but only became established in 1955. Paul Adu was the first indigenous missionary to northern Ghana. He featured largely in the establishment of churches as early as 1939 when he founded a school and church at Atebubu in northern Ashanti. In 1961, he was chosen to re-open the work at Tamale, a predominantly Muslim city. Without discouragement, he began by organizing worship services with some local Akan-speaking people, which resulted in the establishment of the Tamale United Methodist Church.

His success in sharing the Gospel so extensively resulted from patient labor and tact in relating with the people, as he held a sympathetic view towards Islam and relentlessly encouraged Christians to live at peace with Muslims. When faced with the scourge of onchocerciasis (river blindness) in northern Ghana, he determined that one of the ways to win the victims to Christ was to offer blind children education, which resulted in the founding of the Wa School for the Blind using volunteer teachers and not charging tuition. He complemented this program with free health services and basic medicines.

Global Ministries

More recently, Mission Society missionaries Mike and Claire Mozley and UMC volunteers have participated in sharing the Gospel in Ghana. In June 2007, the United Methodist Church commissioned sixteen new missionaries at the

Buduburam refugee camp as part of the Global Ministries program that supports over 200 missionaries around the world with another 700 receiving partial support. Along with Bishop Robert Aboagye-Mensah, the United Methodist Bishop Joseph C. Humper from Sierra Leone performed the "laying on of hands," symbolizing the blessing of God and the mandate of the Church. In the group were six African doctors dedicated to service in the Democratic Republic of Congo, Sierra Leone and Liberia. Their work would be in clinics and hospitals related to the United Methodist Church. One of the doctors was the ophthalmologist, Dr. Ainor Fergusson, stationed at the Kissy UMC Eye Hospital in Freetown, Sierra Leone. Tragically, within a year of his commissioning, he suffered a fatal heart attack. His replacement is Dr. John Buchan, a highly trained eye surgeon from Scotland.

Mozart Adevu

Mr. Mozart Adevu, who coordinates the United Methodist Committee on Relief's Sustainable Agriculture and Development Program in West Africa, grew up tending sheep and goats in Ghana. He studied agriculture at the University of Cape Coast and then earned a master's degree in animal breeding. Unable to find a teaching position, he decided to use his skills in ministry.

"In 2001, I was 'plucked' by UMCOR. Looking back, I believe God was calling me all these years into mission." Today, he trains farmers in six countries on ways to boost food production, cut hunger and malnutrition, and develop local economies. He has also endorsed widespread cultivation of moringa trees, a drought-resistant source of calcium and potassium. "I have a sense of calling to help feed the world and especially to support the less-privileged communities."[17]

Chapter Nine

Cote d'Ivoire (Ivory Coast)

"You have to be with God to learn from God." – Bishop Benjamin Boni

Bishop Benjamin Boni

Historical notes on the arrival of missionaries to Cote d'Ivoire date back to 1914 with the arrival of William Wade Harris. While imprisoned in Liberia for his role in a political revolt, he felt the call to preach in Cote d'Ivoire. Following the establishment of a Christian communion in the area of Grand Bassan, William Platt succeeded Harris in 1923 and the Methodist Church was officially established in 1924. It was related to the British Methodist Church until 1985 when it became autonomous.

In 2004, the General Assembly of the United Methodist Church admitted the Protestant Methodist Church of Cote d'Ivoire as a provisional annual conference with confirmation as an episcopal area in 2008. The Rev. Benjamin Boni, who had been the president of Cote d'Ivoire's United Methodist Church since 1998, became the bishop in 2005 and now leads its 1,018,402 members (estimate from The World Council of Churches).

Bishop Benjamin Boni

Articles by Tim Tanton in *Good News*[18] tell of the rigorous prayer life of the bishop, his wife, M'Gbesso Berthe, and their six children. Prayer begins in the morning at home, continues during the day at the office with the staff and resumes in the evening at home each day. Summarily he says: "You have to be with God to learn from God."

Mr. Tanton continues: "The church has about 700,000 members and serves a wider community of about 1 million, in a country with a total population of twenty-one million. The Cote d'Ivoire conference's main offices are in Abidjan, the commercial capital. About a third of Ivoirians are Christian, a third or more are Muslim, and some twenty percent follow traditional African religions. Methodism is the largest Protestant tradition, and the Catholic Church has the largest Christian presence. The denomination has 900 churches and 100 preaching points, and its membership is growing seven percent to eight percent annually, according to the conference. This thriving church is led by a relatively small number of pastors – about 109 – with help from 6,000 local pastors and 7,000 to 8,000 class leaders.

"(Bishop) Boni also oversees the United Methodist mission to neighboring Senegal which has 800 to 900 members, and Cameroon with about 1,200 members. For those countries as in Cote d'Ivoire, training pastors is a priority.

"**Women and young people are driving the Ivoirian church's growth** (emphasis mine). Up to 60 percent of the church's members are 35 and younger, mirroring the country's demographics, according to the Cote d'Ivoire Conference. Methodism's growth has been accompanied by an expansion of ministries not only into education but also health care and economic development. The church operates dozens of schools, a hospital and other health care ministries. In a country where governmental resources are under strain, the United Methodist Church is standing in the gap to address the needs of the whole person."

Chapter Ten

Kenya

"Believers must . . . be role models and vessels that God uses to bring unity."
– Bishop Stephen Kamyaru M'Impwii

My personal contact with the country of Kenya began in 1990 while doing volunteer eye surgery at Maua Methodist Hospital. I was able to return on three more occasions. It always was a buoyant experience to realize that eight out of each ten people I met were Christian.

The Rev. Dr. Stephen Kamyaru M'Impwii, the bishop in Kenya, is a deeply spiritual leader in a Swahili-speaking nation where a large proportion of the people communicate in English. There are six districts with eighty local churches that have a membership of 30,000 United Methodists. Of the eighty-four pastors, seven are ordained. There is no district office facility, and most of the local churches meet in rented houses or under trees. The government has introduced "universal primary education" for all school-going children. Eighty percent of the 38 million are Christian and ten percent are Muslims. Adult literacy rate is 85 percent with primary education being compulsory. The annual gross national income per capita is $455 or $1.25 a day. The life expectancy is fifty-five years.

Conflicts have resulted in which Kenyans have sought refugee status in Uganda and other countries. As recent as 2008, the perilous state of these people was still being addressed by the United Methodist Committee On Relief. On one occasion, Bishop Felton E. May oversaw the handover of some $50,000 in relief supplies to the local Red Cross. His presence was an encouragement to the more than 1,000 Kenyans seeking refuge in a primary school in Busia, Uganda.

In the Nyanza Province of Kenya, even today 90 percent of the population is experiencing extreme food shortages and poverty. About five percent of the people die each day. UMCOR assists the Coast School for the Physically Handicapped in Mombasa and has partnered with the Emergency Relief and Rehabilitation Program for Nyanza Province, a project of the United Methodist Church, that provides food relief to 20,000 malnourished children, the elderly and disabled, expectant mothers, widows, and internally displaced persons. Relief supplies have included 40,000 bags of maize, 20,000 bags of beans, and 160,000 liters of oil – all purchased in Nairobi for distribution.

Bishop M'Impwii

Bishop M'Impwii oversees this great humanitarian outreach of the United Methodist Church and is one of the leading forces in the Federation of Evangelical and Indigenous Churches of Kenya. In a recent meeting, he spoke on "The Strength and Beauty of Unity of Brethren (Psalm 133:1)."

"Unity in the body of Christ demands individual and collective action in the spiritual realm. It demands that believers build consensus, gain salvation through sanctification, be filled with the Holy Spirit, live at peace with everyone, carry one another's burden and live in harmony. This unity heals relationships at the family, clan and community levels and soothes broken and battle weary hearts (John 12:1-3).

"The unity of believers is maintained by the Holy Spirit who is the agent of new birth (John 3:5). It is the Holy Spirit who transforms believers into brothers and sisters in Christ and unites believers one with another and with Jesus Christ. This unity should be evident in the local church as the Body of Christ. Every believer is a living member of this Body by listening and submitting to the Word, in baptism and Holy Communion. It is God who brings unity to all believers and at all times. This is the essence of the Church Universal. Tribalism, denominational barriers and other forms of discrimination are a travesty to this truth. These divisions strangle unity and bring separation that is outside the will of God.

"Finally, believers must maintain this unity by living a life of purity and righteousness. Confession, repentance and forgiveness bring honor and gives credibility to Christian unity (John 17). Believers must therefore be role models and vessels that God uses to bring unity."

Chapter Eleven

Liberia

"Ganta United Methodist Hospital … (is) a true testament in the health and healing ministry of the church." – President Sirleaf

Bishop John G. Innis

In 1822, some members of the First Contingent of eighty-eight settlers that sailed from Baltimore, Maryland, sought to establish a home for black Americans in the area now known as Monrovia. They had first landed on the Sherbro Island in Sierra Leone in 1820. The Methodists among them found an old building that would serve as their place of worship, and the indigenous people happily offered it to them. The First United Methodist Church resides on that spot this very day.

After the arrival of Rev. John Seys, the missionaries constructed a new building with a cornerstone. The first President of the Republic of Liberia, Joseph Jenkins Roberts, held his membership there as does the present president, the Honorable Ellen Johnson Sirleaf.

Rebuilding through Education

During the civil war, Liberia was ravaged. The United Methodist Church founded Liberia's first primary schools, girls' schools and secondary schools. The 170,000-member strong United Methodist Church has been the forerunner and leader in education as stated by President Sirleaf. President Sirleaf herself obtained a formal education at a West African school founded by Methodist missionaries. She stated: "True to its commitment, the Church in our country has 133 parochial schools serving 130,000 students."

The United Methodist University's educational mission is that of rebuilding a nation severely damaged with schools destroyed, teachers killed or forced to flee the country, and books and educational materials looted. While the United Methodist University only began operations in 2000, two of its colleges have a much longer history. Mr. Jim Gray explains that the Winifred J. Harley School of Nursing, which became a part of UMU in 2001, opened its doors in 1952. The Gbarnga School of Theology began operations in 1959 and joined UMU in 2003.

Healing Ministry

"Ganta United Methodist Hospital…also runs three clinics in other parts of the country. It's…a true testament to the health and healing ministry of the Church….We applaud the work of the Church," declared President Sirleaf in her address to the General Conference in 2008. Built in 1926 through the efforts of medical missionaries, Dr. George Way Harley and his wife, Winifred, during their 35-year ministry, Ganta Hospital is part of a 750-acre compound that includes primary and secondary schools, a nursing school, vocational training programs, a demonstration farm and a leprosy and tuberculosis rehabilitation unit. The complex also serves people from neighboring Guinea and Cote d'Ivoire. Missionaries for Global Health, launched in 2006, supplies the facility with needed medical personnel.

Visiting Ganta Hospital in 1957 during a leprosy conference, I was impressed by the varied emphasis of its program. During the recent war, there was almost total annihilation of the structures that, thankfully, are now being restored.

Bishop Arthur F. Kulah

Memorable among past United Methodist leaders, Bishop Arthur F. Kulah (elected to episcopacy in 1980 and retired in 2000) guided the congregations through much of the difficult and treacherous 1989-2003 civil war. He then served for several years on the important Truth and Reconciliation Commission of Liberia, and in early 2008 resigned to serve as the interim bishop in Nigeria following the untimely death of Bishop Kafas Mavula.

It has been the pattern of his life to respond to important and critical challenges which on occasion have been life threatening. During the early 2000s, he was principal of the Theological School in Freetown, Sierra Leone. On one occasion when I called on him, he came down several flights of stairs to greet Mrs. Gess who was waiting in the car. She never forgot that noble gesture as a caring leader of the United Methodist Church. We were happy that Bishop Kulah was present to participate in the dedication of the Kissy UMC Eye Hospital in January 1984. It was our privilege to subsequently minister to the eye needs of Bishop and Mrs. Kulah.

Bishop John G. Innis

The Rev. Dr. John G. Innis is the present bishop of the United Methodist Church Liberia Conference in West Africa. Frances Porter notes that Bishop Innis obtained a degree in education in 1977 from William V. S. Tubman Teachers' College that enabled him to teach and serve as a principal. In 1985, he was awarded a Crusade Scholarship for post-graduate work at the Saint Paul School of Theology in Kansas City, Missouri, where he obtained a master of divinity degree in 1988. While pastor at Garfield Memorial United Methodist Church in Tubmanville during the height of the Liberian civil war that started in December 1989, the mission station became a place of refuge for thousands of displaced people.

In 1993, rebels raided the campus and Rev. Innis was severely beaten and almost killed in the process. He served as the administrative assistant to the incumbent United Methodist bishop, the Rev. Dr. Arthur F. Kulah, from 1994 until 1996 when he was employed as executive secretary of the General Board of Global Ministries in New York. Rev. Innis had the opportunity to further his academic status during these years. He received a doctor of philosophy in Christian leadership at Columbus University in Mentairie near New Orleans, Louisiana, and a doctor of philosophy in church administration from the Institute of Christian Works, Burlington, Washington.

On his election to the episcopacy in 2000, Bishop Innis was assigned to the Liberia area of the United Methodist Church. In 2003, he was additionally assigned to the Cote d'Ivoire area of the United Methodist Church as the presiding bishop until the election of an Ivorian bishop, Rev. Boni in March 2005. Further leadership included the presidency of the Central Conferences College of Bishops that includes the Philippines, Africa and Europe. His autobiography published in 2003, *By the Goodness of God,* further serves to give background to this dedicated bishop serving within the United Methodist Church.

Reaching Forward

With the growth and support of the Christian Church, Liberia and the African continent are reaching forward with newfound hope after years of violent conflict, corruption and abuse.

Chapter Twelve

Malawi

"And this gospel of the kingdom will be preached in the whole world as a testimony to all nations..." – Matthew 24:14

Bishop Eben Nhiwatiwa

Dr. David Livingston left his imprint in Malawi and today would give glory to God for the great host of people who name Jesus Christ as Lord. I was very much aware of that part of mission history at the time I did eye surgery in Lilongwe, capital of Malawi, in 1998.

The Malawi United Methodist Church is under the episcopal leadership of Bishop Eben Nhiwatiwa. Conference Superintendent Rev. Daniel Mhone reporting on the Methodist tradition in Malawi, notes that it only dates back twenty-three years:

"In 1978, the late Rev. Alufeyo Mpulula and Rev. Max Jawati, both coming from other Christian traditions, worked hand-in-hand with the late Bishop Abel Tendekai Muzorewa of the Zimbabwe Annual Conference to charter the prospects of establishing the Methodist faith community in Malawi. The United Methodist tradition appealed to the Malawian community because of

its focus on an holistic type of ministry and the philosophy of the priesthood of all believers where the laity also participate in the life and ministry of the church, including the decision-making process which in other traditions in Malawi is the monopoly of the clergy."

United Methodist Church Growth in Malawi

- From 1988 to 2000, there were four circuits in the Malawi church.
- From 2000 to 2003, there were eight circuits in the church.
- From 2004 to 2008, there were twelve circuits.
- Since 2009, there have been twenty-two circuits in the Missionary Conference with more than 120 local churches.
- The current membership is 20,000.

The holistic approach to ministry has propelled the growth of the church by the social witness in providing clean water to communities through boreholes and introducing programs of the church, such as adult literacy programs to fight the illiteracy in the country. Additional aid is also provided through the church's Agricultural Clubs that ensure country food security. The women of the Malawi United Methodist Church have also embarked on empowerment programs.

Currently there are no infrastructure developments in the Missionary Conference, such as mission schools, mission hospitals and clinics, or mission farms. Real estate properties are being considered as a source of rental income for church administration.

Chapter Thirteen

Mozambique

"…Our Lord Jesus Christ has and is being manifested through the work of women and men of the United Methodist Church in Mozambique…."
– Anastácio D. L. Chembeze

Bishop Joaquina Filipe Nhanala

My volunteer eye surgery visits to Chicuque UMC Rural Hospital in 1995 and 1998 impressed me with the vitality of the United Methodist Church in Mozambique. Tim, our ophthalmologist son, accompanied me on the latter visit. We worshipped with large congregations in Maputo and Chicuque. The hospital was well staffed with doctors and nurses, Mrs. Beth Ferrell being co-administrator with Mr. Armando Chitata. Bishop Joao Somane Machado and conference personnel were gracious and helpful. Surgery provided physical sight to over fifty patients during our stay. We earnestly prayed that they also would receive spiritual insight into the love of God as revealed in Jesus Christ.

Elected in 2008, Joaquina Filipe Nhanala is Africa's first woman United Methodist bishop. In Mozambique, her priorities are leadership development and self-sustainability for the church and education and health for the country. She leads a denomination of 130 ordained pastors, 150,000 members in 170 congregations, twenty-nine schools, a seminary, agricultural programs and a hospital at Chicuque.

Bishop Nhanala's theological education began in 1985 at the Gbarnga School of Theology in Liberia with ordination following in 1989. She completed her diploma in theology at Trinity College in Ghana until war in Liberia disrupted her studies. She holds a bachelor of divinity degree from Limura University and a master's degree in Bible studies and theology from Nairobi Evangelical Graduate School of Theology in Kenya.

Bishop Nhanala maintains that education opens the eyes and minds of people and is happy that the now stable government is helping the church schools as well as the hospital. She is anxious for the United Methodist Church to become more involved in public solutions to major health concerns such as HIV/AIDS, malaria, tuberculosis and maternal health issues.

Due to her busy schedule, Bishop Nhanala requested Rev. Anastacio Chembeze to submit a description of the United Methodist Church's role in Mozambique:

The United Methodist Church
in Mozambique: 120 Years of Celebration
By Anastácio D. L. Chembeze[19]

This story tells of how our Lord Jesus Christ has and is being manifested through the work of women and men of the United Methodist Church in Mozambique since its inception in 1890 by American missionaries to the present day. This is a story of celebration that should be viewed from points of view of liberation and transformation so that one understands and appreciates how the Gospel has influenced and transformed lives. The story is based on reflections, observations and Christian experiences and evaluates how these factors have contributed to three different areas of ministry: freedom from colonialism, education and heath, and evangelism and church growth.

Mozambique: The Land and the People

Mozambique is strategically located in southern Africa. With a total surface of some 800,000 square kilometers, it is the gateway to six inland countries: Tanzania, Swaziland, South Africa, Malawi, Zimbabwe and Zambia. From south to north the climate is subtropical to tropical. The official language is Portuguese, but there are sixteen main languages excluding dialects. English and French are taught at secondary schools. The predominant religions are African traditional, Christianity, Islam and Hindu.

Mozambique has a population of approximately 20 million people and an administrative division of eleven provinces, including Maputo City, the capital.[20] Its economy is based on natural resources, which include hydroelectric energy, gas, coal, minerals, timber, vast farming land and fisheries. Main exports are prawns, cotton, cashews, sugar, tea and copra; the currency is metical (1 US $ = 33.00 MZM). It is one of the poorest countries in the world and is largely dependent on foreign aid from donor countries, international financial organizations like the Bretton Woods Institutions and the HIPIC initiative of the World Bank.[21] Its GDP per capita is U.S. $900 and has a GDP growth of 6.79%. Due to the impact of HIV/AIDS and malaria, life expectancy is forty-two years.[22]

Mozambique attained its independence in 1975 after ten years of a brutal liberation struggle. The liberation movement Frente de Libertação de Moçambique (Mozambique Liberation Front – FRELIMO) was under the leadership of Dr. Eduardo Chivambo Mondlane.[23] The birth of FRELIMO in 1962 marked a new beginning in the history of the country and a socialist system of governance. The movement advocated for a free and self-governing society whose goal and direction would be determined by its people. It is worth mentioning that throughout the liberation process, FRELIMO received considerable support from some protestant missionaries, namely Methodists and Presbyterians.

A year after independence, the country was confronted with a civil war that lasted for sixteen years, resulting in many deaths and the destruction of infrastructure and the entire economy, uprooting people to different places including neighboring countries. These are typical consequences of conflict in a poor society.

Manifestation in the Sense of Justice

The presence of the Gospel, brought by missionary work, provided a clear sense of leadership. Here we can mention two aspects, national liberation as indicated above, and the influence of Bishop Ralph Dodge who used education as a tool of liberation. The Wesleyan Quadrilateral (Wesleyan theology) served as the guiding principle for Bishop Dodge and his subsequent leaders: the scripture was used as the foundation in close relationship with tradition, reason and experience in church planting and people empowerment.[24]

When Dr. Eduardo Mondlane visited a congregation during a worship service in Cambine, he sang a song that is normally sung at funerals. Motivated by this sense of justice and liberation, he was conveying the message of freedom of kinds of oppression, although people did not understand him until he openly started creating consciousness of freedom and justice for all by forming a liberation movement, which attracted many youth of those days.

Education and Health Care

The Cambine and Chicuque missions are classical examples of educational and health care centers. The idea of teaching the local peoples to read the Bible was a sufficient tool to equip the minds and hearts to understand the basic rights one had to enjoy by understanding the Gospel message. Here the emphasis is on the liberation theology and later African theology. In those days there were pastor teachers who led literacy campaigns through adult education programs that are still in usage. I remember that it was in a Methodist mission that my mother received missionary education and later training in the health school until she became a nurse.

Cambine Mission is still famous and highly respected for its mythical power of transforming people's lives: today there is a theological college, carpentry and agriculture schools, orphanage and other social facilities that make that place so special.

Education was always accompanied with the establishment of clinics and hospitals, which served as compliments for fullness of living. These health care facilities (Chicuque is a good example of a rural hospital and health institute) also served as training centers, and some of them still exist.

Another story is told by Rev. Francisco F. Machava, that after independence, President Samora Machel in his public addresses used to teach people about personal hygiene: he did not understand why the President was so moved to speak on this until he was appointed to a rural congregation where the UMC was not so strong. His observation was that where the UMC had already taught about the basics of public health – how to use latrines, treat drinking water, household cleaning, etc. – while in other places that was not the case. He concluded that such basic education was necessary for everyone. He understood how much the church had contributed to the education of communities and those communities were far different from others whose missionary activity did not penetrate.[25] This is but one vivid example of how the church taught and instructed communities.

Evangelism and Church Growth

When the church was first planted in 1890, missionaries had a high sense of mission in terms of making disciples of Christ and equipping people for ministry and self-sustainability. That was done through the use of local languages to communicate and transform lives. Although their interest of spreading the Gospel to the world came first, it appears that they had the intention of influencing other parts of the world. This resulted in a vibrant, leading and growing twentieth century church. The church, while it understands its mission and clarifies its vision from time to time, is also confronted with various challenges of a contemporary

42

developing world. These challenges include poverty, tropical and infectious diseases, education, infrastructure development, water supply, roads, economic growth, remnants of civil wars and ethnic conflict, etc. In addition, the church is also affected and challenged by the general condition of the continent and, indeed, the world.

In terms of growth, the Mozambique Episcopal Area is constituted by two annual conferences, namely North Save and South Save, respectively. Statistically, the UMC in Mozambique has about 100,500 members, divided into 184 congregations, twenty-five districts, with a total of 220 pastors of which sixty are women. Moreover, there is a new congregation being born in neighboring Swaziland.

As the church celebrates 120 years of ministry, it is proud of having the first UMC woman bishop in Africa, Joaquina Filipe Nhanala. UMC is also celebrating the life of the first African bishop who was ordained in 1964, Escrivão Anguilaze Zunguze. This shows that the Mozambican church under African leadership continues to place emphasis on resources towards education, health care, leadership development, spiritual growth and sustainability for the realization of the Kingdom of God in its fullness.

Challenges and Opportunities

Absolute poverty is the main enemy to the vitality and growth of the church. That is, the growth and sustainability of the church is entirely dependent on its members' living conditions, such as health care, education and development in general so as people have the opportunity to live a dignified life (what the United Nations calls the "attainment of dignified human development"). There's a need to maximize existing resources and leadership, and training of clergy and lay members – just to name a few.

In terms of opportunities, some examples can be mentioned: continuous training of clergy and lay leaders and correct management of their opportunities thereafter, establishment of partnerships within and outside the congregational circles and the country, openness for engagement in social and justice issues.

Heroes in Faith

Currently, the church is engaged in social projects regarding education and training, health care, water and sanitation, agriculture and so on; nevertheless, there is a need to apply and accelerate the implementation of good governance principles with diligence, zeal and obedience to the Lord's command. Special tribute goes to those heroes in faith whose lives have inspired many of us, particularly those who lost and sacrificed their lives and families during the civil war and many difficult times that the church and country experienced. To our brethren around the world for supporting and encouraging us to move forward in good and challenging times, we would like to pay special tribute as well.

Chapter Fourteen

Nigeria

"I thank God today I am a born again Christian." – Mallam Baba Jatau

Interim Bishop Arthur Kulah

This background is not complete, but is recorded as I related to it and remembered it.

The missionary work of the Evangelical Church in Wurkum Land dates back to December 20, 1923, when C. W. Guinter and Ira E. McBride arrived at the Bambur station. Karl Kumm, who had come to Nigeria as early as 1904, accompanied them. Kumm and Guinter had met in the U.S. in 1905. C. W. Guinter then came to Wukari in 1906, staying for three years. While Guinter had wanted to enter Mumuye Land as early as 1916, the British Colonial Office did not permit the request. He tried to enter Mumuye Land again in 1920, but because of unsettlement, withdrew. The territory was closed and became a restricted area by the British Colonial Government. Even in 1953, Mumuye Land was not a responsive area when I made medical visits to Zinna (Zing) and Kassa where Walter and Ruth Erberle were serving.

After the arrival of Guinter and McBride at Bambur in 1923, houses, schools and places of worship were erected. Kura Tella is reported to have been a supervisor at the school being constructed at Bambur, the teachers being Guinter and McBride. By 1927, Kura Tella, himself, was teaching. Mrs. Guinter cared for sick people at the dispensary. Today on that site there is a hospital complex dedicated in 1953 by Bishop Warner.

(I first came to know Kura Tella in January 1953 when he preached at the Bambur church. I did not understand his Hausa but felt the moving of the Holy Spirit as he persuasively shared the Gospel. At the door at the conclusion of the service, I shook his hand and using my new Hausa, said: "Ya yi kyau" [It is good]. He also brought messages to the patients and staff of the Guinter Memorial Hospital.)

The Rev. and Mrs. Victor Walter arrived in 1927 and served until 1935. Rev. and Mrs. John Arnold also arrived in 1927. Their services extended until as late as 1961. I did not have the pleasure of meeting these missionaries. Dr. and Mrs. (Aletha) Arthur Faust came in 1930 and served until 1967.

The devastating small pox epidemic at Bambur in 1927 and the cerebral spinal meningitis outbreak in Bambuka in 1929 underscored the importance of building a dispensary in 1931. New converts called for an indigenous conference. A revival at Bambur enthused the growing church, unlike the resistance that was met in Mumuya Land.

In 1954, I was aware of but did not attend a meeting at Langtang of missionaries and African leaders from the various mission groups serving in the areas surrounding Bambur. Consideration was to be given toward forming an autonomous African Church that was favored by the Africans. Different backgrounds and doctrines of the denominational representatives led to the dismissal of this early opportunity.

Zumuntar Mata

The first women's fellowship began in 1937 when women from Pero and Filiya met with women in Bambur. Full participation of African women started in 1952, the year my family and I first placed our feet in Nigeria. The Zumuntar Mata (as the women's fellowship was called) occupies an important role in the United Methodist Church in Nigeria. It is eminently successful in evangelization with their Christian and compassionate caring for people in births, deaths, illnesses, community disasters, teaching child care and providing for an acceptable social life. They provide music to services and are faithful in leadership roles as they convey the message of the Gospel.

At a Nigerian missionary reunion in 2003 at Lake Junaluska, North Carolina, Pastor Liatu Kane taught the group the Hausa song "Mai Alajibi Allahmu, Mai Alajibi Allahmu, Shi ne farko, shi ne karshe." She was the first woman ordained in the Nigerian United Methodist Church. The mother of ten children, she lost her husband in a 1999 auto accident. Always active in leadership, she affirms the Zumuntar Mata as an important leading force in the growth of the Church. After church each Sunday, they go out to the surrounding villages to sing and witness to the saving power of Christ. Just as the church has had phenomenal growth, so has the Zumuntar Mata. At a recent Majalisa (Zumuntar Mata gathering) held at Zing, there were 28,000 in attendance! The logistics for food and shelter are staggering – and many women were carrying babies on their backs.

Missionary Service in Nigeria

The time of serving for the Rev. and Mrs. (Thekla) Karl Kuglin was 1938-1960. Dr. and Mrs. (Juanita) Wilbur Harr followed the Kuglins. Dr. Harr was my missions professor at the Evangelical Theological Seminary in Naperville, Illinois. Others who followed were:

- The Rev. and Mrs. (Ruth) Walter Erbele (1945-1973)
- Dr. and Mrs. (Bea) Harold Elliot (1946-1953)
- The Rev. and Mrs. (Margaret) Armin Hoesch (1946-1952)
- Ms. Wilma Vandersall (1946-1964) who married Woodrow Macke (1950-1964)
- Lucy Rowe (1946-1953, 1957-1960, 1961-1964)
- Amy Skartved (1946-1962)
- Ms. Dorothy McBride (1949-1959)

Ruth and I – along with our four children – set foot on Nigerian soil in 1952. We served with a host of other new missionaries: The Rev. and Mrs. Duane Dennis, Mr. and Mrs. Eugene Baldwin, Rev. and Mrs. Martin Stettler, Nurse Emmy Tschannen, Nurse Florence Walter, Nurse Ruth Wittmer (Bolliger), Nurse Virginia Draeger, the Rev. and Mrs. Eugene Westley and Ms. Ardis Janke. Dr. and Mrs. Dean Gilliland arrived just after our departure.

All these missionaries have stories to tell. They were "witnesses" known personally.

Dr. Ira E. McBride

I first met Dr. Ira McBride in 1953. I was awed by this senior missionary who, with C. W. Guinter, first shared the Gospel within the Kulung area. Their ministry had been fruitful, with multiple stations ranging from Kirim to Bambuka and Djen. It was a privilege when he invited me to evangelize villages with him because I was aware of his very private nature – and yet he had a compelling drive to evangelize. On those evangelistic occasions, I always carried a Bible. A decade later when our daughters, Mary and Beth, were invited by Dr. and Mrs. David Hilton to spend a Hillcrest holiday weekend at Bambur, some of the people they met remembered their father as "the doctor with the Bible."

Dr. McBride endured privations and perils with his wife, Ruth, from 1923 until 1933 when Ruth died. McBride, himself, had a brush with death from "black water fever," a complication of malaria. His marriage to Betty in 1937 was interrupted by her death in 1941. Betty's sister, Kathleen, became Mrs. Ira McBride in 1946 with whom he shared missionary service until retirement in 1962. Kathleen became ill with cholecystitis in 1955.

Dr. McBride was a spiritual giant. He could be brusque and abrupt like Peter the apostle. To the consternation of indigenous leadership, he might dash into a situation (again like Peter at the tomb) and take control. Nothing could stand in the way of his calling of making known the saving truth of the Gospel. False worship was galling to him to the point of impudence. He could not be patient with abusive pagan practices. It had to be the best. It had to be God's love as revealed in the Lord Jesus Christ.

On a Saturday afternoon in 1953, three male nurses from Guinter Memorial Hospital and I were on a hunting trip into the Lau swamp. We were hoping for meat for the missionaries and the hospital staff whose protein diet was always in question. During the dry season, a four-wheel drive Land Rover could meander in the miles and miles of dried-up swampland where Fulani herders brought their cattle.

Suddenly, we came upon a buck antelope standing on an island of short grass surrounded by taller grass. He was undisturbed by our vehicle. Being careful not to drive directly toward him, at about thirty yards a quick shot from my 30/06 rifle downed the animal. We all rushed to the carcass. As I arrived, I asked "Inna wuka?" (Where is the knife?) as custom has it to drain the blood. There was silence. Could it be that none of us was carrying a hunting knife? I asked again, "Inna wuka?" "Yanna nun" (Here it is) said a voice emerging from the tall grass. It was Dr. McBride who, with a hunting companion had been stalking the same maria on foot, his approach like a true hunter.

Dr. McBride understood and was able to use surveying instruments. At one time he built a telescope on his front lawn that brought the moon to within arms' length. He built missionary compounds and schools in Muri. He knew Hausa and the local Kulung language into which he translated the Gospel of Luke. I count it a great blessing to have known and worked with this able and dedicated man.

Dr. Arthur J. Faust

Another early spiritual giant was Dr. Arthur J. Faust. With his wife, Aletha, he arrived in Nigeria in 1930. He was a persuasive preacher. His organizational and diplomatic skills were apparent from day one. He freely and easily associated with all manner and types of people, maintaining a friendly countenance and a disarming smile. He listened and made decisions in the style of Solomon. His literary ability allowed him to translate the Gospel of Luke into the indigenous languages of both Pero and Zing where he opened primary schools. Later he obtained a Ph.D. degree with research done in the Pero area.

One image of Dr. Faust remains ever in my mind. It was the dry season. New converts were ready for baptism. The Benue River was eleven miles away – and across an extensive swamp. A tiny stream flowed just east of Guinter Memorial Hospital. Along with workmen, Dr. Faust waded in and constructed a temporary dam, filling up a pool the night before the baptismal service. It was carefully guarded, keeping cattle and other animals at bay until after the service. The candidates rose from their immersion a bit muddy but spiritually clean.

Besides his skills with a pen, he handled a 12-gauge shotgun expertly. While driving with him one day, we came upon some bush and guinea fowl. I had not seen a gun in the car, but "lightning-like" it was produced from the side of his left leg. We had delicious fowl dinners that night.

During my three years' tenure at Guinter Memorial Hospital, I was in contact with Dr. Faust almost daily. He was our principal Hausa teacher. He guided the administration of the hospital, which tested his diplomacy to the limit. The nurses and doctors were all strong individualists – and if they had not been, they would not have been where they were.

As late as 1952, a perception still persisted that Sub-Saharan Africa was primitive and savage. The idea was reinforced when we were warned not to do medical clinics in Mumuya Land. Even some of our patients at Bambur came without the benefit of clothing, depending solely on leaves. However, by the end of 1953 we ventured to Zinna (now Zing) and were well received.

These early beginnings foreshadow a period of what was to be an explosive time for church growth in the history of the United Methodist Church.

Mallam Baba Jatau

"Witnesses" form the framework for *Glorious Witnesses for Africa*. One such witness whom I came to know and admire in 1953 at the very beginning of my missionary career was Mallam Baba Jatau, who on April 29, 2009, took the Oath of Office as the 10th Tallah (Chief) of Bambur. Fortunately, Mr. John Auta Pena recognized greatness and wrote a scholarly and magnificent biography of this eminent personality.

In *The Life of Servanthood*, Mr. Pena pens words that are descriptive of the "Baba" I knew and with whom I worked in the early 1950s. I also visited him in Zing in 2002 and learned of his pilgrimage to Israel. Mr. Pena says: "It is an honor to write about the life of a person, who endeavored to build a society that is free, progressive and dynamic, whose tenant is founded on traditional values. He is a man of honor and integrity, humble to the core and soft spoken. He takes into consideration the interest of others, and acknowledges God in his service. His simplicity is worthy of emulation. These summarize the qualities of the traditional rulers. This royal father has been described by many people inside and outside his chiefdom as a **servant** serving humanity."[26]

"Mallam Baba believed the limitless potential of Christianity needed to be unlocked because it is the key to his success."[27] "…It was in the medical field where Mallam Baba showed acts of mercy to his many patients.… This showed how humble he was to the people he served. He was a servant who washed the feet of the people in his domain."[28]

When Mr. Pena congratulated Mallam Baba as "Tallah!!" after his being turbanized on April 29, 2009, Baba's response was: "Say 'chief servant of Bambur,' which is, of course, what I have accepted to do. Pray for me to lead in a humble manner."[29] "I admire Christians, their love towards one another, their faithfulness, their commitment, their zeal to serve God, though persecuted in some instances."[30] "I thank God today I am a born again Christian."[31] "…Baba is humble. He did not allow human ego to distract his attention to achieve his goals in life. His religious belief is admirable. His discipline in Jesus Christ is great and worth emulation. . . . Mallam Baba has and is always thoughtful and taking sides with the oppressed and the defenseless. He is always fighting for the protection of the dignity of mankind . . . he believes in the dignity of labor. Above all, Mallam Baba is frank. He is always fighting for the truth, honesty, nobility, selflessness, patriotism and integrity among his people."[32]

"Wherever Mallam Baba Jatau lived and worked…Bambur, Jalingo, or elsewhere…he aligned himself with the church. When Pastor Ezra Barawani was making it difficult for the church in sessions during which opposing positions were considered an affront to the chairman and insisting on what is "popularly known in politics today as **Tazarce** (tenure elongation) i.e., continuity in office more than the given period(s)," Mr. Pena continues, "Mallam Baba was instrumental in keeping the unity of the church and serving on the Board of Elders for the creation of Gwaten Nigeria Annual Conference. He also maintained a position of non-violence in his approach to struggles. In his usual soft voice, he would say, 'Keep on with the struggle. I am behind you. This is your land…you have no other.'"[33]

It is easy for me to accept the genuineness of these words after having been a part of Baba's life for three years. It is "witnesses" like Mallam Baba Jatau who participated in the glorious growth of the church in Nigeria. Even though Mrs. Gess and I, since our years in Bambur, did not again see Baba's wife, Wardi, we always remembered her as being strikingly beautiful. We were proud to know them and be considered "friends."

50

A peer of Baba in the 1954 Bambur Medical Auxiliary Class was Waikiman of Jen. Imposing, handsome and physically strong (easily carrying me through some Lau swamp patches of water rather than having to remove my boots), Waikiman exhibited a spiritual presence that was riveting. In evangelization to villages, I always was happy when he was a member of the team. With his persuasive voice and intense eye contact, people listened to the Gospel presentation. Other Jenjos also had aggressive personalities, which suited well with Rev. Armin Hoesch, a missionary who worked among them.

So much can be said about Rev. Ezra N. Barawani who followed Bila Auta Jen and Siman Gasiga in the leadership of the Regional Church Council. Pastor Ezra was a mature student of missionary Dean Gilliland. He strongly advocated indigenous leadership and moved to have the expatriate missionaries returned to their homes. His leadership prompted the described schism in the UMCN that involved TEKAN and the government, eventually ending up in the court system where it was dismissed. His support group dwindled over a seven-year period until 1997 when he and the members of his church (EKAN) rejoined The United Methodist Church of Nigeria.

Dr. Dean Gilliland in *Return to Africa* by Esther Megill[34], points to the 1990s as a special decade of growth of the UMCN under the leadership of Done Peter Dabale, acting as a general superintendent under Bishop Arthur Kulah of Liberia who was overseeing the Provisional Annual Conference. In 1992, the Rev. Done Peter Dabale was elected as the first bishop of the United Methodist Church in Nigeria. Evangelism was given priority, although rural health activity was emphasized along with agricultural programs, primary and secondary schools, women leadership, a fully recognized seminary and orphanage care for children of the HIV/AIDS terror.

The aggressive (termed "dictatorial" by some) leadership of Bishop Dabale caused tension that led to confrontations from five districts north of the Benue River. Ethnicity became a factor during the 2002-2006 period. On Bishop Dabale's death, the Rev. Kefas Mavula succeeded him in 2007, who himself suddenly died in January 2008. Again, towering spiritually and administratively, gifted Bishop Arthur Kulah was called upon to pour out his life and his leadership into the challenging, but growing, United Methodist Church in Nigeria.

There may be some disbelief that a church racked with leadership dissention could experience the surge in membership growth that was taking place in Nigeria. Perhaps we should recall that Paul had a serious disagreement with Barnabas about taking Mark along on missionary journeys that led to their parting company. Never in history, however, has there been a more dramatic growth of the Christian Church than during the missionary activity of these two early leaders of the Church.

Accompanying Mallam Baba to the Holy Land was the Rev. Mazadu Bakila on whom I did a cataract extraction with intraocular lens implantation in 1999 with the second eye being done in 2002. Pastor Bakila was looked to for leadership during these stormy days in the church. The chairmanship of the Regional Church Council was placed upon him with the Rev. Peter Marubitoba Dong serving as general secretary. The "staying," dedicated and inspired leadership of Pastor Bakila was crucial during these troubled times.

The third member on the journey to the Holy Land was Mamman Ali Kirim who, as a boy, helped Mrs. Gess and me in our home after primary school hours during the early 1950s. Later he attended the Zaria Auxilliary School, which prepared him for his thirty years of service in rural medicine for the Muri Native Authority. When I last shook his hand forty-seven years later in 2002, he was the chairman of Inter-Religious Affairs for the entire Taraba State of Nigeria.

With the outstanding leadership and witnessing of such men of deep Christian commitment, the Church moves forward.

Chapter Fifteen

Sierra Leone

"For we preach not ourselves, but Christ Jesus the Lord: and ourselves your servants for Jesus' sake." – II Corinthians 4:5 (KJV)

Bishop John Yambasu

The episcopal election of Bishop John K. Yambasu took place December 20, 2008. Energetic and able, he assumed this high-church leadership position in the United Methodist Church in Sierra Leone while it was still emerging from the ravages of an eleven-year civil war.

Born in Bo, his primary and secondary schooling was in United Methodist schools. He received a bachelor's degree in agriculture from Njala University College in Sierra Leone. At Candler School of Theology, Emory University in Atlanta, Georgia, he completed a Master of Theology degree. He was ordained a deacon in the United Methodist Church in 1987 and as elder in 1990. He has served as associate pastor at Trinity UMC in Moyamba; acting pastor and circuit minister at Musselman UMC, Freetown; and acting pastor at Mayenkineth UMC, also in Freetown.

Earlier, Bishop Yambasu taught in schools, which included the UMC Harford School for Girls, Moyamba. He was a senior teacher and school chaplain from 1982 to 1990. From 1992 to 1998, he was the conference director for Christian Education and Youth Ministries of the Sierra Leone Conference. He founded the Child Rescue Centre in Sierra Leone and served as its executive director from 1999 to 2000 when he became a regional secretary for Sub-Saharan Africa under the auspices of the General Board of Global Ministries and Women's Division of the United Methodist Church. His assignment included youth leadership development, education and training with an emphasis on helping young people affected by war. He established a ministry network in UMC conferences that focuses on keeping children safe.

Almost immediately he became involved in analyzing shifting religious and social patterns in West Africa, planning strategies for evangelism and church growth, and mobilizing resources, declaring "Evangelism and mission are inseparable entities in the life and ministry of the Church. There is no evangelism without mission, and there is no mission without evangelism."[35]

Mission Work

Bishop Yambasu leads the United Methodist Church that evolved from the mission work begun in 1855 by United Brethren Church missionaries led by Rev. J. D. Flickinger. They headquartered in Shenge, then expanded to Rotifunk, Taiama, Kono, and throughout the country. The work flourished after the coming of a black couple, Mr. and Mrs. (Joseph and Mary) Gomer from Dayton, Ohio, in 1871. Talented in farming and carpentry, they pioneered a practical Christian lifestyle. Genuinely respected, the Gomers were peacemakers and peacekeepers, effectively witnessing for Christ and the Church.

The dynamic growth of the Church was not without sacrifice. Rotifunk Station, which opened in 1875, suffered the martyrdom of five missionaries in 1898:

- Rev. and Mrs. I. N. Cain
- Marietta Hatfield, M.D.
- Ella Schenck, R.N.
- Mary C. Archer, M.D.

Another two, Rev. and Mrs. L. A. McGrew, were killed in Taiama (as detailed in Chapter Three).

The Rev. Dr. and Mrs. R. N. West arrived at Shenge in 1882 to teach, preach and heal. They were stationed at Rotifunk but he and the Rev. I. N. Cain helped start the medical and evangelistic outreach in Taiama in 1896 where the Rev. and Mrs. L. A. McGrew were ministering at the time of their martyrdom.

Pastor C. V. Rettew

Pastor C. V. Rettew was a schoolboy at Rotifunk at the time of the massacre. Several times while visiting with me, he would recount the circumstances surrounding the death of the missionaries, whom he referred to as "those beautiful people." Tears would course down his cheeks as he described the dreadful happenings perpetrated by out-of-control and screaming groups of men. He lived with great regret that no one protected the missionaries from their terrible fate. Like all the other students, with the coming of the rebels he fled into the bush for protection.

Pastor Rettew and his wife were faithful witnesses of Jesus Christ all the days of their lives. After transferring from Rotifunk to Taiama on a subsequent tour of service, Ruth and I would often hear the tinkling of a little bell. We would smile to each other, knowing that Mrs. Rettew was on her rounds in the village proclaiming the Good News of salvation, open to all who confess their sins and accept Jesus Christ as Lord and Savior.

In a letter from Pastor Rettew in 1961 when he was retired and infirm, he wrote: "Three things are essential for all followers of the Lord Jesus Christ: humility, indiscriminate love for all persons irrespective of color and condition, and a genuine faith in Christ." By running into the bush for protection on that fateful day in 1898, Pastor Rettew was given the privilege of leading hundreds and thousands of people to Jesus Christ as their Lord and Savior. His destiny was not martyrdom but rather life that he might be instrumental in bringing new life to others during the life that he was given.

Rev. D. H. Caulker

In 1910, the Rev. J. Hal Smith and the Rev. D. H. Caulker (from Sherbro Land) opened a mission station in Kono Land at Jaiama Nimi Koro. In 1915, Pastor Smith was accidentally killed. Pastor Caulker capably carried on the missionary outreach. His faith and devotion to the church and school drew many into the Christian fellowship of believers. He ministered not only to Sierra Leoneans but also to "inexperienced missionaries."

In February 1985, seventy years after "Pa Caulker" assumed leadership at Jaiama, Ruth and I made a special 200-mile trip from Freetown to Jaiama to visit him. He was in his 113th year. His countenance was well preserved, his mind quick and his faith strong. After singing a hymn with him, we read from II Corinthians 4:5: "For we preach not ourselves, but Christ Jesus the Lord: and ourselves your servants for Jesus' sake" (KJV). We included verse 17: "For our light affliction, which is but for a moment, worketh for us a far more exceeding and eternal weight of glory" (KJV). In our prayer we thanked God for using him as an instrument of His Grace in establishing the church in Kono Land.

After several pleasantries, we stepped into our car and returned to Freetown over a harsh and bumpy road, convinced that the long trip was well worth it. We had been in the presence of greatness. Several months later, he died. His soul rests in everlasting peace.

Education

The United Methodist Church has long emphasized education. On a medical-surgical trek to Kayima in the far north of Sierra Leone, Ruth and I were surprised to find an active and bustling primary school. With gusto, the students were singing a song we had never heard before. The tune and the words were so clear that we memorized them immediately:

> *They crucified my Savior and laid Him in the tomb,*
> *They crucified my Savior and laid Him in the tomb,*
> *They crucified my Savior and laid Him in the tomb.*
>
> *And the Lord shall bear my spirit home,*
> *And the Lord shall bear my spirit home.*
>
> *He rose, He rose, He rose from the dead,*
> *He rose, He rose, He rose from the dead,*
> *He rose, He rose, He rose from the dead.*
>
> *And the Lord shall bear my spirit home,*
> *And the Lord shall bear my spirit home.*

The words of the teacher were appropriate. It was easy to understand why the Christian faith was attractive to these young minds. However, Gilbert W. Olson notes that the schools are not adequately reaching the tribes people for Christ. More importantly, he states: "The greatest church growth is in people movements, begun in prayer and itineration, and continued by organizing village congregations into sections and parishes, and training volunteer leaders."[36]

Indigenous leaders like Mr. Richard Caulker and the "Max Bailors" along with long-term missionaries Rev. Walter Schutz, Dr. Charles Leader, Ms. Vivian Olson and Ms. Virginia Pickarts emphasized the role of education by establishing and participating in schools and training centers. Prominent schools in Sierra Leone include Albert Academy and Harford School for Girls. Presently, the United Methodist Church in Sierra Leone has 353 primary schools with 65,719 students and 1,624 teachers, and twenty-eight secondary schools with 19,567 students and 730 teachers.

Evangelism

- "The gospel must first be preached to all nations." Mark 13:10
- "They set out and went from village to village, preaching the Gospel and healing people everywhere." Luke 9:6
- "Preach the Word." II Timothy 4:2
- "How can they hear (the Gospel) without someone preaching to them?" Romans 10:14

The United Methodist Church in Sierra Leone has 143 clergy (eighty fully ordained) shepherding a membership of 220,000 parishioners. At the time of my arrival in Sierra Leone in 1957, there were 9,000 communicants.[37] Every aspect of the church's outreach is evangelistic:

Kombe was a blind beggar who had learned to speak English in earlier days. Now he used the gate, leading to the Taiama UMC, to beg for coins to buy food. Compassionate Christians raised money to send him to the hospital in Rotifunk where he was being prepared for a cataract operation. While waiting for the local anesthetic to take effect, we visited with him. I can't imagine how the question came to me, but off-handedly I asked, "Which would be better, physical sight or spiritual insight into the love of God as revealed in Jesus Christ?" Knowing that he was at a Christian hospital in the hands of Christians, he dutifully responded to the latter. But then, he added: "I want to see again, too."

Kombe's operation was successful. After a short period, he was provided with cataract glasses. He left the hospital no longer needing a guide, walking all by himself – walking out of our lives.

A year later I was the guest preacher at the Taiama's "Cathedral in the Bush." It was a vibrant church pastured by the Rev. B. A. Carew who later was elected the first bishop of the UMC in Sierra Leone. People from the cottage (hut) prayer groups in surrounding villages were in attendance for Sunday services. The women and men had strong organizations, the latter conducting a large Lord's Acre project. At the close of the service, communion was served. Pastor Carew announced that those who had committed their lives to Jesus Christ – those whose love and loyalty were to the Lord – were invited to come and kneel for Holy Communion.

Several hundred baptized members out of the congregation of a thousand responded. At the last table, as I was passing the bread, I noticed a man who was healthy looking, well-dressed and wearing thick cataract-type glasses that were used before intraocular lenses were employed. Returning with the cup, the man took it, raised his face and smiled. My heart leaped within me. I was looking into the face of Kombe. He meant what he said when he desired to become a "new creation in Christ."

Once Kombe had been blind and begging. His clothes now indicated that he was gainfully employed.

Once he knew constant hunger. No longer thin, it was obvious that he could afford to buy adequate food.

Once he was a lonely man, now he was experiencing the fellowship of the Christian church.

Once he was without faith or hope. Now, by his kneeling at the communion rail, he was laying hold of the Lordship of Jesus Christ and the promise of eternal life. "If any man is in Christ, he is a new creation; old things are passed away; behold, all things are become new." (II Corinthians 5:17). **Glory! Glory for Africa! Glory for Africa and its witnesses!**

Agriculture and Forestry

The successes of Joseph Gomer in the very early times of the mission to Sierra Leone has encouraged similar programs to the present time. I remember well in the 1960s the work of the Rev. Donald and Mrs. Pletsch at Yanibana. The pineapple cash crop became famous. Helen Pletsch, a registered nurse, conducted a popular clinic. Ted and Hilda Hebel, and Keith and Mary Louise Watkin followed them.

At Manjama, Les Bradford was active in forestry and fishpond farming. His wife, Dr. Winifred Smith Bradford, oversaw a general and maternity program.

Swedish missionaries accomplished a beautiful development at Pa Loko. It was heartbreaking when the church, orphanage and other facilities were destroyed during the decade-long civil war. Redevelopment is moving forward.

Health Program

Rotifunk's Hatfield-Archer Hospital has a long history of service to the country of Sierra Leone. Illustrative Dr. John Karefa-Smart ministered for a time, but it was the career of Dr. Mabel Silver that caused Rotifunk to be considered a premiere hospital. It was destroyed, along with 300 homes, during the 1990-2001 war. Christians from Norway currently are rebuilding and renewing the program.

The Kissy United Methodist Hospital in Freetown, with support from Operation Classroom, is expanding its medical and surgical program. Kissy

Hospital also provides care through a community-based outreach model that sends health workers and traditional birth attendants out into the community. Kissy's HIV/AIDS, malarial and nutrition programs have community components where they provide education through schools and clinics to teach good community health practices. Six rural clinics that serve up to 100 villages are a part of the Kissy health network. These clinics provide lifesaving care to communities that are far from any other medical facility. Regular under-five check-ups and prenatal care help protect some of Sierra Leone's most vulnerable citizens.[38]

The Kissy United Methodist Eye Hospital, adjacent to the general hospital, has been in operation since its dedication in 1984. It followed eye programs that had been conducted at Rotifunk, Taiama and Bo. Support comes from the General Board of Global Ministries through the Advance Special 9229A, Christian Blind Mission International and the Central Global Vision Fund. State-of-the-art equipment makes possible the provision of up-to-date eye care, such as cataract extractions with intraocular implantation of lenses. With this modality, the patient often can manage daily living without additional glasses. Timely clinical care for children saves them from complications and blindness. Outreach programs bring in patients from distant places. Dr. John Buchan, a highly trained ophthalmologist from Scotland, is heading up the program with material assistance from contractor, Roger Reiners, one of the original builders of the facility, and his wife, Melanie, an eye-care professional. They ship containers with supplies, medicines and equipment from Milbank, South Dakota, halfway around the world.

Mercy Hospital, Bo, was established next to the Child Rescue Centre complex. Helping Children Worldwide received a significant matching grant in 2005 to provide primary care for children and adults because of the high child and maternal mortality. According to UNICEF, Sierra Leone's maternal death rate is the highest in the world with one out of eight women dying during pregnancy or childbirth. (About 2,000 deaths per 100,000 compared to eleven in the U.S.). A group from Flores United Methodist Church and the Virginia Conference manages Mercy Hospital.

At Manonkoh, the Doris Acton United Methodist Community Health Center was dedicated on June 4, 2010. Funded by the Lance and Julie Burma Foundation of Minnesota, it provides primary care and focuses on diseases that cause the biggest morbidity and mortality rates in children: malaria, pneumonia, worms and diarrhea.

Manjama Health and Maternity Centre has a long and illustrious history, beginning in the early 1950s as a self-help project with the permission of Dr. Milton E. S. Margai, the first prime minister of Sierra Leone. Medical personnel included Dr. Winifred Smith Bradford, Laura and Joseph Sackey, Ms. Dorothy Gilbert and Mrs. Beth Farrell.

Medical services were begun at Taiama before the fateful martyrdom of Rev. and Mrs. L. A. McGrew in 1898. A detailed and expanded description of the ministry of the Taiama Clinic is available in Lois Olsen's *Contentment is Great Gain*. The program and outreach has been assisted recently by Sierra Leoneans and friends headed by Dr. Michael Pieh, a physician in Michigan, who in his youth lived in Taiama when his father was pastor of the Taiama United Methodist Church.

I first set foot on Sierra Leonean soil fifty-nine years ago. It was my adopted home for fifty-two years, and I ministered there each year except one in spite of the vagaries and dangers of the rebel war. The Lord's calling was to serve in Sierra Leone during the active years of my life. I have come to love Sierra Leone and its people.

We pray that no harm on thy children may fall,
That blessing and peace may descend on us all.
So may we serve thee ever alone,
Land that we love, our Sierra Leone.

– From the Sierra Leone National Anthem

Chapter Sixteen

Uganda (East Africa)

"So they set out and went from village to village, proclaiming the Good News...." – Luke 9:6

Bishop Daniel Wandabula

Bishop Daniel Wandabula was consecrated May 26, 2006, to preside over Uganda and the East Africa Annual (regional) Conference which also includes Burundi, Rwanda and Sudan. The expedited confirmation by vote reflected the desire for development, healing, reconciliation and unity within the church in these strife-plagued countries. In mid-2010, Kampala suffered terrorist bombings from a Somali Islamic militant movement and elements of Burundi and Uganda were engaged militarily with the Democratic Republic of Congo. Years of war in Rwanda, south Sudan and northern Uganda have resulted in many orphans amidst a destroyed infrastructure. AIDS orphans – along with kidnappings, malaria and war-related violence – has led the UNICEF web site to state that the total number of orphans is one million.

For the United Methodist Church to continue to grow, more trained pastors and skilled professionals are needed along with a healing spirit. A consensus developed that Bishop Wandabula is the leader for the new generation with its attendant need for reconciliation.

A ten-year plan is in process to build an "alive" church, one self-sustaining and supportive of its people. It includes areas such as evangelism and church growth, agriculture, disaster management, microfinance, skills training for youth, health and communications.[39]

Bishop Wandabula was ordained in the United Methodist Church in 1994. He earned a master of divinity degree (1997) and a master of theological studies degree (1998) from Garrett Evangelical Theological Seminary in Evanston, Illinois. He holds a diploma in practical theology from the Methodist Training Institute at Kenya Methodist University. Work was also done for a Beeson International Leaders Doctor of Ministry degree through Asbury Theological Seminary.

The logistics and expense of travel make it difficult for Bishop Wandabula, as resident bishop of the East Africa Annual Conference, to visit the countries in this vast area. Problems in leadership that existed prior to Bishop Wandabula's election have persisted and worsened. In Rwanda in 2007, Bishop Jupa Kaberuka was elected and consecrated as the new bishop and legal representative of the United Methodist Church of Rwanda. Also in Burundi, the Executive Committee and the General Assembly of the United Methodist Church of Burundi met and elected Bishop Nzoyisaba Justin. He was consecrated in December 2008 as the new bishop of the United Methodist Church of Burundi and legal representative of the church.

Chapter Seventeen

Zimbabwe

"I pray that God would lay it on the hearts of fellow United Methodists – individuals, annual conferences, institutions – to support their brothers and sisters in Zimbabwe in building a vibrant church that would help transform the African continent for the sake of Christ." – Bishop Eben Nhiwatiwa

Bishop Eben Nhiwatiwa

Bishop Eben Nhiwatiwa leads the 150,000-member United Methodist Church in Zimbabwe. Besides his spirituality, he is well trained, having worked in Africa and the U.S. He was ordained an elder in 1974. He holds a Bachelor of Arts degree from Goshen College and a master's and a doctoral degree from Illinois State University. Bishop Nhiwatiwa participated in the establishment of Africa University from its very inception. He hosted site selection and meetings at Old Mutare Mission where he was serving as pastor-in-charge. On staff of Africa University, he taught pastoral theology. He served as general secretary of the Africa Central Conference before his election to the episcopacy.

In an interview with Hendrix R. Pieterse of the United Methodist News Service, Bishop Nhiwatiwa stated[40]: "The church's greatest resource is its people. The church is filled with people who are very committed to the church and its program and who are willing to sacrifice to take Christ to the next person.

Many pastors are making huge sacrifices to minister in some very challenging and difficult circumstances, and they do marvelous work. They often travel great distances on foot to visit people and hold revivals....

"The Zimbabwe Annual Conference has numerous candidates for ministry but no money to send them for formal training at Africa University or the ecumenical theological college in Harare. The Church is both a divine and a social institution. In its social expression, the Church needs money to operate and offer programs. Money comes from the people. However, the people struggle to survive and are often unable to contribute financially ...(and) the situation (has been) exacerbated by inflation and the devaluation of the Zimbawe dollar. Almost overnight, the cost of seminary or university education shot up tenfold. The conference was forced to focus its apportionment money on providing theological training, with the result that other annual conference programs ground to a vital standstill.

"The church and its programs are continually expanding, but the monetary resources are not matching the church's growth – to the point that the cabinet is forced to stop circuits from being created because the annual conference has nothing in the coffers to support them. Thus, the bishop and cabinet are in the unenviable position of having to actually restrict the development of the church because of lack of monetary resources. The people may be ready and willing to start a new circuit. They are worshiping under a tree, often in great numbers. In Zimbabwe, the harvest is ripe and the laborers are many, but the resources are few. I pray that God would lay it on the hearts of fellow United Methodists – individuals, annual conferences, institutions – to support their brothers and sisters in Zimbabwe in building a vibrant church that would help transform the African continent for the sake of Christ."

Health Care

Zimbabwe has an active medical-dental outreach. Old Mutare – a 70-bed hospital – has a dental clinic, outpatient and inpatient treatment, a maternity ward and a voluntary counseling and treatment unit. It continues to grow. It was Ruth's and my privilege to live with Dr. and Mrs. Tendai Munyeza and their family in 1995 while doing eye surgery. By looking out of the windows of the Old Mutare Hospital, with its outstanding special ward for the care of babies and small children, we could see Africa University being built.

The United Methodist Hospital at Nyadire, with its 240 beds, offers health care to a population of 500,000, serving 150,000 patients each year. Like all other institutions in Zimbabwe, it faces serious social and political challenges but strives to deliver quality health care services and improve the quality of life in the community. However, in order to keep the doors open when the government recently stopped paying its hospital employees, the workers stayed on their jobs in return for one meal a day. The nursing school continues to train the most students in Zimbabwe. Dr. Anand Rao provides Cesarean-section surgeries.

The Mutambara Mission Hospital in Nhedziwa was started as a clinic within the Mutambara Mission Center around 1907. Its 120 beds serve a population of over 120,000 people as it is designated as the district hospital for the entire Chimanimani District in Manicaland Province of Zimbabwe. That means it is the first line referral center for twenty-two clinics and rural health centres in the district, including four rural hospitals.

It has been my privilege to visit Mutambara Mission Hospital on two occasions, the first in 1995 when Dr. and Mrs. Don Rudy and nurse Delphine Jewell were there. The second visit was in 2007 when I was welcomed into the home of Dr. Emmanuel and Florence Mefor. Each time the services of the hospital were impressive and included:

- An outpatient department
- General surgery
- General medicine and pediatric medical services
- HIV/AIDS and home-based care/palliative care services
- Obstetrics and gynecology services
- Holistic care for pregnant mothers. High-risk patients coming from distant locations are accommodated and fed in the "Waiting Mothers' Shelter" when pregnancy is 32 weeks and above. A range of obstetric surgery is available.
- Mother and child health services, including immunizations
- Eye services, including medical and surgical, incorporating intraocular lens implantation. A new eye facility is nearing completion.
- Laboratory services, both hematological and biochemical
- Rehabilitation services
- A school of nursing established in 1994. With the presence of qualified nursing tutors and three doctors, it is being upgraded to train registered nurses and midwives.

Africa University is a United Methodist-African private institution of more than 1,300 students from over twenty of the fifty-four African countries. The 1988 General Conference of the United Methodist Church accepted the General Board of Higher Education and Ministry's proposal for this project. Twenty million dollars is being invested in this much-needed educational center. The groundbreaking ceremony took place April 6, 1991. President Robert Mugabe granted the official charter in January 1992. It is located at Old Mutare, Manicaland, Zimbabwe.

A large cross stands at the entrance to the 1,545-acre campus that has over thirty-six buildings. During my 1995 visit, I was impressed with a room filled with over twenty computers. Email technology was just beginning at the time. With the Internet, world information is now available at the touch of a key. The six faculties are:

- Agriculture and Natural Resources
- Humanities and Social Sciences
- Theology
- Education
- Management and Administration
- Health Sciences

Also included are the Institute of Peace, Leadership and Governance and Africa University Technology Training Center.

Revival!

While serving in Zimbabwe, Anna Morford had the opportunity of attending one of the women's revivals. She alerted me to the article in *Newscope* on September 29, 2010 – "25,000 Pack Zimbabwe Revivals." They come by the thousands, leaving their homes for nearly a week to gather on an open patch of ground. There, they raise their hands above their heads, waving and clapping, singing songs of praise and dancing before the Lord. Many stay up all night in praise and prayer, climbing nearby mountains for private conversations with God during breaks.

Those who want to understand why the UMC in Africa is growing need only attend one of these five-day women's revivals held throughout Zimbabwe in August. In 2010, more than 25,000 worshiped God at one of four revivals held Wednesday through Sunday. "The women's revival is a major event in the Zimbabwe church's calendar. Everyone looks forward to these revivals," said the Rev. Sophrina Sign, connectional ministries director. "A lot of miracles take place, the sick are healed and demons are cast out. The revivals are a climax of a spiritual journey for the church and are also a time for spiritual renewal."[41]

The spiritual preparation begins early. As soon as the names of the preachers for the revivals are announced, teams of intercessors begin fasting once a week, asking for the power of God to be manifested at the gatherings. "First, we pray for purification of ourselves that our prayers may be acceptable before Christ. When we fast, our major focus is on deliverance, healing and winning of souls to Christ," said intercessor Babra Marumba.

With the many outreaches of the United Methodist Church in Zimbabwe, some understanding can be reached regarding the glorious growth of the Christian Church in Sub-Saharan Africa during the 90-year timeframe (1921-2011) selected for this book.

Section III: Co-Workers in Christ

"The one who plants and the one who waters have one purpose, and they
will each be rewarded according to their own labor.
For we are co-workers in God's service..."

— I Corinthians 3:8-9

Everyone Has a Story to Tell

Following in this section are some stories of indigenous Christian leaders and commissioned expatriate missionaries.

They range from church and mission administrators to preachers, evangelists, teachers, agriculturalists, nurses and doctors.

They share their calling by relating times, persons and places of their ministry.

One common theme is expressed: all is said and done in the name of Jesus Christ.

By sharing the Gospel Message through their words and work, lives were changed, becoming new.

"...If anyone is in Christ, he is a new creation;
the old has gone, the new has come!"

— II Corinthians 5:17

Chapter Eighteen

Dr. Thomas Kemper

"…The gospel can transform individuals and the world."

Dr. Thomas Kemper

Representative of the "witnesses" who were a part of the glorious growth during the last ninety years of the Christian Church, and the United Methodist Church in particular, in Sub-Saharan Africa is Dr. Thomas Kemper. Mr. Elliot Wright, author and consultant to the General Board of Global Ministries, did an excellent in-depth interview and write-up of Dr. Kemper, who is the first general secretary of a United Methodist general agency from outside the United States, namely Germany.

Thomas Kemper of Germany is New Chief Executive of United Methodist Mission Agency[42]

A former missionary in Brazil, who has strong United Methodist roots in his native Germany and broad ecumenical and international experience, has been chosen as the new chief executive of his denomination's General Board of Global Ministries, an agency of worldwide scope.

Thomas Kemper, 53, a layman, will assume the new position of general secretary on March 15, (2010). He has led the Board of Missions and International Church Cooperation of the United Methodist Germany Central Conference since 1998. He is also in his second four-year term as a director of Global Ministries, a 190 year-old organization with personnel, projects, and mission partners in 136 countries. He is the first general secretary of a United Methodist general agency who is from outside the United States.

"Thomas Kemper is uniquely qualified and gifted for this position," said Bishop Bruce R. Ough of West Ohio, president of Global Ministries and co-chair of a search committee that presented his name to the agency's executive committee. "His global perspective, missionary experience, sound Wesleyan theology, broad ecumenical involvement and passion for Christ's mission will benefit the General Board of Global Ministries and the entire United Methodist Church as we advance our commitment to be a truly global movement."

The Global Ministries' executive committee elected Kemper on January 13, having been authorized last October to act on behalf of the board, which does not meet again until April 2010. The vote by telephone conference call took place in an atmosphere that included prayer for the organization and for the people of Haiti in the wake of a devastating earthquake. Even as the committee met, the United Methodist Committee on Relief (UMCOR), a unit of the mission agency, was organizing emergency relief assistance for Haiti.

"We celebrate the election of a Central Conference member to head one of our 13 general agencies," Bishop Ough said. "We anticipate the value this will add to the many mission partnerships that currently exist between United States conferences and the rest of our world-wide church." Central Conferences outside the United States, comparable to jurisdictions in the U.S., are organic units of the denomination.

Kemper considers it imperative for the mission agency to hold mercy and piety together and to "help local churches around the globe to feel and see themselves as part of a worldwide family, and to overcome the boundaries of culture, race and denomination in the name of Jesus Christ." He said that he profoundly believes that "the gospel can transform individuals and the world."

The new general secretary will succeed Bishop Joel N. Martinez (retired), who took over the executive position on an interim basis last September on the resignation for health reasons of the Rev. Edward W. Paup, who had served for a single year.

Kemper has traveled extensively, done fieldwork in Africa, worked with Vietnamese boat people in England and can communicate in five languages.

"Thomas Kemper lives the true Wesleyan values of personal and social holiness and is an inspiring person," said Bishop Rosemarie Wenner of Germany. "He reminds us of our Methodist identity: we are a mission movement, combining evangelism and social work. We will miss Thomas Kemper in Germany, and at the same time we are proud to send him to serve as the first general secretary of a United Methodist board from a Central Conference. It is the right time for the General Board of Global Mission to make this step toward more inclusiveness in our collaborative ministry of making disciples for Jesus Christ for the transformation of the world. We need mutual support in living a vital partnership in mission."

Bishop Wenner said that the engagement of the German church's three annual conferences in worldwide mission "increased tremendously" under Kemper's leadership.

Lifetime Involvement in Mission

"My interest in the Christian mission began in my childhood," Kemper said in an interview. "Missionaries would visit the Hamburg congregation where my father was pastor and my mother was involved in the women's mission society. I was excited and challenged by the differing cultural perspectives they represented within our shared faith and Wesleyan heritage."

Kemper and his wife Barbara Hüfner-Kemper spent eight years, 1986-1994, as missionaries in Brazil through the German United Methodist Board of Missions. For six of those years, he taught in the Brazilian Theological Seminary in Sao Paulo and also engaged in ministry with the poor and new church development. The Kempers have three children: Ana, 18; Lena, 17; and Joshua, 13.

A bright spot in his reflections on Brazil is the work he did with Roman Catholic sisters in ministry with the homeless, including the organizing of worship in the streets.

Earlier, he spent almost two years in London working with the German Methodist Mission and with Vietnamese boat people. Kemper speaks fluent German, English, and Portuguese and is competent in French and Spanish.

"My desire to become involved in the international ministry of the church grew in my young adult years," he explained. "It was greatly strengthened in 1976 at a World Methodist Council youth event in Dublin, where I learned why we as Methodists so strongly believe that personal and social holiness hold together. My roommate was from the Methodist Church of Southern Africa. He was white and able to get an exit visa from South Africa, but his friend, who was black, was refused exit. I began to see what it means to struggle for the sake of faith."

Mission Going Forward

Kemper is looking ahead to United Methodist mission in a connectional network as he assumes the leadership of Global Ministries. He believes that his background in a Central Conference outside the U.S. will be helpful in engaging annual conferences in the international nature and scope of mission.

He has high regard for the value of missionaries in facilitating and interpreting mission in the twenty-first century. He has both a practical and theological view of the four focus areas around which The United Methodist Church is now organizing much of its ministry. The four areas stress new congregations, leadership development, ministry with the poor and global health. Kemper is enthusiastic about each of these.

"The General Board of Global Ministries has engaged in each for decades," he said in the interview. "They grow out of the goals of mission, are rooted in the Bible and affect people in all kinds of societies and situations." Kemper would like to put more emphasis on the biblical and theological bases for the focus areas. For example, with regard to health, he would like to focus more on "wholeness and the value of healing" and less on what he calls "technocratic" approaches.

Global Ministries has particular responsibility for ministry with the poor. Kemper has special interests in the ways in which micro-credit and fair trade can contribute to a reduction of poverty around the world. Micro-credit makes small loans available to persons who might not otherwise qualify for loans. Fair trade builds equitable exchange patterns between small producers and consumers.

Kemper said he thinks that Global Ministries can make valuable contributions to all of the focus areas by continuing its commitments to its traditional goals, such as making disciples for Jesus Christ, strengthening congregations, combating racism, seeking peace, providing humanitarian relief and building strong ecumenical relations. A major role of the mission agency, he said, is to "enable and facilitate mission wherever it is already happening."

Kemper earned a Master of Education in adult education at the University of Hamburg in 1982. His thesis topic was "Global Learning in Church Youth Work." Three years later, he received a Master of Arts in sociology from the University of Bielefeld, where his preparation for a thesis in the field of ecology included three months of field work in Burkina Faso in the Sahel area of Africa.

Ecumenical and Denominational Roles

Methodist connectional and ecumenical relations are important to Kemper. After returning to Germany from Brazil in 1994, he worked for six months for the German Board of Mission. Although Methodist, he was offered the post of director for ecumenical learning of the Lippe regional organization of the Evangelical Church in Germany (EKD), an association of Lutheran and Reformed churches. He continued in that role until he joined the staff of the United Methodist Germany Central Conference in Wuppertal in 1998.

During eleven years in the German mission office, he worked closely with the resident bishops in promoting mission partnerships and supervising the missionaries sent and received by the Central Conference. As the mission executive, Kemper had a leadership role in establishing new mission partnerships with annual conferences and mission initiatives in Albania, Eurasia, Malawi and Namibia; introducing new mission fund-raising methods; and starting the Volunteers in Mission program.

From 1999 to 2009, he was secretary of the European Commission on Mission, a coordinating unit for the continental churches of The United Methodist Church and the British and Irish Methodist mission agencies. He held offices in German ecumenical organizations, including the Protestant Development Service (EED), Bread for the World, and the Association of Protestant Missions. He co-founded the Protestant-Catholic Latin American Commission.

Elliott Wright is an author and consultant to the General Board of Global Ministries.

Chapter Nineteen

Dr. Cherian Thomas

"As churches were planted, so were hospitals, and the two complemented each other. Those who were preached to were also healed and those who were healed went home with the Gospel.... It was a period of glorious growth for the Word."

Dr. Cherian Thomas

The meaningful place of health programs in the growth of the church cannot be over emphasized. This has been substantiated in the last ninety-year period being viewed in this book.

Glorious Growth for the Word

Dr. Cherian Thomas, Executive Secretary for Health and Welfare Ministries General Board of Global Ministries, United Methodist Church and Executive Secretary of Health for the United Methodist Committee on Relief (UMCOR), has had a pivotal role in church growth. Dr. Thomas works with more than twenty United Methodist-related hospitals assisting their programs and personnel. (Great numbers of converts to Christianity have their first exposure to the teachings and ministries of Jesus Christ while being attended to in a health facility.)

Dr. Thomas earned his undergraduate and M.D. in internal medicine at noted Christian Medical College, Vellore, South India. Besides having an active medical practice, he was an administrator and the general secretary for the Christian Medical Association of India. Now his work includes coordinating the hospital revitalization program that strengthens the outreach of the United Methodist Hospitals in Africa and Asia, HIV/AIDS ministries in the U.S. and abroad, congregational health ministries and community-based primary health care programs.

It took a missionary who saw a need and could translate her vision into reality. It took a church that believed in the Great Commission and responded to Christ's mandate to heal. It took a sending congregation that supported the missionary and a receiving congregation that welcomed her.

*When these factors were at work, a clinic would spring up and soon would become a health outpost. Then the outpost would become a small hospital, and the hospital would grow to house the thousands who flocked there for help. The patients were mainly women and children – the women suffering and dying from repeated pregnancies and, with their children, prey to malnutrition and a panorama of infectious diseases. Thus, the mission hospital would become the hub of a growing Christian population – a healing arm of the church and a center for care and compassion.... As churches were planted, so were hospitals, and the two complemented each other. Those who were preached to were also healed and those who were healed went home with the Gospel.... It was a period of **glorious growth for the word**. (Emphasis mine.)*

*United Methodist physicians and nurses took up the challenge to provide quality care where none existed, and churches at home raised resources to equip them for the task. Most mission hospitals were born during a fertile hundred-year period from 1850 to 1950, which also connected with the great missionary movement of the churches in Europe and the United States. **More than money or other resources, the churches' greatest contribution to the growth of mission hospitals was a seemingly inexhaustible supply of dedicated women and men.**[43] (Emphasis mine.)*

The need for revitalization in recent years resulted from a slowdown in the medical movement in the mainline churches due to medical personnel opting for short-term mission stints rather than life-long commitments, and in a learning curve where indigenous leadership, sometimes without sufficient experience, gave governance to the programs. Hospitals, with their complex routines and expensive equipment, were de-emphasized with that emphasis being placed on community-based primary health care. The World Health Organization also called for "health for all" rather than a healing ministry for the few at hospitals. Coupled with a decrease of funding and a lack of full-term doctors and nurses, hospitals faced closure.

The General Board of Global Ministries of the United Methodist Church – through its Health and Welfare unit – has launched a Hospital Revitalization Program. Eight hospitals, five in Africa and two in India, already have been assisted in governance, leadership, infrastructure and management – including significant financial support. "Health and Welfare will also coordinate the procurement of equipment, pharmaceuticals, consumables and supplies either from donated sources or at a low cost. Funds will be sought from church sources, nongovernmental organizations, agencies and the government to help hospitals address their priorities realistically, with the goal of sustainability."

Chapter Twenty

Dr. Caroline W. Njuki

"People are watching loved ones die, young people are graduating without employment and there are many who feel no joy and see no future. Fortunately, there is joy in the Church and that's the only refuge. When the Church looks at substance abuse and starts to address it, it has a bearing on so many other challenges."

Dr. Caroline W. Njuki

Dr. Caroline W. Njuki, born in Uganda, arrived in the United States as a refugee. She obtained B.A., Master's and Ph.D. degrees. Her work in the international community included the World Young Women's Christian Association based in Geneva, Switzerland. She has served as UMCOR's Executive Secretary for World Hunger/Poverty, and later on the United Methodist Committee on Relief, UMCOR Unit, as Assistant General Secretary for Health and Welfare.

Her role with the General Board of Global Ministries is Senior International Affairs Officer spearheading program initiatives in development, education, health, micro-economy, gender mainstreaming and HIV/AIDS. She finds affirmation in that the United Methodist Church is recognized as the major faith-based organization on the forefront in advocacy and funding for the HIV/AIDS pandemic in Africa. She has in-depth experience in research, advocacy, project management, policy analysis, programming, gender inclusiveness, public outreach and education, fund raising and grant making. With these qualifications, Dr. Njuki serves at GBGM as Assistant General Secretary, General Administration - Africa Region.

Extensive travel to Sub-Saharan Africa has enabled Dr. Njuki to participate in the growth of the church and be instrumental in supporting the role African women are playing in evangelism and agriculture, noting that about eighty percent of the food in third world countries is produced by women.

We thank God for Dr. Njuki's life-long commitment to Christ and His Church.

Chapter Twenty-one

Rev. Clyde and Gladys Galow

"It is God who provides us with water – cleansing inner refreshment and renewal. It is God who provides us with fire. His Spirit is our source of light, warmth, enthusiasm, energy and empowerment. The Scriptures proclaim both baptisms – with water and with fire."

Rev. Clyde and Gladys Galow

Clyde (the Rev.) and Gladys (R.N.) Galow were co-workers with Ruth and me in Sierra Leone beginning in 1957. Our love for each other has grown over these fifty-four years. During this period, they have witnessed and participated in the wonderful growth of the church. In August 2010, Clyde wrote a card of encouragement to Ruth who had been recently hospitalized and then transferred to a nursing home. We learned also that Gladys was depending on a walker with an extremely painful compression fracture of the spine following the Servants of Sierra Leone Reunion in Cedar Rapids, Iowa, July 30-August 1, 2010. Characteristic of Clyde's promptness and attention to detail, his "Remembering My Baptisms" was the first contribution received for Glorious Witnesses for Africa.

Remembering My Baptisms

It was my special calling and privilege to be appointed as a missionary to Sierra Leone, West Africa for twenty years, 1954-1974 – a servant of the Church there and hopefully an effective ambassador for Christ in many settings: the classroom of the Bible Training Institute; scores of villages, many of which could be reached by bush paths only; youth camps; planning sessions and special events of the Bo Christian Council, the Bo Christian Youth Council, and the national United Christian Council; the pulpits of churches in Bo, Kenema, Freetown, and other towns; annual Mission Council meetings and retreats; the campuses of Harford School for Girls, Koidu Secondary School, Taiama Secondary School, Yonibana Secondary School, Bo Government School, Koyeima Secondary, Union College (for teacher training), and Njala University College; New-Life-for-All events; and annual sessions of the Sierra Leone Conference of the Evangelical United Brethren (United Methodist after 1968) Church.

Over the years in Sierra Leone, it was my privilege to baptize approximately 1,500 believers-in-Christ. Nearly all of these were first-generation Christians and the majority of them had come to know Christ through the witness of laypeople. The hundreds that I baptized in the Taia River at Taiama were given their baptismal teaching by Pastor B. A. Carew or Pastor P. P. Pieh, but I was involved in the teaching of the baptismal candidates at Bo, Mongherie, Koidu, Tungie, Mondema, Magbema, Kissy and several villages on the Yonibana Circuit.

The teaching emphasized that the act of baptism was a threefold celebration: (1) celebrating the gift of God's forgiveness of sins through the atoning sacrifice of Jesus Christ, (2) celebrating God's gift of new birth for new life through faith in Jesus Christ as Savior and Lord, and (3) celebrating the commitment of the forgiven believer to be a faithful follower of Jesus Christ always, in every circumstance of life.

Through instruction, interviews, conversations and prayer times together, effort was made to assess the readiness of the candidates for the threefold celebration.

Pentecost Sunday 1955

My very first experience of conducting a baptismal service in Sierra Leone was on Pentecost Sunday 1955. The congregation met for worship in the Kulanda Town EUB School in Bo, and then we walked together to the stream at the north edge of Bo where the baptisms took place.

About nine weeks earlier we had conducted a week of pre-Easter evangelistic services in the Kulanda Town church with Eddie Smith as our guest preacher. Smith was a professor of mathematics at Fourah Bay College in Freetown, an Englishman, and a keen Christian who knew the Scriptures and who had an evangelistic passion and zeal. He had been invited to preach in Bo during his "spring" recess by Fred Walker, one of our EUB missionaries. The nights of lively preaching with the use of a lively Mende interpreter, accompanied by the work of the Holy Spirit, resulted in conversions and deepening commitments to Jesus Christ. The life of the congregation in the ensuing weeks was aimed at preparing the new believers-in-Christ for their baptisms.

Andrew Allie

Most of those who were baptized on that Pentecost Sunday were adults, but there was among them at least one school boy, Andrew Allie, then enrolled in the Kulanda Town EUB Primary School.

Eighteen months later he was ready to enroll in St. Andrew's United Christian Council Secondary School in Bo, and throughout his years at St. Andrew's School he played an active role in the life of the Kulanda Town Church that later became known as the Leader Memorial Church. After completing his secondary school studies, he served as an assistant to the Reverend Eustace Renner, Principal of the Bible Training Institute, for about one year before proceeding with the encouragement and guidance of Eustace Renner to the U.S. for enrollment at Westmar College in LeMars, Iowa, for four years (1966-1970). Later he enrolled at Evangelical Theological Seminary in Naperville, Illinois, where he received his Master of Divinity degree in 1974.

During his four seminary years, he did a year of internship (1972-1973) in Sierra Leone where he became a victim of political volatility in his homeland. Upon returning to the U.S., he was advised by his friends in Sierra Leone to remain in the United States as his safety in Sierra Leone in the 1970s could not be assured. Consequently, he entered pastoral ministry in the Detroit Conference, serving congregations in Detroit and Pontiac, earning his Doctor of Ministry degree from Drew University in 1985, and serving as the Flint District Superintendent for eight years (2001-2009). During those eight years there was an upswing in congregational growth among the Flint District churches. Their leader was that schoolboy who committed his life to Christ at an ordinary waterside in West Africa on Pentecost Sunday fifty years earlier.

Baptisms on the Mongherie Circuit

On more than one occasion I baptized new Christians in the river at Mongherie, about twenty-eight miles north of Bo. The church at Mongherie was growing steadily under the energetic leadership of S. K. Senesie, a lay evangelist who had been one of my students at the Bible Training Institute. (Several years later I would be mentoring and examining him and P. P. Pieh as they were meeting requirements for ordination.)

On one occasion in Mongherie I baptized a group of village people – who had been brought to Christ through the witness of S. K. Senesie – along with a group of students, mostly Kono by tribe, who had responded to an altar call that I had given some time earlier at the Koyeima Secondary school several miles from Mongherie. At that time, to my memory, there were no secondary schools in the Kono District and the four chief options for continuing education for Kono boys were the government school at Koyeima, the Bo Government School, St. Andrew's UCC School at Bo and Albert Academy in Freetown. Promising Kono girls were directed to Harford School in Moyamba.

Magbema, on the Mongherie Circuit, reached in the final miles by hill climbing along bush paths, was my destination twice. This village lies north of the road to Galu, southeast of Mongherie and northeast of Bo. My first visit there was in the early 1960s and the second visit was about five years later. The church was established there by S. K. Senesie; when I visited the second time, the lay evangelist leading the work there was Alfred M. Dauda, another former student at the Bible Training Institute. Among the persons baptized by immersion during my first visit were two women who later that very day went into labor, each giving birth to a boy. One boy was named Sundayma, simply indicating that he was born on Sunday. The second boy was named Galow.

Mondema

I recall another baptismal service early one morning in a Mende-speaking village midway between Jaiama Nimi Yema and the famous waterfall on the upper Sewa River. It was my first stop on a foot trek from Jaiama Nimi Yema in the Kono District to Mondema in the Gorama-Mende Chiefdom. The lay evangelist at this first stop was John Mayah, one of my former students at the Bible Training Institute; the lay evangelist at Mondema was Abraham Moriba, also a former BTI student. John had agreed to accompany me from his village to Mondema – and two days later back again to his village and on to my parked vehicle in Jaiama Nimi Yema. He had recruited a group of boys to go with us and to carry my loads (a folding cot, a plastic jerrican of boiled drinking water, a suitcase containing some clothing, mosquito net, toiletries, my Bible and a roll of toilet paper – plus a box containing supplies for the communion service at Mondema). The boys had been impressed by the baptismal service. As we proceeded over the bush paths, every so often I would hear them reciting the words: "I baptize you in the name of God: the Father, the Son and Holy Spirit. Amen."

At that time, the Gorama-Mende Chiefdom was the scene of significant church growth, perhaps the most significant church growth in all the nation. God's chosen leaders in this growth were Abraham Moriba appointed to serve at Mondema by the EUB. Conference and Madame Iye who lived in a village about twelve miles from Mondema. Madame Iye, at the time of her conversion from animism to faith in Christ, was an illiterate woman visiting her sister in Mongherie where the Gospel was being proclaimed daily by S. K. Senesie and other Christians. She returned to her village in the Gorama Chiefdom with unbounded zeal to bring her people to Jesus Christ. After a while, the Christians in the two villages – twelve bush path miles apart – discovered each other and began to experience their mutual fellowship in Christ.

I was scheduled to be in Mondema when Christians from both villages were to be there. In addition to proclaiming the Gospel, I had been invited to celebrate the Sacrament of Holy Communion with them, possibly the first time ever that this sacrament was celebrated in that part of Sierra Leone. As I recall, there was a baptized constituency resulting from an earlier visit by a Sierra Leonean pastor, making a communicant fellowship a reality; there would be more baptized believers following my next visit to Mondema.

That next visit was facilitated by the availability of motor-road transport into the area from Blama near Kenema. During that visit I provided teaching for ninety-eight baptismal candidates at Mondema and had the privilege of baptizing them, initiating them into the family of God, the Church of Jesus Christ. I smile when I recall that baptismal experience because Abraham Moriba had chosen a stream site where the bed of the stream was very soft. As I was immersing the ninety-eight candidates, I could sense that my feet and ankles were sinking deeper and deeper into the mud. When the service ended, two fellows had to extricate me from the streambed.

The next day, Moriba and I went on to Tungie by bush path for an evening and morning of baptismal teaching to be followed by an afternoon baptismal service. What a rich experience it was – affirming 118 believers-in-Christ as sons and daughters in the family of God!

Taiama

At Taiama, the baptismal services were held annually on Harvest Sunday (in early December), a time to celebrate the agricultural harvest and the spiritual harvest. Each year, there could be 100, 200, 300 or more new Christians looking forward to their baptisms. These persons came from villages throughout the Kori Chiefdom, the only chiefdom in the land reputed to have at least some Christians in every village.

This phenomenon was largely the result of the faithful efforts of Pastor B. A. Carew and his immediate pastoral successor, P. P. Pieh. However, an ordained missionary was sometimes invited to conduct the early morning baptismal service so that the energies of the pastors could be reserved for preaching and other responsibilities.

I was always mindful at these baptismal services at Taiama of the large rock visible in the flow of the Taia River, the rock on which two of our missionaries, the McGrews, had been beheaded in 1898 at the time of the Hut Tax Rebellion against the British rule – a setting in which being Caucasian was not an asset.

Freetown

While living in Freetown (1967-1970), I had the responsibility of baptizing new members in the Brown Memorial Church at nearby Kissy. One evening I was having a teaching session with several baptismal candidates. Initially, to stimulate thinking and discussion, I asked through my interpreter, for the sake of those who did not speak English, "Who is God?" I was expecting to hear, "God is the Creator" or "God is the one who gives us life," but I did not anticipate the answer given by the illiterate Mende-speaking woman who said, "God is the one who gives us water and fire."

She recognized two of God's gifts that we Americans take for granted – water and fire (matches, stoves, heating systems, electric lights and more.) She possibly had been raised in a village where people had to walk each day to their source of water and then bring the water home, a village where from time to time people had to borrow a bit of fire from a neighbor – or even a neighboring village – in order to proceed with the preparation of a meal.

Her answer was beautiful. It was true in the physical realm and true in the spiritual realm. It is God who provides us with water – cleansing and inner refreshment and renewal. It is God who provides us with fire. His Spirit is our source of light, warmth, enthusiasm, energy and empowerment. The Scriptures proclaim both baptisms – with water and with fire.

Yonibana Circuit

Numerous baptismal experiences on the Yonibana Circuit during my last two years in Sierra Leone flash before my mind. Among them are:

- **Masorie.** The baptismal service at Masorie, immediately east of Mile 91, was one of the integral events in the organization of the congregation there, an event in which several persons of Muslim background presented themselves as followers of Jesus Christ.
- **Rochen Kamandao.** The sprinkling baptism of eight persons in the church building of mud-block construction at Rochen Kamandao was powerful. At the conclusion of the service, the whole congregation escorted the newly baptized believers to their homes in the village, singing all the while, "I have decided to follow Jesus. No turning back. No turning back." That song, which comes from India, was still fairly new in Sierra Leone.

The significance of singing those words while escorting people to their homes lay in the fact that it is in our homes and with our families we are challenged to show that we are followers of Jesus.

- **Rochen Malal.** A baptismal service at Rochen Malal in which a boy with tear-filled eyes said, "Please, sir, my father will not allow me to be baptized" is forever in my memory. I assured the boy that God would continue to love him very much and reminded him that later in life he could choose to be baptized. The situation echoes conversations I have had with adults who inwardly are Christian in their thinking and outlook but who feel they must be nominally Muslim as long as their fathers are living. At any rate, I pray that the boy at Rochen Malal has been able in his adulthood to take a stand for Jesus Christ, knowing him as Savior and Lord.

- **Robange.** A service in the school building at Robange, just a few miles from Rochen Malal, in which eight of the older school boys presented themselves for baptism stands out. Teacher-evangelist Tholley, "Brother Pastor Tholley" in Yonibana, had prepared the way for this service; even the fathers of the boys were present. These fathers were Muslim or Muslim in background, but they were consenting to the Christian baptism of their sons. Afterward, each father stood by his son as the boy was being baptized.

- **Maforkoya.** A number of believers-in-Christ were initiated into the faith and fellowship of the Church during a baptismal service in a very cold stream at Maforkoya near Roruks early in the morning of Good Friday. Three believers I remember especially. One was a young man who, as a Muslim youth, had left Maforkoya to go to Kenema to pursue an educational opportunity. While living and studying in Kenema he had been introduced to Jesus Christ in whom he found his salvation. Upon completing his educational pursuits in Kenema, he returned to Maforkoya where he brought encouragement to the small group of Christians – and where he did not hesitate to share Christ with others among whom were his own mother and his grandmother. So it was that I had the privilege of baptizing three generations of Christians, all in the same hour, all in the same family.

The Church continues to grow in Sierra Leone under the mandate of Jesus Christ: "GO… TEACH… BAPTIZE… I AM WITH YOU."

Chapter Twenty-two

Rev. Joe and Carolyn Wagner

"… I experienced a change in my life. I will tell God thanks. Now I am learning and worshipping at the same time. I can now read and write and by the grace of God, I will continue to live for Him."

Rev. Joe and Carolyn Wagner

Operation Classroom immediately brings to mind Joe and Carolyn Wagner. Under their leadership, this program has been a great blessing to Liberia and Sierra Leone.

Below is a brief story of God working through the program of Operation Classroom. Although the work occurs in Liberia and Sierra Leone, this story relates basically to Sierra Leone.

Operation Classroom

On a November morning in 1986, I received a phone call from Dr. Mark Blaising, the administrative assistant to Leroy Hodapp who was at that time the bishop of the North and South Indiana Annual Conferences. He asked if Carolyn and I would consider becoming the part-time coordinators of Operation Classroom, a new mission partnership program between the churches of Indiana and the UMC secondary schools in Liberia and Sierra Leone.

Dr. Blaising mentioned that he thought of us in that role because of our interest and involvement in missions. Because I was serving a 600-member congregation, I asked how much time this would involve. His response was that he did not think it would be a very demanding task – probably ten hours a week. Little did he realize how quickly this new mission program would capture the hearts and minds of United Methodists – and not only in Indiana – and how it would become a major mission program of the UMC in Liberia and Sierra Leone!

That day, we were leaving to visit the VIM coordinators in the North Central Jurisdiction because we were responsible for the InterSharing program, a forerunner to the North Central VIM program. Three days later, after talking and praying about Operation Classroom, we called Dr. Blaising and told him that, yes, we would accept his invitation to be involved in this new program.

This decision has led us to a 22-year commitment, working to upgrade the secondary education in the UM schools in Liberia and Sierra Leone; assisting the Sierra Leone conference to bring the Kissy Maternity Clinic up to the level of a general hospital; meeting some critical facility needs at the Ganta UM Hospital in Liberia, and training teachers and pastors to become more effective counselors as they relate to those traumatized by the recent civil wars in both nations.

Little did we realize when we said "YES" that our lives would be so changed and challenged as we opened our lives to God's leading in this new ministry! We also did not realize that in the process we were charting a new form of mission.

Assessing the Need

Our first trip to Sierra Leone was in April 1987 where Rev. David Caulker, who served at that time as the conference's spokesperson for the UMC schools, met us. At that time we were focused on plans to upgrade seven schools. On this first trip we became acquainted with the principals of these schools and the church leadership, and became aware of the crucial needs of these schools for even the most basic supplies, chairs and desks in their classrooms. Now, after twenty-two years, we are no longer visitors to Sierra Leone; it has become a second home.

In 1992 when the conflict in Sierra Leone became a civil war, we continued to provide assistance to those schools that were open and to those individuals who were displaced. At one point, we opened a refugee school in Conakry Guinea. Our commitment never faded or waned.

We realized very quickly that it was not "us" but God using us to minister to the children and youth of Sierra Leone. The war caused us to expand our mission beyond schools in accordance with Matthew 25. At the height of the war, we were providing individuals with financial assistance so they could survive. We used a variety of ways to get money to Sierra Leone. At one point we assisted the GBGM in getting funds to specific individuals. Our commitment was and continues –

to serve in the way we believe God to be leading us. We are simply His servants seeking to do our Master's will.

One of the major programs of Operation Classroom is to provide work-study grants (scholarships) to needy students. Each youth is to work three hours a month at the school for his/her scholarship.

Making a Difference, Changing Lives

But has the ministry of Operation Classroom made a difference in the lives of individuals or have we only been doing mission to make us feel good? The answer is – *Yes, we are making a difference.* True, we have provided students an opportunity to get an education, but has it changed lives for the glory of God? We believe the following testimonies reflect that lives have been changed for the glory of God.

A 19-year-old Christian female was anxious to go to school. Her father, who was a farmer and a UM pastor, was killed in the war. Her mother is a petty trader, selling charcoal and palm oil. She lives with her grandmother in Koidu town. She wrote:

> *When I walked to my mother's village, which is thirty miles on foot, and told her about the scholarship I had received from Operation Classroom, my mother and I thanked the Almighty God for what He has done for us. She even came back with me to Koidu to thank the principal. He said she should thank the Lord.*

> *My mother…never went to school. Her mother forced her to get married, and she gave birth to me when she was 18-years-old. That is why I [insisted] that my mother and grandmother send me to school. I want to thank God for what you are doing for me and my family.*

Making Disciples

Making disciples is a primary concern of Operation Classroom. The UM schools have chapel one to five times per week. Many of the schools have activities similar to our Youth for Christ Bible clubs or Young Life clubs. Plans are in the works to have each secondary school have a chaplain.

Making disciples takes many forms. It takes not only the form of teaching, preaching, praying, chapel and Bible clubs, it is also what is involved in the providing of pens and notebooks so the youth can take notes in the classroom. It may take the form of providing chalk for a teacher.

It may take the form of providing a roof on a building or a generator for a school. It may take the form of building a house so a teacher has a place to live with his family. It may take the form of sending a teacher to college to become more qualified for teaching. But you may ask how does that relate to disciple making?

Perhaps these testimonies will answer the question.

I was born a Muslim in late 1983. I began my schooling by attending a Muslim school. Later I became dissatisfied with the Muslim ideology, feeling the learning was of no value to me and I could now apply any knowledge in real life situations. God changed me into a Christian and I joined the United Methodist Church. From that time I am sure I am worshiping God in a true way and getting the education that will be useful to me in my community. I appreciate the Bible and what it teaches. I am thankful to God.

Another student wrote:

Coming from a Muslim home and Muslim school I found things very different in the Christian school. The devotional worship was totally different. There was no recitation from the Koran: no sitting on mats, no bowing down of head on the ground, no more Friday prayers.

The Christian devotion of worship took the pattern of singing praises and the Bible verses were often read and interpreted by the principal.

As a lover of music, the songs really got to me. I loved the music in the Methodist Hymnal. Soon I joined the school choir. I had a great desire to listen and to associate with other youth grew higher and I grew to love the activities in Xian worship. (Brima was baptized and became a United Methodist.)

Another girl wrote:

I must be very thankful to the United Methodist Mission for changing my life and I am also grateful to my sister and her husband for helping me to enter the United Methodist Primary and Secondary Schools. (With) the help of God, they took me from my village and put me in school.

My life started to change when I stopped tapping palm trees and started going to church. From that time I experienced a change in my life. I will tell God thanks. Now I am learning and worshipping at the same time. I can now read and write and by the grace of God, I will continue to live for Him.

Another student wrote:

The work-study grant has made a very great difference in my life in such a way that I no longer become frustrated to pay my school fees. Before this time, I have been finding it very difficult to get my school fees but I must confess that the compassionate gift from Operation Classroom has served as a solution to the payment of my fees.

The tasks I do perform for my fees are fetching sticks to mend the fence that surrounds the school compound and I undertake cleaning exercises to beautify my school. I also fetch stones to the site where the rehabilitation exercises are said to be commencing on the school library. I also form school fellowships to sing to the glory of God.

Yes, Jesus has made a difference in my life because since I came in contact with Jesus my life is no longer been compared to that of the man who does not have the conviction that Jesus is Lord and that He has the final say. I also believe that Jesus Christ is the solution to all problems that may come my way.

These are just a few of the testimonies of the changes in students' lives and demonstrate the importance of the United Methodist schools. The schools always have been used by God to reach youth. Operation Classroom is committed in keeping that tradition.

During the war, we were visiting a UM church in late June. The pastor announced that they were taking a "thank offering" for having lived through the first six months of the year. This is only one example of the vibrancy the church.

At the 2010 annual conference, the Rev. Isaac Ndanema, aged 100, was recognized and honored for his work in evangelism. During his ministry, he started fourteen United Methodist Churches.

It has also been a joy to see the church grow. The church has stayed vibrant throughout the war years. Recently, the church been invited by three paramount chiefs to establish a church in their area. Some of these are heavily Muslim areas and the paramount chief is Muslim.

The church continues to reach out in ministry and evangelism.

Chapter Twenty-three

Dr. Gideon A. Avar Ophthalmologist, UMC Eye Centre, Zing, Nigeria

"What would have happened to thousands of people who are now seeing and going about their normal activities if there were no eye surgeon at Zing?"

Dr. Gideon A. Avar

Dr. Gideon Avar, eye surgeon at the UMC Eye Centre in Zing, has for the past two years held an eye camp in one of the church areas. With the help of Iowa health care professionals, eye surgeries have been performed on over 125 patients as well as performing eye exams on another 1,000. This year (2010), Dr. Avar wants to hold another eight-day eye camp in the Bambur area. In order to allow Nigerians access to free eye care, Iowans are requested to underwrite the cost of the surgeries – $150 per eye. In 2009, $5,000 was sent for the eye camp. Can we help the blind to see physically (and spiritually) in 2010? You bet!

Giving the Blind a Chance to See

I was at the United Methodist Church in Nigeria (UMCN) Rural Health Program, Zing Taraba State, Nigeria barely three months when Dr. Lowell Gess visited Zing to see with his eyes the newly constructed Eye Centre building complex. The central unit of the Eye Centre building was built with an estate grant of Mr. Reuben Schneider, a farmer from Paynesville, Minnesota, and commissioned by the late Bishop D. P. Dabale in 2005.

As a medical officer, I wanted to become a cardiologist. However, I discovered that there was a need for an ophthalmologist at the Eye Centre, which was depending largely on visiting surgeons who came to perform eye surgeries during eye camps. It was Dr. Lowell Gess and Dr. S. Kiru (formerly the medical director, ECWA Eye Hospital Kano) who inspired me to become an ophthalmologist. I completed my postgraduate training in ophthalmology in 2006 and started work at the Eye Centre in 2007. In 2007, we performed 314 eye surgeries. It is amazing how our eye surgeries have increased since then to 1,032 in 2008 and 1,344 in 2009.

The passion for doing eye surgeries and giving blind people an opportunity to see was passed to me by Dr. Lowell Gess. What would have happened to thousands of people who are now seeing and going about their normal activities if there were no eye surgeon at Zing? Patients now come from neighboring states to Zing for their eye surgery. We are now doing small incision cataract surgery with very good visual outcome and quick visual recovery. We hope to do more in the field of pediatric ophthalmology and also upgrade to Phaco emulsification in future. Our School Eye Health Program will be started very soon.

Thank you, Dr. and Mrs. Lowell Gess, for inspiring me and for transforming the socioeconomic lives of thousands of poor people who were blind but now can see.

Dr. Gideon Avar was named the outstanding ophthalmologist in 2009 by Christian Blind Mission International, which helps support over a thousand projects in over 100 countries of the world.

Linda Rowe in her article, I/Eye Care, *writes: Each year I go to see the eye doctor to check the only pair of eyes I have! Has my vision changed in a year? Do I need new glasses? Do I have cataracts or glaucoma? I care about my eyes. In Nigeria, caring for one's eyes is difficult due to lack of good sanitation, poor diet and scarcity of eye doctors.*

Quack "doctors" will come to a village stating that they are able to care for eye problems, like removing cataracts. Taking the villagers' money, they poke the cataract, breaking it up but fail(ing) to remove it, often causing complications that can lead to blindness...a tragic happening, but true![44]

92

Chapter Twenty-four

Lois Olsen

"...But godliness with contentment is great gain." I Timothy 6:6

Lois Olsen

Lois Olsen was born in 1925 in Arcadia, Wisconsin. She earned a Bachelor of Science degree at the University of Wisconsin in 1949. She received a State Certified Midwife degree from the Central Midwives Board, London, England, in 1951. Previously she had undergone Chinese language study at the Yale University Institute of Far Eastern Languages from 1949-1950. She served in Sierra Leone with the Evangelical United Brethren Church from 1952-1963, and then taught nursing as a volunteer in other countries. An exciting account of her experiences is found in her book, Contentment is Great Gain, *Leone Press, P.O. Box 93395, Milwaukee, WI 53203-0395.*

Contentment is Great Gain

Of all my memories of Taiama, I think the best are of the church in that village. When I arrived in 1952, we were still worshipping in the old building, which was just behind my house. The new building was under way, and we soon were able to worship in that great building. While the old building was crowded on any one day, the new building could seat 900. On the day of dedication, there were probably 1,200 people in attendance. For those who couldn't be seated in the sanctuary, they crowded around the windows in order to participate. Although several villages had small chapels and had small gatherings, they all belonged to the Taiama congregation.

On a Sunday morning, many people walked in – some as far as twenty miles – to come to service. The power behind the church was Pastor B. A. Carew. Of the many innovations, he was the one who originated and accomplished them. He was elected the first bishop in what became the United Methodist Church denomination in Sierra Leone.

The services were long, often two and a half hours. On Communion Sunday, they were apt to be three hours. The service was almost entirely in Mende, the local language. I was told that Pastor Carew spoke a classical Mende. His original tongue was Temini, but he had learned Mende very well. There was lusty singing accompanied by a lusty pump organ. Most of the hymns were English, but had been translated into Mende. There were several men in the congregation who had a gift for composing local songs. One of the best was a blind storyteller, Matthew Mwami. I heard that he went from village to village telling stories, and ending always with the great story of redemption. When the sermon was long and people were nodding, Pastor would stop the sermon and ask Matthew to start a song, waking up the sleepers and the service would go on.

Pastor organized a literacy institute that met in December. Only the men were included, twenty to thirty learning how to read mostly in Mende. At one point, Pastor's wife Betty Carew and I started literacy classes for women. There was one woman who was very bright and made excellent progress until her husband sent me a note saying that she should learn to do something useful. I taught her how to knit.

Pastor also developed a crop-tithing program. People who had farms and grew crops and those who cultivated gardens were encouraged to bring a tenth of their harvest to the church. When sold, the money was used to meet church expenses.

In the early years, we followed the United Brethren tradition of baptism by immersion. The United Brethren dedicated but did not baptize children. When adults made the decision to be baptized and join the church, they were immersed in the Teye River. The candidates to be baptized wore white gowns. The congregation gathered at the church and then marched the four blocks to the river, singing a hymn. The candidates then went into the river and were baptized. On one occasion, Pastor was joined by a bishop who was visiting us from the U.S.

Pastor Carew had a unique ability to link Christian theology and practice with those of the traditional religions. For instance, he related the communion practice with the Mende tradition of people eating with their ancestors.

Since so many of the people walked long distances to come to church, Betty Carew would cook a hot meal that was served to the parishioners before they left for home.

Village Clinics

In my youth, I had heard Nora Vesper talk about how she conducted village clinics in Sierra Leone. This I wanted to try. The first time, Abraham Lavaly and I went out on bicycles with our medicines and supplies on the back of the bicycles. Unfortunately, we started in February, which is the height of the hot, dry season. After about the third time, I decided that it was just too hot to make the trip. I learned much later that Miss Vesper had been carried in a hammock. Wise lady!

After I got a vehicle in 1960, we went to the clinics by car. We first started with two villages, Largo, about ten miles to the north and another village five miles to the south. Several of the staff went with me. But I soon found that two clinics were too many and we dropped the south clinic. We attended the Largo clinic for about three years. As in Taiama, we treated the school children for free. We also had a prenatal clinic and a big baby clinic. We held this in the village court barri.

After about two years, the village elders decided we were making so much money that they would have to charge rent for the court barri. It was never a moneymaking experience. I paid for the petrol. I had someone cook for us and I paid that woman. I decided that if we could not use the barri, we would have to stop coming. What confusion! For several weeks, I had representatives from six other villages come and ask if we would start a clinic in their village. The women in Largo wouldn't let that pass. They put such pressure on the male elders that that the men had to relent and invited us to move back.

Largo was right near the borderline between Mende-speaking and Temne-speaking people. My Mende staff spoke very little Temne and I spoke even less. So I offered to give five pounds to the first staff person that could run the clinic in Temne. Before long, I had picked up more Temne than any other member of the staff.

Missionary Illness

I had been at Taiama for about sixteen months when I was requested to go to Rotiifunk. This was where our main mission hospital was located. There were, in addition to the African staff, an American doctor, nurse, and lab technician as well as a British midwife. Dr. Silver, the doctor, had had a serious heart attack several months before and was carrying a limited load. The English nurse, Betty Beveridge, and an American nurse, Ruth Harding, had developed an illness that seemed to have no diagnosis or cure. In fact, an honest diagnosis was never made, even though blood samples were sent to Nigeria and to Tulane University in Louisiana for a diagnosis. The nurses were totally bedridden, having trouble eating and sleeping, with elevated temperatures.

I had been asked to come to Rotifunk to both help care for the sick women and run the hospital and clinic. Rotifunk was not Taiama. I was not happy. But I was needed to help. Dr. Silver was always available for advice and the African staff was competent. Esther Megill, the lab technician, was also of tremendous help. To make matters worse, Rotifunk was in Timini Country and I was only used to speaking Mende.

At first, Dr. and Mrs. Leader were there to help with numerous tasks on the compound. They were on their way home to the United States, but stayed to give assistance. However, Mrs. Leader had been ill as well; so after a month, they went on their way home.

Dr. Silver had made us promise that we would not send this information to the U.S., realizing that if the mission board were aware of the problem, they would insist the nurses also be sent home. My family was very upset. They assumed that I was ill. Why else was I in Rotifunk? This was probably the most difficult period I had while being in Sierra Leone.

Finally, Ruth Harding left by ship accompanied by at British missionary. On our American Thanksgiving Day, Dr. Silver and Betty Beveridge flew back to London. Dr. Silver had been awarded the MBE (Member of the Order of the British Empire) by the Queen of England, the first American in Sierra Leone to be granted this. This had been presented privately due to the emergency. Esther left, too. I went back to Rotifunk for another two months.

There was plenty of reading material. One of the articles I read was the account of the five missionaries who had been massacred in Rotifunk in 1898. I should have found something better.

In December, Gertrude Bloede arrived. Gertrude and I had known each other in Wisconsin. She was on her way to Nigeria, but stopped several months in Sierra Leone. In January, I was able to return to Taiama.

Both nurses eventually recovered at their homes and lived fairly long lives. Betty ultimately came back and started a school of midwifery. Dr. Silver felt that there was a high incidence of whatever the organism was. In August of that year, I succumbed to a ten-day spell of the same thing, but recovered without problems.

Independence

April 17, 1961, was Sierra Leone's Independence Day. The British had been rulers in parts of Sierra Leone since 1810. Independence came without battles or troubles. The British left and the Sierra Leoneans took over. The new Prime Minster was Dr. Milton Margai, a medical doctor and United Methodist who had long worked in the provinces.

I decided to stay in Taiama for the celebration, which lasted ten days. A cow was killed and I got a nice beef roast. I got a special Independence Day dress. We had a special service in the church.

On the night before Independence Day, the British flag was lowered and the new blue, white and green flag of Sierra Leone was raised. On the very day, there was a march that passed by with children, Boy Scouts and sports teams. By this time, my dispenser, Abraham Lavaly, was the assistant chief, and he took the salute from the marchers. The new national anthem was composed by John Akar and is based on the hymn "Old Hundredth." It is easy to sing and the tune is easy to remember.

Visit of Queen Elizabeth II

Queen Elizabeth and Prince Phillip made an official visit to Sierra Leone in November of 1961. Although the most elaborate ceremonies took place in Freetown, the couple visited all three provinces. At one point, the Duke traveled alone to Kono.

As missionaries, we had all been invited to some events. I was to go to Bo. I took the whole staff from our compound. Abraham Lavaly, as assistant chief, was traveling with Chief Gbappe. We were to leave at 6:00 a.m., but at 3:00 a.m. the yardmen were up, ready to go.

We had a delivery. After that – and when we were just ready to leave again – we admitted another woman in labor. Tator Bagrrey, the midwife, did a quick delivery and by 8:30 a.m., we were on our way. Bo was fifty miles from Taiama.

The missionaries were invited to the reception at the Bo Town hall. I was fortunate to sit on the seat next to the aisle, and could have touched the Queen, as she was so close as she moved towards the stage. There were a number of speeches and gifts given to the royal couple.

In the afternoon, the Queen was dressed in a royal gown and sat under a canopy, flanked by her husband and Dr. Margai, the Prime Minister, There were fifty-two chiefdoms in the province, and all fifty chiefs were presented to the Queen. Most of the chiefs were carried in hammocks to the royal couple, accompanied by members, all male, of their chiefdom. When they got to the canopy, they got out, bowed to the Queen and presented a gift.

We were sitting on a hillside behind the area of presentation. In the evening, Dr. Silver, Dr. Charles and Bertha Leader met the royal couple.

I try every year, on April 17, to remember the joy of living in Sierra Leone.

Chapter Twenty-five

Donald and
Lilburne Theuer

"...This was a serious moment, a moment of solemn expression, the result of an expanding Christian commitment. ...This was the moment when the young men declared that their lives would become what God wanted them to become..."

Donald and Lilburne Theuer

Don Theuer (with his wife, Lilburne) served as a business agent and treasurer for the West African Mission of the Evangelical United Brethren Mission in Freetown, Sierra Leone from 1958-1964. Lilburne was hostess of the Mission House, caring, listening, feeding and housing missionaries. After Don died, Lilburne married Bill Senn whose history included living in five different countries (Chile, Uganda, Greece, Ecuador and Kenya). Lilburne cherishes an article written by Don after retirement from mission (written in 1964) entitled "Train Up a Child." Her history to missionary status is most "interesting."

As a youth, Lilburne was careful NOT to commit herself to full-time Christian service; all ministerial students were "off" her list as potential future husbands. A husband was not to have red hair and but should be tall enough so that she could look up when being kissed.

Don Theuer in college fit all those requirements – majoring in business, dark brown hair – and standing 6'2". Within five years, Lilburn was in Sierra Leone with her missionary husband at the Mission House in Freetown, Sierra Leone, the mother of a little red-haired daughter – and her tall husband, Don.

In 1989, Lilburne and Don returned to Sierra Leone as volunteers, caring for the eye doctors coming to the Kissy UMC Eye Hospital and participating in the business side of the hospital. Theirs was a meaningful ministry to West Africa in helping the Church grow.

Train Up a Child
by Donald Theuer

It was a hot summer evening.

Three young men stood at the altar rail in the tabernacle at Linwood Park, Ohio. Three young men who had been the closest of friends for years. They had common memories of ball games, amusement parks, juvenile practical jokes and "doing the town." These memories were in the background, unimportant now. There had been times when the tabernacle services at Linwood were mere jokes to these boys; the sawdust and sand at their feet was funny . . . they laughed when the lights went out during a storm. "Let's sit at the edge so we can leave early."

But this was a serious moment, a moment of solemn expression, the result of an expanding Christian commitment. Perhaps none of the three standing there could say when they had become Christians. They were examples of "born" Christians to whom the "born-again" aspects came so naturally as to defy specific timing. This was the moment when the young men declared that their lives would become what God wanted them to become, including, perhaps, engaging in full-time Christian vocations.

The consecrated homes and family life experiences of these young men played an important part in their decision. In my home, participation at church was a major portion of my life. Sunday school, worship service, Sunday evening and mid-week service was a foregone conclusion. My mother and dad's talents were used in the service of the trustees, choir, WSWS and other organizations.

Regular financial support of the church was a priority item in our budget. I was urged, from as early as I can remember, to use the weekly envelope and to give a portion of my allowance.

Family devotions were part of a daily schedule. I can recall that the Bible, with the Messenger folded inside, was within reach at Dad's regular place at our table.

Our family was always interested in missions, so we often entertained missionaries in our home. The worldwide Church was a common topic of conversation.

I do not recall ever feeling that these activities encroached upon the desires of a growing boy for time to play ball, fellowship with Dad or school activities. It would seem that Mother and Dad had found the "formula" sought by Christian parents everywhere for I did not, during college or national service, feel a need for rebellion.

Mother and Dad's personal examples of Christian living and service were highlighted by a deep love and devotion for us. The freedom we had to form our own decisions did not mean that we were unaware of their feelings. Usually a stern look was all that was needed. The results of the combination of love, heartache, freedom and discipline which Mother and Dad were able to instill into our family attitudes can be seen in my brother's years of missionary service and a sister's happy and successful family life and devoted service to her local church.

What about the three young men standing at the altar? Where are they today? One is a successful pastor in the Ohio East Conference; the second, after spending many years in musical evangelism, finds it necessary – because of a physical ailment – to restrict himself to a few hours each day at a desk keeping a religious record company in operation; and I and my family are happily serving our local church after having been privileged to spend six years in Sierra Leone taking an active part in the worldwide mission of the EUB church.

Chapter Twenty-six

Dr. Donald Rudy

"The mission work in Africa was absolutely wonderful, in spite of being hard and challenging. God gave me the strength to do it. THANKS BE TO GOD!"

Dr. Donald Rudy

Donald B. Rudy, M.D., was called to be a medical missionary to Africa at an early age. His service was in Portugal and Rhodesia/Zimbabwe.

Working for the Lord

Dr. Rudy writes: "The United Methodist Church in Rhodesia/Zimbabwe is now over 100 years old. Originally, it was assigned a district in eastern Rhodesia, but by 1975 had grown to also include the western part of Rhodesia. One of the early Christian missionaries was Dr. Gurney, a medical doctor who attracted many to the church after he successfully operated on a woman who had been gored by a cow. She survived her abdominal wounds, prompting many people to believe on Jesus."

"I had two years of surgical training before going to Africa. However, I had to do all sorts of surgery because there was no one else to do it. We had to perform up to twenty emergency Cesarean sections per month, many hysterectomies because of fibroid tumors, ovarian cystectomies, throidectomies and fracture work. We had many malnourished children who stayed in the hospital for a month or more to recover. Many had Kwashiorkor, a protein-calorie deficiency, which caused generalized swelling of the body.

"I remember a 10-year-old girl, skin and bones, who always followed me around on my pediatric rounds calling me 'chiremba wangu, chiremba wangu,' my doctor, my doctor. We became close to our HIV/AIDS and TB patients because they stayed six months or longer in the hospital. One young woman, about twenty years of age, had a rough course with frequent high fevers, diarrhea, as well as TB. She became terminal and as she was leaving to go 'home,' I hugged her and told her she was like a cat with nine lives. She agreed and said that this was to be her ninth life. She had become a Christian while in the hospital and was not afraid of death. She knew where she was going and was happy. Most of my time in Zimbabwe was spent working at Mutumbara in southeastern Zimbabwe where I was medical superintendent.

"The mission work in Africa was absolutely wonderful, in spite of being hard and challenging. God gave me the strength to do it. THANKS BE TO GOD!"

Chapter Twenty-seven

Gertrude Bloede

"My father was very glad to have me go as a missionary. He said when I was born, he gave me to God to use as He wanted."

Ruth and I kept in contact with Gertrude over the years up until her recent going to Glory on November 1, 2010. We were amazed at the clarity and beauty of her writing and the sharpness of her intellect. God used her in marvelous ways for His kingdom building.

Doing God's Work in Sierra Leone
by Rachel Colliver, Otterbein Homes
Used with permission. Originally published Winter 2010.

At ninety-eight years old, Gertrude Bloede's memory snaps to recall names, dates and places from the 1940s and 1950s like it was yesterday. Leaning back in her recliner at Otterbein Lebanon Retirement Community in Lebanon, Ohio, she told her story:

As one of the first midwives in Sierra Leone as a missionary, her experiences are as rare as a true albino moose. The daughter of an evangelical pastor, Bloede was born in 1911 in Wisconsin. After graduating from high school, she earned her bachelor's degree from North Central College in Naperville, Illinois. She went on to the University of Minnesota for her nurse's training. Graduating in 1948, she spent the next year working at a Kenosha, Wisconsin, hospital.

Then an encounter with Dr. Mabel Silver, the doctor in charge of an Evangelical United Brethren (EUB) missionary station in the West African country of Sierra Leone set the course of her life. Dr. Silver told her a missionary who had been there thirty-five years was retiring and they needed a nurse to take her place. In order to go, Bloede had to be appointed by the EUB mission board and receive midwifery training.

On September 21, 1949, she and eight others sailed to England where Bloede spent the next year being trained in nurse midwifery. She arrived in Freetown, Sierra Leone, in January 1951 and traveled to Rotifunk, located in the country's southern province.

While Bloede worked in Rotifunk at the main hospital, the long-time missionary she had replaced was called back into service for one year and stayed to help for five years at the Jaiama station, a nine-hour drive from Rotifunk. They were short-staffed and every person was needed.

The very first missionaries who came to Sierra Leone had come in 1855 and a centennial celebration was being planned for 1955. Considering her tenure, the missionary was then asked to leave the Jaiama post and become a member on the centennial committee. The call came for Bloede to once again step into her shoes, where she served for the next ten years.

"I was so fortunate when I got to Jaiama because I'm no cook," she shared conspiratorially. "I don't know anything about keeping house and cooking." She didn't have to with two special people around. One was a cook, who had worked for missionaries for twenty-five years.

"He knew more about cooking than I'll ever know. He kept me fed the entire time," she said.

She also had a houseboy, who attended the local secondary school. Bloede paid his school fees and bought his uniforms and he kept her house clean and did her washing.

Except for a three-year leave of absence to care for her ill mother, Bloede was in Sierra Leone until 1965.

"One of the doctors from Rotifunk was supposed to come visit us every six months. That was mostly theoretical," she said. "They did come once in a while."

For Bloede, sometimes the hardest part of her job as a missionary was not the physical work that drove her from morning until night, but a deeper feeling of regret that because of her intense work schedule, "I felt sometimes I wasn't as good a Christian witness for my Lord as I should have been. God was using me and he helped me."

For example, she said, if certain medical emergencies arose, instead of acting themselves, the pupil nurse midwives were instructed in their training to send for medical aid.

"Well, I sent for heavenly aid when I was out there," she said. And then she did what she knew she could do to help save lives. Nurse midwifes were not supposed to do breech deliveries, Bloede said, but it had been included in her training in Britain.

"I think because they knew I was going to Sierra Leone," she explained. "I was going to Africa as a missionary and medical aid wasn't always going to be around."

For a time, another nurse midwife was assigned to help her, but that wasn't always the case.

"Breeches seemed to just follow me," she said. "My very, very first delivery in Rotifunk was a breech! And in Jaiama, it always seemed the breech deliveries came on my turn."

The most memorable one for her involved the wife of the main helper, whose baby had a severely difficult face presentation. Bloede was at Rotifunk all by herself.

"There was no way to send for medical aid," she said. "I don't think in all my life I ever prayed or worked harder at the same time for so long. But I tried my level best and I worked and I worked and prayed. And finally, thank God, He helped me flex the head and the baby was born in the usual position. I just know it was the hardest delivery that I ever did."

At Jaiama, with eight African helpers, Bloede was in charge of the dispensary and was the acting doctor. The clinic also had a 12-bed maternity unit. Under her direction, the frequency of pre-natal and well-child clinics held weekly was increased. The need for help grew dramatically during the time she was there, so much so she could barely keep up toward the end. She was thankful an African-trained midwife came to help from Rotifunk.

"When I first got to Jaiama, if they had five deliveries in a month ...," she shrugged. "By the time I left on the 22nd of May 1965, we'd already had some 30 deliveries (that month)."

Toward the end of her time in Jaiama, she hardly slept. On call 24 hours a day, seven days a week, sometimes she didn't have time to eat or sleep.

"When you work like that, you get worn out," she explained. Telling the mission board she could not serve any more time in Sierra Leone, she volunteered to work in one of the missions in the United States. She was assigned for work January 1, 1966, at the Red Bird Mission near the Cumberland Gap in Kentucky. For the next fifteen years, she devoted herself to serving others, helping to increase the services and clinics available just as she had done in Sierra Leone.

Right before her move to Otterbein Lebanon in 1984, Bloede had the opportunity to take a trip back to Sierra Leone. A doctor at the Kissey eye clinic in Freetown pointed out a helper there and said, "Do you remember him?"

Now a grown man, the baby born at the time of the hardest delivery she had ever made was now serving in the eye clinic himself fitting eyeglasses.

On that trip, she and ten others spent one week in Liberia and one week in Sierra Leone.

"I got to see David 'Old Pa' Caulker in Jaiama. At 112 years old, he was the oldest pastor in the whole United Methodist Church. He could talk eleven languages and he came with the very first missionary to Jaiama. At the time they came, they had to carry everything over land," she said.

Bloede said her life's work as a missionary fulfilled her father's dream. He always wished he could go to Sierra Leone and see the work done there, but never was able to make the trip.

"My father was very glad to have me go as a missionary," she explained. "He said when I was born he gave me to God to use as He wanted."

Chapter Twenty-eight

Jane Eberle

"We have different gifts, according to the grace given to each of us. If your gift is ... teaching, then teach...." – Romans 12:6-7

Jane Eberle with kids

Teachers have a tremendous impact on their students morally as well as intellectually. Our children loved Jane as their teacher. We thank God for Jane's willingness to cross oceans to serve Him by teaching others.

Called to Africa

KRMS (Kabala Rupp Memorial School) was the beginning of my teaching years. That was 1959. Nine school years were spent there, and with furloughs, that brought the time up to 1970. During various times, I taught grades 5-8, 4-6 and 7-9.

I didn't think it was a problem that the school generator only ran a few hours in the evenings. Our refrigerator ran on kerosene. Then there was kerosene for the burners for cooking and the wood stove. We also had kerosene lamps.

Our house was well built and had indoor plumbing. Living conditions were great. The pupils and the other staff members lived in the dormitory of the boarding school.

KRMS was a great setting for teaching. It was super to have science class take us on a hike to "middle peak" above Kabala.

The teachers could help with Sunday school classes. Sometimes we could attend the services at the Kuranko-speaking church at the bottom of the hill.

A special happening each year was the all-school program. Thankfully, talented art pupils could make the stage scenery look professional. And the parents were the audience.

I remember one year, for a change, each of my classes went on a short walk – then we ate our picnic supper out on the trail. The fifth graders chose a flat, large, shortish rock to be their tabletop and place to fix their hotdogs. The fifth graders scrambled up the rock, but I, the teacher, couldn't make it until some pulled me from the top and others pushed from the bottom. Thanks, kids.

Eighth grade graduations were what I would call a "fancy time." Decorations were made to follow a certain theme and there was a special dinner for the eighth graders and staff members and a program. The last item of the evening was the presentation of the diplomas.

KRMS was an example of a school-type family with respectful pupils.

During the long school break, I had the opportunity to visit in the homes where other EUB families lived. (Later on the name changed to UM – United Methodist.) I also taught classes at the Sierra Leone Bible School camps at Moyamba and Bo. Shenge, Mt. Leicester and Hamilton Beach were places to spend some holiday time. Thanks to the Glover family who accompanied the KRMS teachers, we got to walk to and climb Bintumani Peak. To have Easter service on Bintumani was very special.

Thanks to God for the Sierra Leone years of my life!

Nigeria

In 1970, I was transferred to Nigeria to teach in the middle grades – various subjects – at Hillcrest School at Jos. There were a lot more groups of people involved in this school. There were day-school pupils as well as boarding school pupils. I had to think about pupil discipline rather than just attending to the preparation of material and teaching.

I was glad that in my reading classes we could work up plays to perform for another class or so.

Being interested in AV (audio-visual) materials, I volunteered to take care of the AV room and equipment.

People came to the school auditorium on Sundays for the church service. There were opportunities to be a part of small group Bible studies during the week.

After two years at Hillcrest School, I was given a short course in bookkeeping from the missionary going on furlough and I became the mission treasurer/

business manager. Duties were: to go to the SUM headquarters and make radio contact with the bush stations, keep the account books, buy supplies requested at radio time, meet the mission airplane and Nigeria Airways when visitors were coming.

Lorry drivers needed to be contacted to come to Sprite Lodge (UMC Jos headquarters) to load up supplies – mainly for the hospital. There were drums of gasoline and kerosene and large boxes that had made their way from Lagos after getting off the ships. Another assignment was to take my turn staying a few hours on certain evenings at Boulder Hill Hostel where Church of the Brethren and UMC high school pupils boarded so the house parents could have a night off.

This sort of a one-year position extended to five and a half years. It was interesting work with lots of variety. Finally, a properly trained accountant came, which was necessary so the work of training a Nigerian church person for the treasurer work could begin.

Then, in 1978, it was time for me to be called out of Africa.

Chapter Twenty-nine

Dean and Ramona Spencer

"As Jesus was walking beside the Sea of Galilee, he saw two brothers, Simon called Peter and his brother Andrew. They were casting a net into the lake, for they were fishermen. 'Come, follow me,' Jesus said, 'and I will send you out to fish for people.'" – Matthew 4:18-19

Dean and Ramona Spencer

Impressive were the many ways in which called missionaries ministered in and through the Church. The Spencers took up the specialty of establishing printing services at the Albert Academy in Freetown. Their work included woodworking and casting. The work of their ministry continued even after their departure from Sierra Leone.

"Tell God Tank-ee"
Albert Academy, Freetown, Sierra Leone, West Africa, 1958-1968

The Spencer family arrived by ship at Freetown on January 14, 1958, having spent three and a half months in England. It was there that Dean attended a training college for teachers of manual arts to learn the British philosophy of education in that field. Albert Academy in Freetown had been asking for a manual arts teacher for some time. Dean had finished an M.S. in Industrial Arts from Oregon State University and was assigned to the school.

Dr. Richard Kelfa-Caulker, principal of Albert Academy, and Don Theuer, the mission's business agent, met us. Dr. Kelfa-Caulker had been overseeing the manual training program for some years. The print shop utilized handset type and supplied churches, church schools and hospitals with their printing needs. The wood shop made furniture – tables, chairs, school desks, church pews, bookcases, closets and burial caskets. Schoolboys worked in both shops, learning elementary skills and earning money for school fees. Upon arrival, we were dismayed to find the type trays falling apart and the print shop's roof falling in.

We were hosted for several days at the mission house where Don and Lilburne Theuer with their daughter, Marilyn, resided. At our first meal – our first experience of eating papaya – one of our co-workers said, "Of course you will be sending your children to the American Mission Boarding School?" That was the wrong thing to say to me at that moment. Our children, Gwen and Tim, had just had their fifth and third birthdays.

We moved into a two-bedroom house about three blocks from the school compound. The main floor was on the second level with a small covered veranda at the front, which almost overhung the busy street. We woke up every morning to the sound of people walking and greeting each other: "Kusho! How de body? Tell God tank-ee," and to the sound of rushing water hitting the bottom of buckets at the standpipe on the corner across from our house.

Some of our neighbors included the missionary chaplain, Vernon Phelps, and his wife, Mary, and their two small boys; the older African couple in the one-room thatched hut across our back fence under a huge palm tree; the small bar on the corner of Circular Road and Berry Street which played a record of "Hang Down Your Head, Tom Dooley" over and over, and the government primary school play yard across the street. With the average temperature at 80 degrees plus and open house windows, each day was full of sounds.

With funds allocated through the Sierra Leone Conference of the Evangelical United Brethren Church, the print shop was enlarged and re-electrified with the help of a Scotsman – employed by the UN to train electricians – and his students. A new four-story classroom building with a chapel/assembly room was also being finished, mostly paid for by British development funds.

Dean taught mechanical drawing and metal work including casting. Among other things, they cast C-clamps, handles on knife blades, school and church bells, and aluminum signs. Francis Kangaju continued to direct the print shop. Richard Carew and Clarence Davies conducted the wood shop program. Mr. Carew, with conference support, attended Stout State in Wisconsin for a time for further training.

In 1961, just after independence (and the Queen's visit) Stan and Helen Trebes, printers from San Diego, came to oversee and upgrade the printing program. They had obtained a linotype from England. Eventually, the manual arts program was upgraded so that credits could be earned and applied to the engineering program at the University College of Sierra Leone at Fourah Bay.

Teachers at the school, in addition to up to six missionaries that came and went, included U.S. Peace Corps and Great Britain and Canadian-equivalent Peace Corps program volunteers. There were also others from Great Britain, Jamaica, and India, as well as other local West African countries. When we arrived in 1958, 250 boys attended Albert Academy, including Muslim students. When we left in 1968, 750 boys and a few girls attended. There were not enough teachers to accommodate the number of qualified students who wished to continue their education.

Sometimes, a daughter of the Kelfa-Caulkers, Velma, who was about eight would visit and read children's books to the students, including Beatrix Potter's and Noddy books. Very few children's books written by African authors were available in the late 1950s. Velma later told me that the reason she became an English teacher was because of those books.

After being principal of Albert Academy for twenty years, Dr. Richard Kelfa-Caulker became the Sierra Leone high commissioner to Britain, and then at independence in 1961, he became the Sierra Leone ambassador to Britain, the Sierra Leone ambassador to the U.S., and later the Sierra Leone ambassador to the UN. Les Shirley (with his wife, Grace) was the interim principal until Max Bailor, Jr., became principal.

Others who were co-workers during our time in Freetown were Vivian Olson, in the Freetown office; Hank (Gene) Baldwin, business agent, and wife, Jean, and children; Rev. Howard Mueller, chaplain at Albert Academy, and wife, Mary, and their two little girls; and Rev. Russell and Nellie Birdsell and daughter, Sharon, of the United Brethren Mission who were neighbors and good friends.

Most of the time we attended church at King Memorial EUB where Dr. S. M. Renner was pastor. Daniel Fungbahun from Taiama was ready for secondary school when we arrived in 1958. Lois Olsen, the nurse at Taiama, recommended him to us, as he needed to work to pay his school fees. He was a fine young man. After finishing at the Academy, he went on to a two-year agricultural school upcountry, and then received a conference scholarship to attend the University of Illinois around 1970. He eventually became an assistant to the minister of agriculture in the Sierra Leone government (the government collapsed during the civil war). As of 2003, it was reported that he worked for the Department of Education of the United Methodist Church in the Bo region of Sierra Leone.

The missionary chaplain, Vernon Phelps, and his wife, Mary, were teaching at Albert Academy when we arrived. Vernon, with schoolboys, would go out into the community around the school on Sunday mornings and gather up to

100 children for Sunday school in the chapel. Ramona would meet with several schoolboys during the week to go over lesson material. The boys did the actual teaching in Krio.

One Christmas, many of the children and Academy boys put on a program in the new chapel of the Christmas story that had been written by Esther Megill. The chapel had open jalousie windows on both sides and a platform at one end. The school choir marched around the outside with candles singing carols including one in Calypso, "Christmas don cam and we no die-o." Mary Phelps directed the children's choir, each child dressed in white surplices and wearing silver tinsel halos. At the side of the stage, a Krio mother told the story to her children, as other Academy boys presented a pantomime including shepherds in the fields, no room at the inn, the star, the manger scene and "We Three Kings of Orient Are." Children and their parents of the community filled the chapel. I remember it as a glorious, almost magical evening. The Academy boys were very good actors.

Vacationing on the "Bumpe Evangel"

Dean built a river boat for the Rotifunk Hospital staff to use on the Bumpe River that was about 58 miles upcountry from Freetown. During a vacation time when our kids were home from boarding school, we decided to use the boat for a trip to Shenge down the coast to the south. Dean and Jim McQuiston had once made the trip from Lumley Beach near Freetown in a smaller boat. Shenge is the place where the EUB mission was first started. (When we decided to take our children, Gwen and Tim, on a river and ocean trip, no one advised us against it or seemed to question the wisdom of it. Looking back, I think I would never have attempted such a thing again.)

At Rotifunk, a lot of people attended the dedication ceremony of the boat before we left. It was late, about 2:30 or 3:00 in the afternoon. The boat, called "The Bumpe Evangel," had a roof over it, was about 16' long with a 10-horse motor. And, of course, it carried extra fuel, oars, life jackets, water, food, flashlights and many other items. The temperature that day was in the mid 80s. The sun was bright.

About 7:00 p.m., it was twilight and we had reached the mouth of the river with the tide coming in. It got dark quickly as it always does near the equator. There was no moon. It was hard to keep our orientation. There were fish traps – chicken wire strung on poles on and near the beach – and the tide covered them up. We got inside of one and could not find our way out. Finally, we packed down the top of the chicken wire fence, lifted the motor and went over the top.

Going in a southerly direction, we could not tell how far we were from the shore – whether the shadows were from tall trees and we were far out, or if they were from short bushes and we were close to shore. A fisherman in a dugout canoe with a lantern was the only reference point we had. The children went to sleep in the bottom of the boat. My heart was beating fast and I was very scared. Dean just thought it was a great adventure and was totally confidant. I held the flashlight at the front of the boat. Large rocks protruded from the water. Fluorescent light shined in the waves at the prow. We managed to miss all the rocks.

The Yawri Bay shoreline is shaped like a large crescent. We were heading for a gap between Plantain Island, about a mile offshore, and the beach at Shenge. A slightly lighter area showed up on the left – a gap in the tree line. Dean thought at first it was where we wanted to go, but then realized it was the mouth of another river emptying into Yawri Bay. We had quite a bit further to go.

Finally, the treeless gap between the island and the mainland showed up. We went towards the beach, pulled the boat up onto the sand, woke up the kids and started the climb up the bank toward the rest house. It was 10:30 p.m.

A watchman slept under the old house (which was built up off the ground). He did not know we were coming, was frightened and would not come out. We did not have a key and had to break in the door. We had brought a small pressure stove, and with water and dry milk, made cocoa. By the time we had shaken the dust from the mosquito nets, made beds, brought everything from the boat and climbed into bed, it was past midnight.

During our time there, we called on the Paramount Chief, Madam Honoria Bailor-Caulker, the wife of Max Bailor, Sr., the director of the hundred or so West Africa Mission (EUB) primary schools in the country. His first wife had died, leaving several children, one of whom – Max Bailor, Jr. – eventually became principal of Albert Academy. Chief Honoria, tall, regal and most gracious, invited us to a thatch-roofed shim beck on the beach. Two men in livery approached with machetes and a basket of husked coconuts, saluted, clicked their heels, then chopped off the tops of the jelly coconuts and handed them to us to drink the milk.

We later made a boat trip to Plantain Island a mile off shore. It was a beautiful sunny day. The water was very clear. We visited the ruins of slave pens on a small peninsula where the ocean was about to cut through. This is one of the places where slaver John Newton visited. He eventually wrote the words to *Amazing Grace*.

One day, Dean went hunting for monkeys that were getting into the orange trees with some schoolboys and local men. Also, they caught moray eels, which somebody ate.

After several days, we packed up, got back into the boat, back across the bay up the river to Rotifunk. We saw crocodiles sunning on the bank.

This was the same river in which Rev. Ira E. Albert drowned. There were those who wished to commemorate him and his service by building a school around 1904. Because of this and the work of many people since, some 2,000 students attend Albert Academy today. There are now 300 United Methodist primary schools and thirty secondary schools in Sierra Leone.

We have been – and continue to be – greatly blessed because of our experiences and friendships. We are grateful to the churches and people who supported us. We thank God for the privilege of being part of the great host that worked together for His kingdom, which continues to grow.

Bishop Gaspar Joao Domingos, pg. 19

Bishop Jose Quipungo, pg. 19

Bishop Katembo Kainda, pg. 22

Bishop Ntambo N'kulu Ntanda, pg. 22

Bishop David Kakeumba Yemba, pg. 22

Bishop Benjamin Boni, pg. 29

Bishop John G. Innis, pg. 33

Bishop Eben Nhiwatiwa, pg. 37 and 63

Bishop Joaquina Filipe Nhanala, pg. 39

Interim Bishop Arthur Kulah, pg. 45

Bishop John Yambasu, pg. 53

Bishop Daniel Wandabula, pg. 61

Dr. Thomas Kemper, pg. 69

Dr. Cherian Thomas, pg. 74

Dr. Caroline W. Njuki, pg. 77

Rev. Clyde and Gladys Galow, pg. 79

Rev. Joe and Carolyn Wagner, pg. 86

Dr. Gideon A. Avar, pg. 91

Lois Olsen, pg. 93

Donald and Lilburne Theuer, pg. 99

Dr. Donald Rudy, pg. 102

Gertrude Bloede, pg. 104

Jane Eberle with kids, pg. 108

Dean and Ramona Spencer, pg. 111

Roger and Sylvia Burtner, pg. 117

Hank and Jean Baldwin, pg. 121

Billie LaBumbard, pg. 125

Virginia Pickarts, pg. 127

Rev. Donald and Helen Pletsch, pg. 131

Rev. Alfred A. N. Karimu, pg. 134

Rev. Alice Fitzjohn, pg. 136

Dr. John Buchan, pg. 152

Roger and Melanie Reiners, pg. 155

Dr. Lowell Gess and Vivian Olson, pg. 157

Dr. Emmanuel and Florence Mefor, pg. 160

Letticia Williams, pg. 168

Esther Megill, pg. 170

Rev. Angie Myles, pg. 173

Ruth Gess and Rev. Doris Caulker, pg. 176

Bishop Joseph Humper, pg. 178

Anna and Virginia Mariama Morford, pg. 186

Dr. John Karefa-Smart and Dr. Lowell Gess, pg. 191

Rev. Katherine Horn, pg. 194

Rev. Etta Nicol, pg. 202

Rev. David H. Caulker, pg. 204

Rev. Vernon and Mary Phelps, pg. 209

Rev. Dr. Crispin and Teresa Renner, pg. 206

Dr. Allen Foster, pg. 212

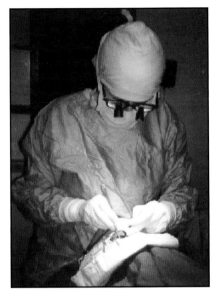

Dr. Marilyn Scudder, pg. 214

Dr. Jeanette Troup, pg. 216

Billy Graham, pg. 219

Dr. James and Martha Foulkes, pg. 222

Dr. Subramaniam (Kiru) and Raji Kirupananthan, pg. 228

Dr. Gizella Baghy, pg. 230

Dr. Istvan Patkai, pg. 234

Arrival in Africa, pg. 244

Our family photo, pg. 274

Chapter Thirty

Roger and Sylvia Burtner

"Did not the Book you brought teach 'thou shalt not kill'? And further, that all of us are Brothers, one Family under one Father?"

Roger and Sylvia Burtner

Roger Burtner has lived an unpretentious Christian life. He refrained from being set apart by not wearing a robe when preaching or leading worship, and refused to be addressed as "Reverend." His uniform as a CROP/CWS Regional Director was a denim blazer and denim trousers – but with a white shirt and tie to "bridge the troubled waters." He and his wife, Sylvia, did and continue to do, all that is possible to fight against unbelief, poverty, disease, malnutrition, illiteracy and hunger.

Mai Gari and the Fleeing Ibo

On the night that I met him, it was dark – but the days were dark, too, in the mid to late 1960s. Nigeria was being torn asunder by violence.

Mai Gari was holding up a lantern on that June night of 1966. He was welcoming us back, showing us the compound, which was to be our home for the

117

next three years. Those years were to redefine our understanding of life and death, commitment and service. Those were the years in which we learned much about war and refugees, fear and courage.

Mai Gari taught us how much "risk" can mean. He brought us that message in his humble, effective way – he lived it!

Arrival

We had traveled a long, long way on that sunny day in June, and so had our new friend and brother in Christ, Mai Gari. So had Nigeria! It had been a week of fateful-hateful days during which the flower of sacrificial love had blossomed here and there by God's grace.

Our journey had begun at Lankoviri where Tim and John (our junior high-aged sons) and I had picked up our International Scout, which had rested on concrete blocks for our furlough year. We had traveled about 180 miles, across gravel roads between Lankoviri and Pero ("Filliya" on the Exxon map). Ninety miles up the road we stopped in Numan to purchase fifty gallons of petrol.

Some distance out of Numan, we discovered the drum was leaking so Tim and John took turns holding a finger over the hole until, hours later, we pulled into the Sudan Interior Mission Station at Kaltungo. We stopped there to shift the petrol to a sound drum if possible. Our friend, Tom Sinn, a teacher on the secondary school staff, was there to help us.

I found Tom by his dining room table, sitting and staring as though in a trance.

"Tom! What's wrong?" I cried out.

"Roger! Are you not aware? They are killing Ibo people everywhere!"

"No! Oh, no! We have been on the road all day and did not know!" I replied, remembering, very painfully, the *New York Times*' headline: "Civil Disturbances Shake Nigerian Cities." This I had read on the Pan Am jet as we left JFK Airport just the day before.

Tom continued, "I watched five Ibo students mercilessly beaten and killed here on our compound yesterday. The mission flew Doris and our kids out this morning, along with all the women and kids. These are bad days, Roger, very bad days!"

It was hard to comprehend, even that close to the situation, seeing terror etched on Tom's troubled brow. We were to more fully understand that following October 1st. At that time, Sylvia and I were in Kano where the riots claimed the lives of thousands of Iboes. They were being killed in retaliation by Hausas and Fulanis avenging the death of Sir Ahmadu Bello and other high-level northern Nigerians who had been killed by power-seeking Ibo army officers earlier that year. It was especially hard to accept the fact that Christian soldiers trained at Sandhurst in so-called "civilized" England had killed these Muslim leaders.

Night was coming rapidly as it does in the tropics, and early as it does, where days and nights are of equal length all year around. Tom's new drum held the petrol securely as we applied our energies to the final thirty miles of our trip. It would take two hours to get to Pero, which we hoped would be home for the next three years. Many thoughts churned in our heads and hearts while the petrol sloshed continually. We traveled sometimes at five miles per hour, in low range, sometimes fifteen, and occasionally for a moment up to twenty-five. Finally, we were there!

Mai Gari

"Sannu da Zuwa! (Greetings upon your coming!)," a little man with a lantern called out. That night I met Mai Gari, our mission station guard.

About a year later, he trusted me enough as pastor and friend to tell me the following experience that had been his on the day we had met:

There had only been three Ibos in Pero, all of whom were well known and all reasonably appreciated. On the day of the riots, however, all three had been hustled to the village market area and had been abused. Striped of their clothes, one had been beaten to death by the angry crowd.

Suddenly, the other two burst free from their captors! One fled to the hills east of Pero; the other ran at a frantic pace through the village and up the road to the mission compound.

"Mai Gari! Mai Gari!" he had cried. "Will you not help me?!"

It was a momentous request. Coming up the hill was the angry mob!

"Quickly! Into my house!" I had cried. And within moments, the mob was upon me!

"Mai Gari! Where is he? The dirty Ibo?" (They were cursing him in Hausa.)

"Would I not tell you if I only knew?"

"Mai Gari! Does he hide within your home?" they asked.

"Am I so foolish as to hide the hated Ibo in times like these?" I had asked. With that, the crowd moved on, looking frantically for the Ibo who was indeed hiding in my house! That night, I gave him my own robe to dress

him as a man of the north, and the old carpenter fled on foot. He began the 300-mile journey to the south, to the tribal lands of his fathers called Biafra.

As Mai Gari ended his story, we stood for a moment in awesome silence. Then I asked him, "Why? Why would you take such a chance? Why risk your own life and the lives of Dija and your children? Mai Gari, that mob might have killed you, too!"

Mai Gari, who was a quiet man, thought for a moment and said, "Did not the Book you brought teach 'thou shalt not kill'? And further, that all of us are Brothers, one Family under one Father?"

This answer made me quiet.

How much, I wonder, will I risk?

Chapter Thirty-one

Liston E. (Hank) and Louise Jean Baldwin

"Lord, please let Christ's love for these people be evident through my actions of this day."

Hank and Jean Baldwin

Hank and Jean made a tremendous impact on the life and growth of the Christian Church in West Africa with their varied, essential and anointed skills. Most of all, they lived and worked to share the riches of Jesus Christ and the bountiful new life in Him.

Miracles

"The Lord works in mysterious ways." I believe that one could safely change that to, "The Lord works in miraculous ways," or so it seems in our case. Picture a young man in rural Ohio with a yen to help black people although not a single one lived in his county, and a young lady in urban New Jersey who wanted to be a missionary nurse to Alaska from the moment she was saved. Getting them to be missionaries together in Africa is a story of miracles that only the Lord could manage. And that's not all. They were just two of a flood of post-World War II missionaries with a vision of bringing Christ and the new life that Christ represents to Africa. I am sure that each of those missionaries can attest to the miracles that were needed to make them ready and to get them to that place of service.

Now back to our miracle: The boy from Ohio met the New Jersey girl when her parents moved to Ohio. They began seeing each other as she entered a nursing program and he worked in a factory as an engineer. Their relationship developed into love and they wondered how they could marry and still work toward their individual goals of service. They decided to trust the Lord to lead them and they married.

Then other miracles began to happen. Jean met a nurse while training at Cincinnati General Hospital who was a friend of retired EUB Sierra Leone missionary, Dr. Schutz. She arranged for us to have an interview with him. He assured us that there was a need for engineers in the mission work in Sierra Leone and that a nurse-engineer combination could be very useful and he arranged an interview with EUB Board of Missions Director, Dr. Heinmiller in Dayton, Ohio.

Another miracle: Dr. Heinmiller said "Yes, indeed there was a need for engineers and nurses in Africa but the priority at the moment was not in Sierra Leone but in Nigeria." He also said that our Baptist background would be acceptable and he agreed to recommend us to the Board of Missions. Another miracle: we were accepted with the condition that Jean successfully pass the Nursing State Board Exam and then go to Minneapolis for a special course in anesthesia. She passed and on December 5, 1952, we left Ohio for Bambur, Nigeria.

In England, we caught up with Dr. Lowell Gess, the surgeon and director of the new Guinter Memorial Hospital in Bambur. Together with his family, we traveled to Lagos, Nigeria, and finally, in the first days of 1953, to Bambur and our new life in the mission service. The next thirty months were filled with successes and failures, exhilaration and despondency, and victory and defeat as we labored there with the others in conditions and cultures that were completely foreign to us in an effort to be a witness there for Christ.

"Actions speak louder than words." This is the axiom that motivates many of the missionaries working in the health field in foreign lands. The very basis for providing health services in the mission field is the Christian ethic of helping the sick and the poor. For newcomers like ourselves, with little knowledge of the culture and language of the area, our main avenue of witness was by our everyday work among the patients in the hospital and the people of the neighboring villages. We hoped they could see the love of Christ in our lives and actions.

Our major activities were as follows: Jean would go to the hospital first thing in the morning to find a line of patients already waiting. Some were holdovers from previous days, while others were new, having arrived on foot in the night from villages as much as thirty or mores miles away. She would perform the initial screening, treating the minor cases while passing the more serious ones on to the doctor on duty. This would usually occupy most of the morning. After that, she would give the anesthesia for the surgeries that were scheduled by the doctor. In the late afternoon she would return to the hospital for rounds. She would also take her turn at being on call at nights.

My job was to try to keep water and electricity available for the compound and to do minor construction and repair on the grounds. I was also responsible for keeping the mission books.

Our daily prayer was, "Lord, please let Christ's love for these people be evident through my actions of this day."

One of our disappointments on the field was that we were not blessed with a child of our own. It became evident that we would have to adopt children in order to make our family complete, so when our term was up we left the mission field with the intent to pursue that purpose at home in the States. We settled in Seattle where I pursued a business degree at the University of Washington and Jean gave anesthesia in an oral surgeon's practice. Our daughter was adopted there. After graduation we moved to Rochester, New York, where I was employed as an administrator with the DuPont Co.

More miracles happened. We adopted a baby boy and then two years later another. Then it was Dr. Heinmiller calling again. We need you and your wife in Sierra Leone, will you go? How could we say "no"?

I left my job and we moved to Dayton where I enrolled in a couple of courses at the Bonebrake Seminary as we prepared for our new assignment. I would be the business agent for the Sierra Leone Mission and we would live in Freetown. My main responsibility was to prepare the local EUB conference leaders to administer the conference's portion of the mission annual budget. The mission board felt that it was time, after more than a hundred years, for the local conference to administer its own budget and business affairs. I was to be the last fulltime missionary business agent in Sierra Leone. In addition to her family responsibilities, Jean was to be available to give anesthesia at the Rotifunk Hospital when needed. We arrived in Freetown on June 5, 1962, with our three children aged six through one.

Part of my duties was to meet new and returning missionaries and help them get their luggage through customs and secure the supplies they needed as they went to their stations up country. Not long after we arrived, who should show up but Dr. Gess and his family returning to Sierra Leone for eye service at Taiama. (Our families and two or three other missionaries were privileged to have worked in both EUB African mission fields.)

This situation was so very different from our experience in Nigeria. First of all, we had a family this time. We lived in a modern house in the capital city and had most of the normal conveniences that this type of location provides. Secondly, we were working with Sierra Leonians who had the benefits of over a hundred years of missionary presence in their country. The church, schools and medical works had long been established and the fruits of these labors were visible in the many Christians there. Many of the country's leaders had been educated in mission schools and received advanced education in the U.S. and/or Britain. This applied to the church leaders as well, and they brought their energy and convictions to the work of developing the Christian Church in their country. Thirdly, the country had just recently received its independence from Great Britain and there was enthusiasm and hope for the future in the air.

We were different, too. We were older and the intervening years had helped us be more patient and accommodating as we worked with our colleagues both white and black. During our term, we had to experience what so many of our colleagues in the mission work go through when they have to send their young school age children to a mission boarding school at a location distant from their homes.

One of the highlights of my work during the term was working with Sierra Leonian leaders like Bishop Carew, Dr. Max Bailor, and my favorite of all, Dr. Pa Renner, pastor of the Freetown EUB Church. Jean, besides her occasional trips to the Rotifunk hospital to give anesthesia, especially enjoyed working with the Women's Missionary Society of the Freetown Church. One of the things our children remember most about our stay there was the steaming dish of jollof rice that Mrs. Renner occasionally sent home with us after Sunday service.

Our term ended all too soon and we had to make plans for our family and ourselves. We decided that we would like to settle down in one place so as to give our children a stable environment for growth and education. For ourselves, we decided to work toward careers in college teaching. We earned the graduate degrees required and began our new professions at the University of West Florida in Pensacola, Florida, in 1969. We retired in 1994. Our children presented us with six grandchildren and the oldest of these has given us two great-grandchildren.

We have enjoyed going to the reunions of both the Nigerian and Sierra Leone Mission workers and renewing, once again, be it just for a few days, the comradeship we had with our fellow workers in Africa all those many years ago.

Chapter Thirty-two

Billie LaBumbard

"So send I you to bind the bruised and broken, O'er wand'ring souls to work, to weep, to wake, To bear the burdens of a world aweary – So send I you to suffer for My sake." – Margaret Clarkson, 1954

Billie LaBumbard

Billie LaBumbard ministered in Nigeria from 1970 to 1974. The years following were spent in mission programs with the Wisconsin Conference of the United Methodist Church. She also has been engaged in world mission trips.

So Send I You

My preparation for Nigeria began at Stony Point, New York. I then went to England to study Hausa at the School of African and Oriental Studies in London. Second semester, I traveled to Liverpool for a course in tropical medicine.

In the spring of 1971, I traveled to Bambur, Nigeria. I lived in a duplex near the Guinter Memorial Hospital (GMH) with a German laboratory technician named Ulrike Morgan. In the first year, I traveled the area around GMH with Dr. Joyce Matthiesen to survey the life, morbidity and mortality of the residents. I worked with the United Methodist Women.

I was considered a "rebel" missionary because I went to all tribal dances and ceremonies to learn the customs and the language. I helped supervise the village clinics, counting medicines to prevent "loss." I also taught the community health section of the Dispenser's training. I served as the interim Director of Nursing at GMH while the German director was on leave. We had a war on troublesome insects.

In my final year in Nigeria, 1973-1974, I organized and taught women. I trained trainees for short courses covering topics such as Bible stories, how to make water straining bags, hand sewing, disease prevention (especially malaria), nutrition and latrine preparation and use. Each participant, Christian or Muslim, was to teach three people in her village what she had learned. A graduation certificate was given upon completion.

My years in Nigeria were a blessing to me and I hope to others. They set the pattern for my life in mission work that continues today.

Chapter Thirty-three

Virginia Pickarts

"Then I asked, 'When are you going to become a Christian?' 'Now!' she said."

Virginia Pickarts

Students remember the names of favorite teachers all their lives. As a teacher at Harford School for Girls in Moyamba for forty-one years (the longest teaching commitment of any UMC missionary in Sierra Leone), Virginia is remembered by thousands in Sierra Leone. Her serious commitment to the Lord Jesus Christ did not go unnoticed. Thanks to Virginia's faithful service, many outstanding Christian women – in all walks of life – became leaders in Sierra Leone.

Girls of Harford School

I finished Westmar College with a B.A. degree in 1949. The following September, I was on my way to London with seven other missionaries. Five of us were teachers trying to learn about the British educational system since we would be teaching in British colonies – three of us in Nigeria and two in Sierra Leone. I was sent to Harford School for girls in Moyamba, Sierra Leone. At that time, the school was in the process of becoming the only girl's secondary school (high school) in the interior of the country. As the elementary classes were dropped, the secondary classes were added.

Harford School was and is an abounding school. Students come from all over the country, and even from surrounding countries. Being in a British colony, English was taught – first in the elementary grades and on into high school.

Because of the reputation of the school, many Muslim as well as Christian parents sent their daughters there.

Humu, Mabinty and Iye

It was an ordinary afternoon after school was out for the day. Eight-year-old Humu (she was not attending school) came to the house to sell peanuts (called "ground nuts"), which her mother had roasted. She was very alert and cheerful. When we asked by she was not in school, she said she couldn't go because of her mother's "foot" leg. Her mother had had an ulcer – which hadn't healed – so her leg had been amputated below the knee. We wondered if Humu would be allowed to go to school if her fees were paid for her. So, with interpretation in the main language of Mendi and the mother's language of Temne and mine of English, we talked to the mother, as she was the head of this extended family. Her husband – and the children's father – was deceased.

At first, mother Iye said she needed Humu – but she would allow her six-year-old daughter, Mabinty, to go. Then we asked if both girls could come, with the understanding they could sell after school. Finally, Iye agreed, but they were not to become Christians, as their late father had been a Muslim.

We helped to tutor Humu and she soon was in her rightful class. Both Humu and Mabinty were doing well in school.

Harford School for Girls was primarily a boarding school; as such, those students had a strong Christian atmosphere around them. They had rising bell, prayers and chapel services before attending classes. For evening vespers and Wednesday night services, they attended the church that was near the campus. They also attended Sunday services, which were open to all. In addition to all of that, Bible knowledge was part of the curriculum. (As you can see, most of the students could fairly easily accept Christ as their Savior by the time they left school.)

Seeing how her daughters were progressing in school, Iye finally gave her consent to their becoming Christians. She even allowed some of the students and me to hold Christian services on her large veranda each week. Iye and I became friends! Even with her handicap, she would walk a quarter of a mile to visit me. Sometimes, she would bring some of the children from her extended family. One weekend, she and some of the children came and we visited, drinking an orange drink made from oranges from our orange tree and eating cookies.

That day, I asked her, "Iye, what have the Muslims done for you?"

"Nothing," she said.

"What have the Christians done for you?"

She began to name quite a few children who went to school because they had Christian scholarships from the churches in the U.S.

Then I asked, "When are you going to become a Christian?"

"Now!" she said. That took me by surprise; it had been seventeen years of hearing about Christ before she accepted Him.

In the Bible, Paul helped the Philippians jailor and his household to accept Christ. Not only did Iye accept Christ, her sister, mother and some of the children were baptized.

Some years later, Iye's mother – "Mama Fatu" – died. We Christians thought she should have a Christian burial. The men of the family who were Muslim disagreed. The day of the burial, they came to the house with their drums. They did, however, allow the Christians to sing and pray in the house where her body was lying. We eventually had to leave, but I sat on the veranda and wiped a tear from my eye.

Some weeks later, Pa Sulley sent me a letter. In it, he said he saw how I loved them, for I had a tear in my eye. Because of that, he and his son were going to become Christians. I left Sierra Leone after that, but I am told he continued in his Christian faith.

Namisa

Namisa was in eighth grade. She was from a Muslim background, but because the school had such a good reputation, her parents wanted her to attend there.

Namisa became sick and had to be admitted in our local hospital. Her parents were notified and a representative from the family came to take her home. She died on the way. We feared the family would blame us for her death.

Her father came to the school to thank us for the way we had taught Namisa. Whenever she went home for the holidays, she was helpful, kind and assisted with caring for the younger children. She always carried a little black book with her. Her father did not know what it was, but Namisa had liked it. They buried the book with her. Her "little black book" was her Bible.

Because the school had helped Namisa so much, instead of blaming the school for Namisa's death, her father wanted to send her sister, Martha, to school.

Zainab

Zainab was from a Muslim family. Her parents wanted her to have a good education, so they sent her to a boarding school. She was not to sing Christian songs or say Christian prayers.

The longer Zainab was at Harford School, the harder it became for her to keep silent when others were singing. Finally, she thought she had the answer. She would be a Christian at school but a Muslim at home. That way her father would not know what she was doing. She was never really happy.

One day, when she was at home during her vacation, the local church bell was ringing and she went to church. Her father discovered what she had done after she came home and threw her out of the house.

She came back to school and told the principal she could not attend. Her father had disowned her and she had no school fees. The principal showed her a letter she had just received. The American lady who sent it said, "I don't know why I feel compelled to write and send you this check." Zainab looked at the letter and check – it was the exact amount for the school fees. Now Zainab could believe the Bible, which said "Before they call I will answer."

After some time, she was allowed to return home. One Sunday, when the church bell rang and Zainab was still sleeping, her father sent one of the children to waken her so she wouldn't be late for church.

Chapter Thirty-four

Rev. Donald and Helen Pletsch

"Why did you come to me?" I asked. He replied, "You are the only one who cares."

Rev. Donald and Helen Pletsch

Ruth and I were happy to be a part of Helen and Don's life in Sierra Leone by assisting as a doctor and nurse as their family "increased in number." Helen, as a registered nurse, proved to be the perfect patient.

"I Hear You Are Going to Africa"

A beautiful young woman, who later became my wife, had made a commitment to Jesus Christ to become a missionary nurse. I was attending Agricultural College where my professor of crop science was talking about world hunger. He turned to the class and said, "You guys could do something about that." It took more time to convince Helen to marry me than it took both of us to decide to apply to become missionaries.

"I hear you are going to Africa." Those words, at a district youth gathering, were how we learned about our missionary appointment. I went home after the meeting and told Helen that she should pack our suitcases. So began the most incredible experience of our lives. Carolyn, our eldest went with us, much to her grandparents chagrin, and Sue and Steve were born while we were there.

Agricultural and Community Development was the title under which we served. We arrived in Sierra Leone in 1962 to find that Les and Winnie Bradford had blazed a well-marked path, but were also a tough act to follow. Les and Winnie's sense of humor carried us through more than one rough patch. Yonibana, in Temne territory, was our place of residence.

During one of our early years, the Conference was held in King Memorial Church. I was sitting toward the back of the church next to the aisle. The pastors processed and as Dr. S. M. Renner passed me, he whispered, "How is the new pastor of Yonibana circuit?" God seems to break news to me in strange ways! The headmasters, the local evangelists, the interpreters and the dedicated lay people made possible a powerful Christian witness in the many villages of the area. J. F. Tholley, M. B. Kamara are only two of the many co-workers who lived their Christian faith in ways that I hadn't experienced up to that time.

Communion services in Makundu, or in another village, at 6:00 a.m. on Sunday morning were meaningful times of worship. I was always impressed by the number of people who would come to those early services and not complain about the time of worship.

One Sunday evening, in Rochen Kamandao, we celebrated the completion of the "Lord's Portion Project." We sang hymns by lantern light as one after another of the farmers came forward with their offerings. One man in particular came forward and, Leone after Leone, made his offering. As I recall, it was about fifteen Leones in total. His offering reminded me of the widow's offering who gave all she had. His generosity has been a guide for me from that moment on.

A number of projects deserve to be mentioned in the agricultural and community development area. They include Helen's backdoor clinic for women and children; the growing of rabbits and the raising of chickens; the introduction of chemical fertilizers; the planting of oil palms and fruit trees; the distribution of improved varieties of rice; the digging of wells; the development of small pineapple plantations and a short-lived experiment of exporting pineapples to England. Many, if not all, of the projects were in response to the needs identified by the communities in which we worked. Helen's medical work was an opportunity to share Christ's love through the treatment of malaria, ulcers and other physical needs.

Fertilizer usage in our area of Temne country went from five hundred pounds to over five tons and became known as "powerful medicine." The fertilizer demonstration plots helped convince the farmers that fertilizer more than paid its way in an increased yield of rice. Fertilizers, along with improved varieties of rice, in some cases increased harvests enough to reduce, or eliminate, hunger in many households. The 4H rice clubs also helped promote the growing of improved varieties of rice. A different twist on these clubs was that the fathers of the children also wanted to be members.

While building schools and church renovation were not in our job description, they became part of the job because that was a need many communities identified for their village. The preaching of the gospel by pastors, missionaries and lay people demonstrated their strong faith in Jesus Christ. Rev. Clyde Galow would preach at every opportunity. He developed a strong evangelistic outreach in the Yonibana secondary school and surrounding villages during our time there. Dr. S. M. Renner preached from the Paramount Chief's veranda one night, stating that the Christian faith was different from the Muslim faith because of Jesus Christ, God's Son. Lay people who would ride for miles on the back of a motorcycle to preach in villages where there was little, if any, Christian witness, made a strong impact on the people and on me.

I recall the pastors' retreats where pastors and missionaries met together, shared in the leadership and in breaking bread together. For me, it was an opportunity to learn and grow in my relationship with Christ.

One day, I was under my Volkswagon van, attempting a necessary repair when I heard and then saw a pair of sandals close by. I let on that I didn't hear his greeting. However, he wouldn't go away. I finally gave up, crawled out from under the van and asked the man what he wanted. He said that he wanted me to build a school in his village. I said that I hadn't come to Sierra Leone to build schools and asked him if he had talked to the pastor. The man said that the pastor couldn't help him. I then suggested that he go to the chief. He said that the chief couldn't help him. "Why did you come to me?" I asked. He replied, "You are the only one who cares." It is my prayer that the man's visit was not in vain.

Two boys, in particular, spent a lot of time in our home. Sahid A. Konteh became a plumber and is very active in Boughman Memorial United Methodist Church in Freetown. Momodu Kamara now lives in Cedar Rapids, Iowa, with his family and is active as a lay preacher in the local United Methodist churches. We appreciate them both and their commitment to Christ, and are grateful for the contributions they have made to our lives.

In response to the question, "What did you do over there?" while on deputation, I responded by saying that we tried to do what the questioner would want to do if he or she was there. In my best moments I might have added that we tried to do what Christ wanted us to do!

A gradual realization that a full stomach was important, but not sufficient for a fulfilled life, became a call to preach the gospel of Jesus Christ as an ordained pastor. To each of the missionary family members with whom we worked, we owe a tremendous debt of gratitude, for those relationships continue to this day. Paul, in writing to the Christians in Philippi, says, "Now unto God our Father, be glory forever and ever." (Philippians 4:20 LAB)

Chapter Thirty-five

Rev. Alfred A. N. Karimu

"Jesus replied, 'Let us go somewhere else – to the nearby villages – so I can preach there also. That is why I have come.'" – Mark 1:38

Rev. Alfred A. N. Karimu

The Rev. Alfred A. N. Karimu is a distinguished leading pastor and official in the Sierra Leone Conference, United Methodist Church. He recently authored a book, The United Methodist Church in Sierra Leone: 1900-2010, *with special reference to education and culture. It is fascinating reading. About his early life, he writes the following essay:*

For many years now I have been meandering through the Christian ladder, (the ladder of faith). I find it somehow difficult to narrate the whole story of my Christian life because of the number of years involved and the way I have been able to reach where I am now in my faith in Christ Jesus our Lord.

As a little boy, I attended church services together with my grandmother in the early 1950s. An evangelist, whose name I cannot remember now, used to go to our village once every month. We sat under a hut covered with thatch. We sang choruses in Mende, and a passage was read to us from the Holy Bible.

I never understood some of the deeper meanings of the Bible. One thing we were taught was that Jesus Christ was the Son of God and that He died for our sins – but He rose again from the dead by the power of God. When we were asked if any of us would have offered himself/herself for the sin of another person outside himself /herself, we said no. That showed the magnitude of love Christ had for us.

For some years, I did not know the name of my religion, i.e. "Christianity," for those formative years I understood my religion as the "Church." It was then I came to know that the church was the place of worship for Christians. Some of my contemporaries, together with whom I attended church later, went to other faith religions.

In the town, we went to church every Sunday as opposed to once every month. We learned a number of Bible studies and Bible verses. Some of these verses were learned by rote. Our missionary friends witnessed to us from time to time and they also extended kindness to us.

By and large, I came to know Jesus more through the lessons I learned in Sunday School. I made sure that I attended regularly and punctually. Later, as I advanced in education, I became a Sunday school teacher and a Sunday school superintendent.

I am grateful to the following people for helping me in my Christian journey: Mr. and Mrs. P. J. B. Baimba of Daru in the Eastern Province, Mr. Tom Patton who was my principal, Pa Moinama Johnson, the late Philip Johnson and Mr. S. B. Johnson, Rev. Dr. Billy Simbo and a host of others. The Christian journey is best enjoyed in companionship with other believers.

Chapter Thirty-six

Rev. Alice Fitzjohn

"I remain grateful to God Almighty for what He has done in my life and has allowed me to use the talents He's given to make a difference. Indeed, nothing happens by chance. God is Supreme. He ordained what should be. May God's name be glorified!"

Rev. Alice Fitzjohn

Rev. "Alice" Fitzjohn's contribution contains such a wealth of information that no attempt was made to shorten its length. Thank God for women in leadership such as this in West Africa.

My Membership in the United Methodist Church

The Early Days

It is a privilege and honor for me to write an account of my long-standing relationship with the United Methodist Church Sierra Leone Annual Conference, West Africa. Historically what became the United Methodist Church (UMC) by a merger of similar protestant denominations, the Evangelical United Brethren (EUB) and the Methodist Church in St. Louis, Missouri in 1968, extended the boundaries of the EUB that had been a merger of the United Brethren Church (UBC) and the Evangelical.

As a child of the Methodist manse, I was very much involved in church matters. Sierra Leone, at the time I was growing up, was outstanding in religious developments. The witness of the protestant churches was distinctly strong.

The Catholic Church, which came in later than the English and American missionaries, also engaged in Church and educational programs. All missionary churches effectively reached the interior of the country, i.e., the provinces, in order to establish churches, schools and medical programs (hospitals and health centers).

My father, the late Rev. Melville Wellington Cole, served the English Wesleyan Methodist mission from Sierra Leone as a missionary in West Africa – in the Gambia and Nigeria – where I was born. In 1932, my family returned to Sierra Leone where I completed my education at the Freetown Secondary School for Girls (FSSG), a non-denominational school established by a Sierra Leone Board of Trustees. Mrs. Maisie Ejesa Osora, an English wife of a Sierra Leone Anglican priest, was the first principal and Mrs. Hannah Benka Coker (twelve years after the start of the school in 1926) developed the program from nursery classes to school-leaving certificates. Upon graduation from high school in December 1942, I entered the Women's Teacher Training College (WTTC) in January 1943.

In 1940, the United Kingdom parliament had passed the Colonial Development and Welfare Act, intending to grant scholarships to students from West African countries and other British colonies for further education in British universities. I was one of ten Sierra Leonean women students who were admitted to British universities in the 1943 academic year. Five of us from the FSSG (my school) and the Annie Walsh Memorial School (another principal girl's high school) received our teacher education at Homerton Training College, Cambridge University. This was wartime Britain and we were not exempted from hardships and hazards. Fortunately, we gained the United Kingdom Teachers' Certificate (UKTC) and returned to Sierra Leone in 1945 to serve in our alma maters.

The ten UK-trained teachers were well received in Freetown, Sierra Leone. I believe we made a difference. Apart from teaching, we were invited to speak in churches, youth clubs and social events that took place at the British Council.

Meeting Willie Fitzjohn

My relationship with Rev. William Henry Fitzjohn, acting principal of the Albert Academy, started with a letter he wrote inviting me to the Albert Academy to visit a project he had in the school library. The young man, who handed me the letter, was interested in my positive response to this invitation because he was a family friend. I consented and went to the Albert Academy to see Rev. William Fitzjohn's project.

Interestingly, Rev. Fitzjohn had been told about my responsibilities at the FSSG where I taught mathematics, English language and English literature to school certificate (seniors) classes. He had started the program at the Albert Academy and he wanted me to see his choice of books in his school library. After the official meeting, I was invited to the principal's home to meet Mrs.

Violet Fitzjohn, William's mother, a gracious elderly lady who told me she had recently lost her husband, Rev. T. J. Fitzjohn. She also told me that she knew my own father, Rev. Melville Wellington Cole of the Methodist church. So much happened from that November 1946 meeting.

In January 1947, the Minister's Fraternal of the protestant churches met in Bo and my father was in attendance. Rev. John Karefa-Smart, Rev. William Fitzjohn and Mr. Frank Anthony also attended these meetings. These three friends, who were also relatives and colleagues – "old boys" of the Albert Academy – met my father and I believe they told the old man that they had met his daughter, Alice, the FSSG school teacher.

On my father's return to Freetown, he told me he had met the three American-trained young men in their flashy neckties! I told my dad that Karefa-Smart and Anthony had got to know me through their own sisters and had entertained me in the dining car on my train trip to Njala via Mano to see my older brother, Melville Cole, the meteorologist.

My father was district superintendent of the York Methodist Church. The district includes Hamilton, Sussex, Kent and the Banana Island churches. My father and my stepmother, Mrs. Muriel Cole, enjoyed the seaside areas and they would invite family members for weekends to attend special church programs. My grandmother, Mrs. Nancy Mousa, lived with me at 117 Circular Road near the Albert Academy School. By the end of January 1947 she had met William Fitzjohn. My grandmother told me she was impressed with William's respectable mannerisms. The rest is history. We were married on June 7, 1947, after a brief engagement.

Our wedding was on a Saturday so that students and teachers from the Albert Academy and FSSG could attend. We were married at Brunswick Memorial Church in York (formerly a slave pen) where my father was pastor. The officiating ministers were Rev. Dr. J. F. Musselman of UBC, Rev. W. B. Marke of Wesleyan Methodist Church; Rev. Dr. Karefa-Smart was best man. My two bridesmaids, like myself, were UK-trained teachers – Murietta Metzger and Judith Thomas. After a brief honeymoon, I was at home in the principal's house with my husband, Rev. William Henry Fitzjohn. The staff, student body and helpers gave us a warm welcome. Our union brought the EUB and the Methodist church closer together; later, I would tell my children that the union of their father and I foretold that of the Evangelicals and Methodists.

Albert Academy, Harford School and American Missionaries

I was very much impressed with extracurricular activities at the Albert Academy. The shops – printing and woodwork, the science laboratories – indeed personified an all-American system of education. At the end of the senior year, there was the important celebration of graduation exercises with presentation of diplomas. On the Sunday after, there was the baccalaureate service at the King Memorial (now United Methodist) Church.

At the Albert Academy, the boarding home offered a very special training ground for future leaders. Here, the boys learn to live in a community where one is expected to give the highest service with faith, hope and love. Prayer is central in the boarding home. Rising-up bell was followed by prayer, domestic duties, prayers in chapels and then classes. Then there were mealtime prayer and study hall prayers. Boarders attended Sunday services marching in line from Berry Street to the King Memorial Church. Special mid-week services were important celebrations during Lent, Holy Week or Advent.

The school started an acapella choir when Rev. Solomon Caulker returned from the U.S. and became a lecturer at the Fourah Bay College, University of Sierra Leone. Rev. William Fitzjohn introduced the Cambridge School Certificate Examination to the senior class. These academicians were pleased with the sense of unity and brotherhood that existed, as the students came from different provincial towns and villages as well as Nigeria, Liberia and Ghana.

As a preacher's wife, I supported the work of the mission with women, youth and children. Worship at King Memorial was similar to Wesley Methodist Church were I was confirmed. We attended mid-week prayer meetings on Wednesday evenings. Men, women, youth and children, choir members and church stewards all developed their groups for Christian service in building the Church of Christ.

The Sierra Leone Annual Conference, with headquarters in Freetown, was the umbrella that covered the entire ministry of the mission. The district included the western area, eastern province, northern province and southern province. From that time, the programs of Christian education, health and welfare and church development have grown from strength to strength.

When I met Rev. William Fitzjohn, I learned firsthand information about the United Brethren church that later merged with the Evangelical so that UBC became EUB. Dr. and Mrs. J. F. Musselman were at the end of their sojourn in Sierra Leone and they knew my parents. Rev. and Mrs. Walter Schutz were successors to the Musselmans. Ms. Vivian Olson was a great administrative secretary organizing the women's work and educational programs in our twelve major districts. Rev. and Mrs. C. W. Leader were stationed in Taiama which I had visited before I met my husband; my brother, Melville, was stationed at Njala as a meteorologist. Other missionaries who served in Taiama were Rev. and Mrs. Jim McQuiston, Lois Olsen, Metra Heisler, and Dr. and Mrs. Lowell Gess. The pastor and wife of the Calvary EUB church in Taiama, Rev. and Mrs. B. A. Carew, served a wide district. Taiama was a center for education and medical programs.

I did my best to get to know the missionaries, the preachers' wives, and women workers for the WSCS, WSWS, and recently, UMWO.

Shortly after we were married, my husband brought me home to Yoyema where his mother was at home with her mother, Katie Caulker, who had recently

139

died. I met my aunt in-law, Madam Lily Carpenter, who had cared for her mother, Katie Caulker, when the Rev. and Mrs. T. J. Fitzjohn had served in the Rotifunk church. On our visit to Moyamba to see Paramount Chief Julius Gulama, we were carried by hammock bearers for five miles from Yoyema to Moyamba. We received a royal welcome similar to our Yoyema welcome. Chief Gulama had known my husband William as a young teacher/preacher serving in Moyamba before he left Sierra Leone to further his education in the U.S. in 1939.

We visited the Harford School for Girls, which had been established in 1900. Ms. June Hartranft had succeeded Ms. Naomi Wilson, who had served as the principal of Harford for thirty years. I fell in love with Harford in 1947, little knowing that I would return in 1965 to teach alongside my husband, the first African principal of Harford School, from 1965-1971. I served as acting principal in 1971-1972. My last three years as a high school teacher of math and English were spent at Harford from 1982-1985.

Moyamba has been a fertile area for the development of the mission of the United Methodist Church. Rev. J. K. Fergusson, the district superintendent, and his wife, Mrs. Sarah Fergusson, a Harford alumna, were very busy in their station. The primary school was enlarged and June Hartranft Memorial School was established in 1968 (the Moyamba Boys' Secondary School was also established during Rev. Fergusson's superintendency).

Harford School has done outstanding work in the education of the Sierra Leone woman. Thank God for the American women missionaries who were pioneers in the difficult but challenging work of training rural girls into ladies of high esteem and competent devotion to duty and excellent academic achievement. No wonder Harford girls (Harfordians) are in so many professions, just like their American leaders who made a difference in their lives. After Ms. Naomi Wilson and those before her who had laid the firm foundation, we were blessed with Ms. June Hartranft as principal and other staff members - Ms. Virginia Pickarts, Ms. Wavelyn Babbit, Ms. Florence Barnhart, Ms. Ethel Brooks, Ms. Elaine Gasser, Ms. Betty Esau, Ms. Arabella Enyhart, Ms. Mary Alice Lippert, Ms. Marilyn Kopp, Ms. Anna Mae Morford, Ms. Cora Schofield, Ms. Jody Dyer, Ms. Marsha Nolte, Ms. Judy Lamm, Ms. Dettie Nelson, Mrs. Susan Matthews, Mr. Jayboy Matthews, Mr. John Hunter, Mr. Dave Figi. And there were Sierra Leoneans: Mr. Vandy, Mr. John Yambasu, Ms. Doris Caulker (Lenga Koroma), Ms. Elsie Mae Myers (Kallon), Mrs. Florence Johnson, Mr. Johnson, Ms. Mamie Kamara, Ms. Annie Lefevre (Bangura), and several other Harfordian alumnae, who came back to give service to their alma mater, as well as Ms. Balkie Kamara and Ms. Amelia Fitzjohn. Following Dr. Fitzjohn, the first Sierra Leonean Principal, we have had Mrs. Elsie Mae Kallon, nee Myers, Mrs. Doris Lenga Koroma, nee Caulker, Mrs. Etta Nicol, nee Kallay, and Mrs. Lucretia Sheriff, nee Gbogba, all Harfordians.

Today, we can proudly say that the Harford School for Girls, Moyamba, has produced talented women leaders who have given faithful service to Sierra

Leone. The missionaries had dedicated their time, talent and possessions to make their students succeed in their quest for learning. We are proud of the women paramount chiefs who received their education at Harford – Madam Ella Koblo Gulama, Madam Honoria Bailor Caulker and Madam Doris Lenga Caulker, newly installed Paramount Chief of Shenge. Harford girls are in all the professions (among them education, theology, diplomacy, politics, medicine, engineering, sciences, business and more), and like the Albert Academy alumni, they are making a difference in the development of independent Sierra Leone.

Coming to America: Part I

The years 1948-1949 found me in the U.S. when I came to join my husband who had already arrived in the States in order to continue his studies at Teachers' College, Columbia University, in New York. By this time he had received an M.A. in education and was halfway towards achieving an Ed.D. I also enrolled at Teachers' College and took classes in American education and culture, as well as teaching English.

My first home in the U.S. was in Toledo, Ohio, where Mr. And Mrs. Elmer Ward met me at the bus station after I had traveled from Norfolk, Virginia, for many hours. I had sailed from Freetown to the port of Norfolk in 1948. Mrs. Inez Ward was president of the WSWS in her United Brethren Church. The pastor, Rev. Roy Cramer, was my husband's seminary colleague. He and his wife, Charlotte, had cared for my husband during seminary days. These wonderful friends in Toledo opened their homes to other Sierra Leoneans after accepting us as their friends. Madam Ella Gulama and Mrs. Eula Hatib were invited to Toledo after their official visit to the U.S. Other friends who were hosted included Sister Olive Johnson, Chief Nursing Officer of Sierra Leone, and Mrs. Ada Awoonor-Renner of Freetown who was visiting her two sons who were studying in the U.S.

Mrs. Ward was a missionary at heart. She learned about the work of the missionaries in Africa and she encouraged her members of the WSWS to support the work in Sierra Leone. My husband and I shared the news of the good work of the UBC and EUB missions and that inspired the churches in the Sandusky Conference in Toledo.

The time we spent away from the university was with Willie's seminary colleagues, as well as retired missionaries who had served in Sierra Leone. We were invited to speak in their churches. Dr. and Mrs. Robert Parsons, former missionaries in Bunumbu College, Sierra Leone, invited us for a visit to the Kennedy School of Missions, Hartford Seminary in Connecticut in the spring of 1949. Rev. and Mrs. Robert Etter of the EUB church in Lancaster, Pennsylvania, invited us to speak at a Sunday celebration after which we visited Isaac Long's Band in Lancaster. There, Martin Boehm and William Otterbein had embraced each other as brothers. Thus the UBC church was started.

Dr. Parker Young and wife, Helen, who were married in Sierra Leone and had served at Harford and Bunumbu College in the 1930s, had invited us. Dr. Parker Young was pastor at Woodville United Brethren Church in Ohio. One of the members, Sandy Price, was a successful businessman who responded to the call to do missionary work in support of the UBC mission in Sierra Leone. Sandy Price visited Sierra Leone a few times with his grandson and was a volunteer in mission, giving financial support to several projects. Later on, when the new church in Dworzak Farm-George Brook (a neighborhood in Freetown) was completed in 1964, it was named Price Memorial United Methodist Church after Sandy Price.

We also visited the EUB church in Richland Center, Wisconsin, where two women pastors were in charge. To see Rev. Mayte Richardson and Rev. Sara Moer sharing news of the work of church building was truly impressive. Thirty years after this notable encounter, I also received my call into the ministry in 1979. (After five summer sessions – meeting every August at the Bible Training and Vocational Institute (BTVI) in Bo – my classmates and I received our ordination at the Sierra Leone UMC Annual Conference at the King Memorial Church in February 1984.)

Our daughter, Amelia, was born on August 24, 1949, during the peak of my husband's work to complete his dissertation for his doctoral program at Columbia. Yet, Amelia's father successfully combined childcare duties and daily trips to the library. Fortunately, he completed with great commendation his certificate that was signed by Dwight D. Eisenhower, president of Columbia University. I felt really blessed to have been present at the side of my husband during the time he did his research and writing and to have given him my support. Now, with baby Amelia, parents, friends and family in Freetown, Sierra Leone, greeted us very warmly when we arrived in December 1949.

Service in Education, Diplomacy, and the Missions

Fourah Bay College. My husband was invited to be a member of staff of the teacher-training department of Fourah Bay College under Ms. Elizabeth Hirst. She was an asset in education, putting a vital program together for the enhancement of Fourah Bay College, the oldest university in West Africa (established in 1827). Willie wasted no time in making those students, who belonged to the Evangelical United Brethren Church, feel as if they had a special counselor in their lecturer and preacher, who would also give them an uplifting Christian education for their future careers. In fact, our home soon became a meeting place for many smart young students after the fashion Willie had lived as a student in America.

Leading to the Foreign Service. For the next ten years after our return from the U.S., my husband and I gave our best service to the church and teaching Sierra Leonean young adults, boys and girls. We traveled extensively for the church in

Sierra Leone and raised five children during this time. From 1959-1964, the government of Sierra Leone appointed my husband to diplomatic service, first to open our embassy in Washington, D.C. from 1959-1961, and then as High Commissioner to the Court of St. James in London from 1961-1964.

Harford School for Girls. On our return from London to Sierra Leone in 1964, we served the Sierra Leone Annual Conference. Then in 1965 we accepted the principalship and vice-principalship of Harford School for Girls, which at that time had been in existence for sixty-five years. Mr. and Mrs. Baldwin, the EUB missionaries in charge of the affairs of the program in Sierra Leone, had discussed the proposal of inviting the Fitzjohns to head the Harford School. We considered it a privilege that the entire family of seven children, coming home with their parents, would live in the large missionary residence on the campus. Rev. and Mrs. Don Appleman and family, who previously resided in the mission house, assisted our family in getting adjusted to living on the Harford campus.

During our first year, funds were provided through the Ministry of Education for the construction of two classrooms on the other side of the main quadrangle, which comprised of ten classrooms. Work continued on the fencing of the entire school compound, as did leveling of the playing field for track and field events. Later, a school bus for Harford Girls was purchased with support from the missions; it allowed transport for the girls and staff to Freetown and within other provinces for educational trips.

Harford School has a beautiful history and stunning grounds. Harford School for Girls was named for Lillian Resler Harford, a dedicated Christian woman and a staunch supporter of the women's missionary society. She helped raise funds for the education of women and girls in the mission fields.

Four years after Harford's inception, the UBC established the Albert Academy for the Christian education and training of young men. The church had a vision of preparing young men and women who would become future leaders to give competent service both to the government and the church.

When we arrived on Harford's campus in September 1965, we fell in love with this renowned school built by American missionaries who had developed a wide curriculum of education similar to their American system. We developed four areas of instruction so that Harfordians would achieve high academic results in science, arts, home economics and business studies.

Between my husband and me, we gave ten years of leadership to Harford School in the 1960s, 1970s and 1980s, with the support of a good academic staff, bursar, matrons, domestic staff and school prefects.

The boarding home comprised three buildings on campus for the junior, intermediate and senior students. The library was well stocked, and the science and home economics laboratories were well equipped. Four hundred students, the majority of which were boarders, looked immaculate in their blue uniforms with white trim, black shoes and white socks, straw hats and hat bands or blue berets embroidered with the school crest as they came through the main gates when all schools in Moyamba would parade the main streets to celebrate national events. The Harford school choir would always bring back trophies from singing competitions – an annual event which was conducted in Freetown. However, our sports teams were not as swift in track and field races held in Bo at the Coronation Field or in Freetown at the Brookfields stadium.

Today we can proudly say after Rev. Dr. William Fitzjohn and his wife Alice served at Harford, former Harfordians later succeeded them. Dr. Fitzjohn served as principal from 1965 to 1971, when he was assigned by the Government of Sierra Leone to be High Commissioner to the Republic of Nigeria where he served from 1971 to 1976. I succeeded him as acting principal until 1972. I had the full support of the teaching staff matrons – Ms. Mary Weaver, Mrs. Elizabeth Hatib, Mrs. Amy Challe – and Mr. Thomas and Mrs. Berma Dudley, missionaries representing the General Board of Global Ministries. Missionaries to Harford School had dedicated their time, talent and possessions to make their students succeed in the quest for learning.

Ms. Marilyn Kopp, missionary from Illinois, an English teacher interested in library and basketball, succeeded me as acting principal in 1972 when I left Sierra Leone to join my husband in Nigeria. Harford School excelled in the 1970s and the transition was smooth to the first alumna principal, Mrs. Elsie Mae Kallon. Next came Mrs. Lenga Koroma, Mrs. Etta Nicol and then Mrs. Lucretia Sheriff, the current principal. Harford girls, like the Albert Academy alumni, are making significant contributions in the development of independent Sierra Leone.

Missionaries to Education, Medicine and Other Fields. Among Americans who have served Sierra Leone, the Annual Conference of the United Methodist Church has given outstanding leadership in the development of the Republic of Sierra Leone. Missionaries who came to serve in the 1940s through 1960s were indeed trailblazers. The Peace Corps volunteers then arrived in the 1960s along with other international contract teachers. Together, with the Sierra Leonean educators and other public servants, Sierra Leone celebrated its independence on April 27, 1961.

When I joined the UMC (then UBC), the missionaries were pioneers in most district headquarters, supervising education, medical and welfare programs. Sierra Leonean superintendents were leaders of the district programs. The first EUB bishop, the Rev. B. A. Carew, had served in the Taiama District for years. Following in the steps of Rev. Dr. Charles and Mrs. Bertha Leader, and Rev. Jim and Mrs. Nancy McQuiston, were Rev. Dr. J. K. and Mrs. Sarah Ferguson who served in the Moyamba District. Rev. Tom F. and Mrs. Regina Bangura served in the north. Rev. William B. and Mrs. Priscilla Clay served in the Rotifunk area. Rev. Dr. Sylvester M. and Mrs. Martha Renner served in the Western area, where Pa Renner was pastor of King Memorial UMC for many years. Other Sierra Leonean ministers that I recall were Rev. and Mrs. S. H. Gorvie in Bonthe District, Rev. and Mrs. J. B. Rogers in Bo District, Rev. and Mrs. Vincent in Kenema District and Rev. and Mrs. J. S. Kamanda.

In the mission house in Freetown, Rev. Dr. and Mrs. Schutz succeeded Rev. Dr. and Mrs. J. F. Musselman. Rev. Dr. and Mrs. L. O. Shirley served the Albert Academy, as well as the conducting the administration of the Conference. Mrs. Grace Shirley, a music major, taught at the Albert Academy. A new residence for missionaries was built at King Street, Wilberforce. Ms. Vivian Olson, who had arrived in 1947, occupied the King Street house. She gave outstanding service over the years until her retirement in the 1990s. Mr. Don and Mrs. Lilburne Theuer were missionaries who served in the administration in Freetown. Ms. Jeannette Schendel was one of the administrative officers in the Freetown office.

The medical program of the UMC was second to none. The Rotifunk hospital, named for slain missionaries during the 1898 Hut Tax War (the Hatfield-Archer), had grown beyond the Sierra Leone limits under the management of Dr. Mabel I. Silver. Dr. Silver took care of gynecology and obstetrics, maternal and child health cases and folks with serious health problems. Members of my own extended family received healing and became proud mothers of healthy babies under her care.

The hospital laboratories were effectively organized by missionaries, who had specialized as well as with help from locally trained technicians. Esther Megill was an outstanding team leader of the laboratory specialists that supported Dr. Mabel Silver in her busy program. Dr. Winifred Smith and husband, Mr. Lester Bradford, were married in Rotifunk in the 1950s. She joined the staff at the Hatfield-Archer Memorial Hospital and Mr. Bradford was an agricultural and development director. Ms. Lois Olsen, a qualified nurse and midwife, was also a member of this remarkable team.

Dr. and Mrs. Don Pletsch from Canada arrived on the scene in the 1950s and they served in the Northern District in Yonibana. Don Pletsch introduced milking goats in his program and Mrs. Pletsch, a qualified nurse, took care of the sick. Missionaries in Kono included Rev. and Mrs. Fred Gaston, Rev. and Mrs. Fred Walker, and Rev. and Mrs. Jack Thomas. Some of these colleagues went as far back as seminary days in Ohio with Willie.

Willie Back to Church Service. In 1977, Bishop B. A. Carew, our first Sierra Leonean bishop, assigned my husband to Brown Memorial Church Kissy, as well as to train ministerial students at the conference program and theological education by extension. At Brown Memorial Church, Kissy, Rev. William Fitzjohn was appointed the pastor in charge while serving the theological training program with students from all over the country.

During the month of August, ministerial students from all the country attended classes at the Bible Training and Vocational Institute (BTVI) in Bo. On completion, successful students were ordained at the Annual Conference in February of the following year. They were ordained deacons and commissioned to preach. Missionaries who served at the BTVI included Dr. and Mrs. Clyde Gallow and Rev. and Mrs. Jack Thomas. Sierra Leonean clergy Rev. and Mrs. A. J. Fahn Smith and Rev. and Mrs. Eustace Renner also served the BTVI.

United Methodist Church Sierra Leone Conference. May 31, 1981, was a Sunday and it turned out to be a day I will never forget. After morning worship service at King Memorial UMC at which the preacher was my husband, Willie, Ada and Max Bailor and the two of us went over to the parsonage, which had been recently vacated by Rev. Dr. S. M. Renner's family. The Fitzjohns had been assigned to that residence, as Rev. Fitzjohn was to be the new pastor of Kissy Memorial and the district superintendent of the western area.

The following day, however, June 1, 1981, my husband suffered a stroke and he remained in a state of coma for four days, waking up in the intensive care unit of the Connaught Hospital in Freetown where he received very good medical attention. After three weeks, he was discharged but was not able to assume normal duties as a pastor.

Rev. David Caulker was the preacher assigned to King Memorial, and he and his wife Mrs. Mamei Caulker (music teacher at Harford School) moved into the parsonage. The Bishop Rev. Dr. T. S. Bangura and several clergy, as well as missionaries and volunteers in mission, continued to pray for my ailing husband. They paid visits to the Fitzjohn residence on Syke Street, which greatly encouraged their colleague and mentor.

To make a change of atmosphere, we moved to Moyamba where I could serve at Harford School and give my husband the opportunity to meet old friends of former years. He had served as teacher and scoutmaster in the UMC schools; so many old acquaintances visited us. Madam Ella Koblo Gulama visited our home next to the Moyamba Hospital.

At the time, I was halfway through my ministerial training at the BTVI (where we spent the month of August every year). In Moyamba, the Rev. S. K. Senesie was pastor in charge of Trinity UM Church in Moyamba and was our district superintendent. I had the privilege of serving with Rev. Senesie who assigned me to preach at Rotifunk, pastored by Rev. W. B. Claye. I also preached at Sembehun and Yoyama, the latter being my husband's village home where the T. J. Fitzjohn Memorial Church is a new addition.

After my ordination in 1984, I felt like I was receiving the baton to continue in the race Willie had ably started in the 1940s. We returned to Freetown in July 1985 as I retired from teaching secondary school, which I began in 1945.

My next station was pastor-in-charge at Baughman UM Church in Brookfield with the Rev. Dr. F. B. Davies, associate pastor. My next appointment was at Price

Memorial UM Church, George Brooke. I served there for four years and Rev. Henry Jusu, Rev. E. M. Jimmy and Rev. Bob Sam Kpakra served with me. It was an ideal mission church with a well-organized primary school on both sides of the church. King Memorial Church was our mother church and Rev. D. H. Caulker and his associate pastors involved us in ministry. The UM men's organization, the UM women's organization, youth groups and the children's ministry in the western area were outstanding in church growth and development projects.

UMCOR. Operation Classroom, the PA LOKO Extension Ministry supported by the Swedish UM Church Partners, made our UM Church Sierra Leone Annual Conference stronger in witness to Christ's Church.

When my husband died on December 20, 1989, Bishop Bangura, Rev. Caulker, Rev. Crispin Renner and western area pastors were very supportive of my family. When my six children, who were abroad, came home for their father's funeral that took place on Sunday, December 31, 1989, they were satisfied with what brother Walter had set up by way of funeral arrangements. Indeed, God's plan for a remarkable celebration of His servant's home going was in order.

In December 1990, I retired from active service. There were two of us retiring – Rev. Isaac Ndanema and myself. The chapel at the Pa Loko Retreat Center was packed full as arranged by the bishop and the conference. The bishop presided and sent us with much encouragement.

My Work as a Clergywoman. Theological training produced the first female ministers, Rev. Mary Fofana and Rev. Mary Johnson, who had previously worked as leaders of the WSWS. I was the only female in my class of eight who received ordination in 1984.

The Women's Division of the General Board of Global Ministries (GBGM) is the head of all women's mission, united under the United Methodist Women. At each quadrennial, an assembly of thousands of female delegates meet at the appointed convention center. I received my first invitation from the Women's Division of the Board of Mission to represent the Sierra Leone WSWS. At the assembly in Philadelphia in April-May 1982, ten of us women from ten countries in Africa met in New York City at the headquarters of the GBGM where the Women's Division gave us a warm welcome. Two young ladies, staff members, were in charge of us, and they took us to our hotel in Manhattan. Ms. Andrea Stevens briefed us on our program and our hostesses took us to their homes. Ms. Genefer Brooks, a Caribbean American ministerial student, was my hostess at her home in Jamaica, New York. She guided me around to and fro the assembly in Philadelphia. The theme for the conference we attended in 1982 was "The Women at the Well," and Bishop Marjorie Swank Matthews was the keynote speaker.

A young WSWS scholarship holder and I were invited to bring greetings to the assembly, each of us speaking for five minutes. My brief message was about how the UMC had impacted my country, Sierra Leone. It was a pleasure to meet so many missionaries who had served in Sierra Leone – some were on furlough leave, others had returned home and had settled in other assignments in the U.S. Among the ten delegates from Africa were Mrs. Leah Tutu, wife of Archbishop Desmond Bishop Tutu from South Africa, and Rev. Amina Isaias, the first ordained Mozambiquan clergywoman. It was interesting for me to meet the future bishop of Mozambique, Rev. Machado, who in 1984 was one of the eight planners sent by GBGM to discuss how the meeting to be held in Harare, Zimbabwe, to plan the Africa University by GBGM was to be conducted.

I had just been ordained at the Annual Conference in Freetown in February 1984 when the invitation came from the GBGM to the bishop of the Sierra Leone Annual Conference – Bishop T. S. Bangura – for me to serve on the planning committee of the proposed Africa University. This meeting took place in December 1984 at the Millimani hotel in Nairobi, Kenya. The team of eight planners included Bishop Alfred Dorocimpa of Burundi, who was the chairman. Rev. Dr. Richard Tholin, Dean of the Garrett Evangelical Theological Seminary was the secretary. Liberia was represented by Rev. Dr. Brewer of Gbanga Theological Seminary, Dr. Yemba from the Congo, Bishop Machado from Mozambique, a delegate from Angola and me. At the Millimani Hotel we discussed the plans to host a meeting of sixty persons at the Jameson Hotel in Harare, Zimbabwe, the following summer. After a week we were back in our countries.

In June 1985, delegates from GBGM and GBHEM – and other UMC leaders – came together to deliberate on the establishment of a United Methodist University in Africa. The outcome was to build the proposed institution of higher learning to be named "Africa University at Old Mutare, Zimbabwe." Sierra Leone, Liberia and Angola had hoped to have the university in their countries. By divine intervention, during the past twenty years Africa University has proven to the world that God used the UMC in the U.S. to plant the idea that has blossomed over the years and has united other nations.

In 1986, the GBGM sponsored the African clergywomen at their first assembly that took place in Nairobi, Kenya. Delegates came from Liberia, Congo, Angola, Zimbabwe, Sierra Leone, Burundi and Mozambique. A young clergywoman, Rev. Kathryn Nikerson, was our chaperone and the representative of the GBGM.

Our African clergywomen assembly in Nairobi, Kenya, coincided with the World Methodist Conference, which meets every six years. Bishop Leontyne Kelly of the California-Nevada conference was keynote speaker at the assembly. The African clergywomen were invited to the grand opening of the World Methodist Conference at the gigantic Kenyatta Conference Center. What a spectacular parade to watch all the different banners from all parts of the Methodist world.

Then to listen to our first black woman bishop, Bishop Leontyne Kelly, speak at that gathering was a moving experience for us.

The next day after the opening of the World Methodist Conference, our leader from the U.S., Rev. Kathryn Nickerson, arranged the inaugural of the African Clergywomen Association with Bishop Leontyne Kelly presiding. Fifteen clergywomen from seven countries in Africa formed the first organized African Clergywomen's Association launched by Bishop Leontyne Kelly in June 1986 at the Millimani Hotel in Nairobi. It was a solemn occasion because women spoke French, Portuguese and English. We were united in love to serve our Lord and Savior in building His Church on earth. The first executive included President Muriel Alice Fitzjohn (Sierra Leone), Vice President Marie Smith Eastman (Liberia), Secretary Motumbo Ilonga (Congo) and a treasurer who was a delegate from Zimbabwe. It was proposed that we meet every two years and the four-year assembly should be held in a different country.

After my ordination in 1984, I served at Trinity UMC in Moyamba until 1985. My next appointment was pastor-in-charge with Bishop Baughman of the UMC in Freetown. My next charge was Sandy Price Memorial UMC, George Brooke, Freetown, from 1986 until 1990.

In 1987, the GBGM invited me to cover the newly established Operation Classroom at the Indiana Conference, U.S. My host and hostess, Rev. Dr. and Mrs. Frank Messenger, had given excellent service to the mission in Sierra Leone and they supported the new Operation Classroom project. Operation Classroom was gathering momentum, which continues in ministry under leadership of the Rev. Joe and Carolyn Wagner. I was invited to bring a message of hope and gratitude to these dedicated UMC mission-minded churchwomen who wanted to make a difference in the education of children in Africa. The Messengers took good care of me as I undertook nineteen speaking engagements in ten days in several churches in the Indiana Conference.

At the end of that period, Rev. Sue Messenger and I went off to attend the clergywomen's consultation held in McAffee, New Jersey. Rev. Mary Fofana and Rev. Mary Johnson came over from Sierra Leone to join us. We were all dressed in gara (tie-dyed) outfits and Rev. Sue Messenger and other ministers, who had served in the Sierra Leone Annual Conference, had on the same outfits. It was the first of many clergywomen consultations that I would be privileged to attend. To see more than one thousand clergywomen worshipping together and attending different sessions over a long weekend was truly inspiring.

On my return to Sierra Leone from Indiana and New Jersey, there was so much to share with my growing congregation at Sandy Price Memorial Church. At this time, my husband had become incapacitated by a stroke. However, I kept up my usual duties in addition to preaching and organizing programs for my United Methodist women, United Methodist men, youth and children. Church Women United brought all protestant women together, and we celebrated seasonal programs as planned.

UMC in Sierra Leone: Recent Strides. I am amazed at the great strides taken by the UMC, Sierra Leone Annual Conference. The growth and development of the medical program continues. The most impressive development I would submit is the Kissy UMC Eye Hospital, which is the brainchild of Rev. Dr. Lowell Gess. God laid it on his heart to help the people of Sierra Leone fight blindness and eye disease. After a first missionary tour to Sierra Leone (1957-1960), Dr. Gess studied ophthalmology so that he could fulfill his dream to care for Sierra Leone's eye patients. From 1964-1967, with his wife Mrs. Ruth Gess, a qualified nursing sister, Dr. Gess worked tirelessly at the Taiama Eye Program. He also extended the Taiama Clinic to Bo 1972-1975.

It was a dream come true when the Kissy UMC Eye Hospital was launched in 1984. I consider him God's special envoy to the people of Sierra Leone for deliverance from blindness as God had ordained. My late husband and I received treatment from Dr. Gess in the 1950s. He told me I had astigmatism in my left eye and prescribed my first pair of glasses. Dr. Gess shared his vision with people in the U.S. and mission-minded Christians have carried the work forward to the glory of God. The Kissy Hospital and Eye Clinic are a blessing to Sierra Leone because the UMC is making a difference there year after year. Dr. Gess has a wonderful team of volunteer ophthalmologists and medical personnel who take turns volunteering their services to the Kissy Eye Clinic and hospital every year. Mr. Roger Reiners, who was one of the original Kissy Eye Hospital builders, and his wife, Melanie, continue annual visits for oversight of the eye work and provision of containers of supplies.

It was my pleasure to participate in the Volunteers in Mission program (VIM) by offering hospitality and onsite visits during the 1980s. The Fitzjohn Memorial Methodist Church in Yoyema (built in memory of T. J. Fitzjohn, father of my late husband) was constructed by missionaries – Dr. Tom Dudley and his wife, Berma Dudley – who were based on the Harford campus in the 1980s. I believe Tom Dudley as well as local builders contributed to this wonderful worship center that to this day serves the Christians in Yoyema village. Here, my family spent rainy season vacations whenever we were in Sierra Leone.

Back to America

Here I am again in the U.S. I have lived here for the past twenty years after my oldest child, Amelia Fitzjohn Broderick and husband, Sylvester Modupe Broderick, invited me to join their family after my husband died in December 1989. I settled with them and their daughter, Vania, and son, Ahovi, in Silver Spring, Maryland, in 1990.

I became a member of Colesville UMC, in Silver Spring, Maryland – part of the Baltimore-Washington Annual Conference – in 1990. In 1991, I was invited to be a mission interpreter for a great rally, "Mission '91 – Just the Beginning." It was through this medium I was able to tell the Sierra Leone story and about how the UMC has impacted my people all over Sierra Leone and how it has undergone many changes since my childhood.

At Colesville, I served on the church council of administration, missions, United Methodist Women, prayer ministry, and visitation to the sick and shut-in.

The Sierra Leone community received me warmly in the Baltimore-Washington metro area. I have been invited to preach, officiate at weddings, funerals and participate in alumni association activities. In 2003, the Sierra Leone community gave a surprise dinner to honor me as the "Mother of the Year" on Mother's day. Out of this gathering, they started the "Mummy Alice Scholarship Fund" (MASF). In November 2005 when I turned 80, my family organized a Thanksgiving service in my honor. Guests were invited to contribute to the established MASF in lieu of birthday gifts. This Fund is very active and scholarships have gone to the four girls' schools where I had taught English and mathematics for more than thirty years. Three deserving students from each of these four schools – Harford; FSSG (my alma mater); St. Joseph's Secondary School, Freetown, and YWCA Secondary School, Freetown – receive scholarships each year. The 2010-2011 academic school year will be the fifth year of granting these scholarships.

Sierra Leoneans in this Diaspora are doing well to hold onto the good relationship between their country and the U.S. "Friends of Sierra Leone" (returned Peace Corps volunteers and others), a group of which I am a member, has been very forceful in strengthening the ties between the two countries and in promoting Sierra Leone-related issues to policy makers.

I thank God for the opportunities I have had to attend UMC General Conferences, clergywomen consultations, United Methodist women assemblies, schools of Christian missions and "Servants of Sierra Leone" meetings. It is gratifying to be in touch with so many wonderful missionary friends of former years – some were my colleagues, others I recognize as my mentors whom the Lord has graciously preserved to this day.

I plan to visit Sierra Leone during summer 2010, since my last visit was in 2004 when I witnessed the 100th anniversary of the Albert Academy. I plan to stay for the 50th anniversary of Sierra Leone's Independence on April 27, 2011, by the grace of God.

My relationship with United Methodist Church is by no means by my own design. No one can tell what the future holds. I just remain grateful to God Almighty for what He has done in my life and has allowed me to use the talents He's given to make a difference. Indeed, nothing happens by chance. God is Supreme. He ordained what should be. May God's name be glorified!

Chapter Thirty-seven

Dr. John and Anne Buchan

"Amazing Grace, how sweet the sound, That saved a wretch like me.
I once was lost, but now am found; Was blind, but now I see."
– John Newton, 1773

Dr. John Buchan

When Dr. Buchan wrote the article below, he expressed hesitancy about the interest others might have in his situation. He felt that his four-year commitment to caring for the eye needs of patients in Sierra Leone was a drop in the ocean in the light of others who have given decades or even their entire lives in mission service. He expressed it in this way: "Like caring for a child for a few months who is waiting for adoption, one is not providing the depth of parenting and commitment that is really needed in that child's life, but one can do something to help that child adjust."

That "something," as Dr. Buchan moves forward in the name of Jesus, is preventing blindness in children suffering from diseases and infections and restoring sight to the blind – by the thousands.

"Was Blind, But Now I See"

With my wife and three small children, I accepted the offer of support from CBM (Christian Blind Mission) to work as an eye surgeon in the developing world wherever the need was most pressing. There was surely nowhere more in need of support than Sierra Leone, which, despite a population of nearly six million, has less than 200 doctors in total and only two national eye surgeons!

Having arrived in Freetown, Sierra Leone, in June 2009 at the start of an initial four-year term of service as the "doctor in charge" of the Kissy UMC Eye Hospital, it quickly became apparent that we were just another link in the long chain of those to take up the yoke here. The hospital, established by Dr. Lowell Gess twenty-five years previously, has seen literally dozens of workers come, mostly from the U.S., to maintain the service, provide sight for the blind through cataract surgery as well as hope for those in distress with the full spectrum of other eye problems.

I reflected on the legacy of these twenty-five years of input from various – mostly short-term – medical workers coming to Kissy. So many people, often at such personal expense, coming to give what they can. What is the sum of all the efforts that have been made?

Certain things have not been achieved. It would be fair to say that the meticulous working practice of the health care systems of Europe and North America from whence most volunteers at Kissy Eye Hospital had come has not rubbed off. There is a progression, though slow, of the recognition of the need for safe and sterile operating conditions, and the subsequent improvement in outcomes. The very best is prayed for each patient. Hopefully, Sierra Leone will continue to rise from its low ranking of the UN Human Development Index.

But undeniably what has been left behind is a large number of formerly totally blind people who have walked into the clinic here wondering if their other eye can have something done for it. Another larger number of formerly blind people who have returned to their villages to live out their days seeing as they were created to see, giving thanks to the God who made them and for the care they have received. To have lost your sight must be terrible, but to have had it restored to you surely gives people cause to know that there is a God who is active through his people to reach down in mercy. The God who opened the eyes of the blind is still at his work through the hands of his people who are willing to go.

In Freetown, we find that many patients are already Christians. When we pray for each patient before operating, there is often a good "Amen!" coming from under the drape. One lady continued to pray quietly but audibly as I started to operate; her prayers got louder as I proceeded, despite adequate anesthesia, until by half way through she was claiming "The Blood of Jesus! The Blood of Jesus!" Whilst I realize that the blood of Jesus cleanses us from personal sin, the fallen state and many of the consequences of sin, it is not going to stop me making inappropriate holes in the back of her lens capsule if she does not lie still. We are not likely to lead to greater faith or fervor in prayer by the eye care service here, but we can at least remind her through sight-restoring surgery that she has a Father who loves her, and brothers and sisters who are prepared to reach out to provide care through donations that support this hospital, whether from Central Global Vision based in South Dakota, CBM based in Germany, or the General Board of Global Missions based in New York.

So whilst many witnesses whose stories are recorded in this book have given their lives to bringing the Good News to the continent of Africa, there are many who have given just a few years, or a few months or even weeks to that cause. I myself may well be amongst their number if four years proves enough. It reminds me of the Christmas story where some bring a lamb, others bring gold; neither are needed by the Baby who was the Creator of the universe, but both are a delight to that Baby and his Father as signs of obedience to God as shepherd and wise men brought what they had to offer.

Chapter Thirty-eight

Roger and Melanie Reiners

"Each patient receives prayer prior to receiving surgical intervention and each member of the staff, through their witness, adds credence to the message."

Roger and Melanie Reiners

Some answers to the previous contribution of Dr. Buchan's feelings about the brevity of mission service can be found in the following deeply spiritual testimonies of Roger and Melanie Reiners.

Growth of the Church in Sierra Leone
by Roger and Melanie Reiners

Roger and Melanie Reiners have had the privilege to be associated with the Kissy UMC Eye Hospital in Freetown, Sierra Leone, at some level through part-time mission work for the past twenty-eight years.

Roger first went to Sierra Leone in 1982 as a part of a mission work team from our church dedicated to erecting a building for the medical eye care program of Dr. Lowell and Ruth Gess at the Kissy UMC Eye Hospital. After his return, he often spoke to the fact that even short-term mission service changes how you live your life forever. His commitment to the work there has never wavered; Roger returned for the thirteenth time in 2010. Joined by his wife, Melanie, in 2004, they have continued their commitment to the eye care program at Kissy, making

155

eight of those trips together. They serve in overseeing the physical condition and maintenance of the buildings, the maintenance of generators and other equipment, securing some of the medical supplies needed to keep the hospital operating at the highest level possible and providing staff administrative support whenever possible. They have developed a shipping ministry through which needed medical supplies can be transported efficiently, effectively and economically from the U.S. to Sierra Leone.

What observations can be made from short-term mission work relative to the growth of the church? When patients arrive at the Kissy UMC Eye Hospital for care, Christian, Muslim and those of other tribal beliefs are treated equally in all respects. All are exposed to the story of God's saving grace through Jesus Christ during the opening devotions held in the outpatient building each morning. Each patient receives prayer prior to receiving surgical intervention and each member of the staff, through their witness, adds credence to the message.

It has long been documented that persons who come to Christ in a third-world, developing nation, most often as a result of a medical emergency (the number may be as high as 80 percent!). It has been our privilege to witness this power. On one of his most recent trips, Roger had the opportunity to offer surgical care to a man of the Muslim faith who was employed at the airport. The surgery was critical to his being able to continue working and, in turn, to support his family. Following successful surgery, this man has returned to work and his gratitude is evident through his transformed demeanor. The restoration of "physical sight" is vitally important, but no one can truly measure the value of the "spiritual sight" gained as a result of Christian medical missions.

Although measurement of statistics is difficult, at most – in a developing nation recovering from a horrendous civil war – one only needs to travel to villages throughout the country to feel the resultant impact of medical missions over this past quarter century. Whenever the name of the Kissy Eye Hospital is mentioned, someone attests to the excellent care they or their family members have received and, most times, through the care delivered by Dr. Lowell Gess either at Kissy or in any of the other locations within the country in which he served during his fifty-plus years of service.

Our commitment to the continuance of premier eye care through this wonderful facility becomes deeper with each visit. We have seen the positive result of medical missions in the area of eye care and know with confidence the contribution this ministry has made to the growth of the Church in Sierra Leone. To God Be the Glory Now and Forever!

Chapter Thirty-nine

Vivian Olson

"To God be the glory, great things He hath done.
So loved He the world that He gave His own Son.
Who yielded His life, an atonement for sin.
And opened the Life-gate that all may go in...."
– Fanny Crosby, 1875

Dr. Lowell Gess and Vivian Olson

Vivian Olson first went to Sierra Leone in 1947 as a missionary teacher and served thirty-three years in many roles. Her longest term of service was at the Bo Bible College, which is now part of the UMC Child Rescue Center. I remember her as an intense and accurate bookkeeper for the missionary office, rescuing us in our work in Rotifunk, Taiama and Bo. In 1986 after years of retirement, she returned to Sierra Leone as a volunteer bookkeeper for the Kissy UMC Eye Hospital. The hospital was very busy during her seven-month stay, as everyone wanted to "see Vivian." Her impact on the growth of the Church ranged from the pastors of the conference to women in huts in far places. She loved Sierra Leone and Sierra Leone loved her.

To God Be the Glory

The Lord has been most gracious and has blessed me with experiences as a missionary in West Africa. On January 3, 1918, I was born to my parents, Henry E. and Anna Peterson Olson, at a home in the sand hills and which he had homesteaded. As part of a family of eight children, four boys and four girls, we were influenced by our Christian parents, the Depression and rural schools. Mother lead me to accept Christ using John 3:16. This gave direction to my life. In 1928, we moved to a farm in western Nebraska where I sensed God's call to missionary service through our pastor's messages and the Girls' Guild, where every time it was my turn to lead it would be a lesson on mission work in Africa (Sierra Leone).

After seven years of teaching in rural schools, the way opened for me to attend Moody Bible Institute. They emphasized self-governing, self-disciplining and self-propagating of those we ministered to. I prayed that the Lord's choice might be made by the first response to the three mission boards to which I applied; our own United Brethren in Christ was the first to answer. Many times over the years I have been thankful that the Lord directed in that way because of the blessings of support from the churches here in America which became United Methodist after a merger.

The years from 1947-1955 and from 1970-1979 were spent in the business office in Freetown with some ministry to women's groups where later churches were formed. The years 1955-1970, I had both Bo and Freetown addresses with about three months a year spent in the business office in Freetown and nine months with teaching at the Bo Bible Training Institute. From Bo, I had women's village meetings in Bible lessons, used flannel graph charts on malaria and other health issues, provided child care, baked bread in iron pots over a fire among three stones, made soap and sewed simple baby dresses. Then in the evening we would have Bible films projected by the energy from the car battery. Students from the Bible Institute were very helpful with these women's meetings. Doris Lenga-Koroma, Zainabu Renner and Zainabu Kallon were most helpful as well as other pastors' wives and teachers. We shared together in presenting the Good News of salvation in Christ.

At the Bible Training Institute, students were equipped to go to the villages on Fridays and Saturdays to share the Good News. Later, the students were assigned to establish churches in the villages from where they came. What a blessing to hear their reports and to hear them heartily sing, "To God be the glory, great things He hath done. So loved He the world that He gave His own Son. Who yielded His life an atonement for sin. And opened the Life-gate that all may go in...." I was greatly blessed by visiting in their homes and churches throughout the area where we had churches in the lower two thirds of Sierra Leone.

At one annual conference, six of those being ordained as ministers had been in my classes at one time or another. Oh what a blessing and thrill to see them taking their places of leadership! God so richly blessed me through their ministry and through that of Dr. Sylvester, Martha Renner and Bishop Benjamin and Betty Carew. There were many opportunities to be an encourager for those in the United Christian Council, United Church Women and other groups that bound Christians of all backgrounds together. My greatest joy and blessing was in the fellowship and ministry with the African and missionary families, one in Christ.

Beatrice Fofanah, who is in charge of the women's ministry for the conference, each year sends reports, pictures and the women's monthly Bible lesson guides which they prepare. Battiloi Warritay visited here recently and is gathering material for a book about his father who came from a strong Mandingo Muslim background and became a Christian minister with wide influence to his relatives. These, and so many others, have been great blessings to me as they have shared the Christian witness and honored Christ as Lord and Savior. They are just a few among the many.

Rev. David Caulker and Rev. Alfred Gbaya frequently call and minister to my spiritual needs.

159

Chapter Forty

Dr. Emmanuel and Florence Mefor

"Emmanuel, (borrowing words from Jesus Christ) replied to the nurses, 'You do something to help him.'" (Matthew 14:16)

Dr. Emmanuel and Florence Mefor

The report below reveals the difficulties and challenges that are faced by missionaries serving in the healing ministry in the name of Jesus Christ. While they prepare for all exigencies as best they can, they still depend upon the power of God to overcome.

In late April 1995, I arrived in Mozambique following my acceptance by the government of Nigeria to participate in its program "Technical Aids Corps" as a medical general practitioner. The Technical Aids Corps program is one in which the Nigerian government assists fellow developing countries all over the world by sending and sponsoring Nigerian professionals with technical-know-how to work in those countries.

In late 1995, I met Dr. Lowell Gess for the first time in Hospital Rural de Chiquque (Chicuque Rural Hospital), and again in 1998 as he recounted in his book, *Mine Eyes Have Seen the Glory.*

Mozambique 1995

I arrived in Hospital Rural de Chicuque in September 1995, having been reassigned there temporarily from a clinic about two hours north of Chicuque.

160

Dr. Annette Gonsalves was the medical director. Dr. Roberto Codeiro, Beatriz Birchal, Paul Wolff and Bryan Stone were the other doctors working in the hospital. Roberto and Beatriz were Brazilians and Persons-in-Mission of the United Methodist Church.

Paul Wolff, a missionary of the German Board United Methodist Church, had already gone on holiday to Germany. He has been taking care of the obstetrics and gynecology section of the hospital. Bryan Stone from the U.S. was the General Board of Global Ministries of the United Methodist Church Missionary and the general surgeon. I had come to stay in his place for the period he was to be in the States.

I really felt at home compared to my former place of assignment because Chicuque is a mission hospital, the type of environment I was used to back in Nigeria.

In the next two weeks, it was so busy. I had done an average of four cesarean sections daily, eight normal hernias, one obstructed hernia with bowel resection and anastomosis. Thanks to the good operating theatre team – which included Mr. Samuel Ngila, the nurse in-charge of the theatre; Mr. Yusuf, the anesthetist, and the late Helena.

About four weeks into my stay, I had one of the occasional calls at the pediatric ward to review a neonate with a history of vomiting after feedings. The only positive finding on examination was weight loss and a palpable mass midline in the supraumbilical region. Laboratory investigations were normal. I made a diagnosis of pyloric stenosis and decided the child needed surgery. While rehydrating the baby, I had a hard time convincing the theatre crew about the possibility of a successful surgery, more so as I was seen as general practitioner than a specialist surgeon. Another apparent reason was the possibility that they had never witnessed the surgery I wanted to perform.

However, we went on with the surgery (Ramsted's operation) to relieve the pyloric obstruction. We were done in about fifty minutes and the baby began breastfeeding the next morning. The baby's recovery was uneventful and had no additional vomiting.

July 1997

My two-year contract for the National Technical Aids Corp ended May 1997. Bishop Simao Joan Machado was very eager and willing to give me a place in the hospital as Person-in-Mission (PIM) in the hospital. This I happily accepted and we talked about bringing my family to Mozambique from Nigeria. I left for Nigeria to report the end of my service and my experiences.

In July 1997, we left for Mozambique by Ghana Airways via Johannesburg, South Africa. I had my temporary resident permit for Mozambique. The church administration had agreed with Ghana Airways that they would allow my wife,

Florence, and our three children (Chukwuebuka, then nine; Osita, then seven; and Anulika, then three) on the plane since the flight booking was done from their office in Maputo. The flight was uneventful to Johannesburg.

The situation turned sour when we were to board a connecting flight for Maputo using Linhas Mocambique (Mozambique Airlines). The South African immigration services would not allow Florence and the children to board the flight unless they had visas. God being with us, we were able to contact the church office late that evening to make arrangement to get a letter faxed from Mozambique immigration to their South African counterparts confirming that visas will be issued at the port of entry in Maputo. Having done that, we proceeded to Maputo the next day.

Mozambique at that time was just few years out of their approximately thirty-year war (fourteen for Independence and about the same for civil war). The young and middle aged were born into war and never knew anything about peace, only knowing violence. So people usually settle scores by violence. Besides the above mentioned conditions, my seven years in Hospital Rural de Chicuque was characterized by a lot of surgeries to repair traumas due to violence, injuries from gunshot wounds, thoracic and abdominal knife-stab injuries, land mine injuries and vehicle accidents requiring orthopedic surgeries like amputations, external fixations and Perkins traction.

Jos Plateau State, Nigeria, March 2003

In March 2003, we arrived in Jos, Nigeria. We met George and Nancy Carew, missionary couple of the UMC assigned to Jos. We spent a couple of weeks trying arranging for the children's admission at Hillcrest School in Jos before moving to our assignment in Zing. The children got placement in Hillcrest School, but the two most senior had to repeat one year each. They had similarly repeated one year each when they were to adjust to the Portuguese school system.

Our reassignment to Zing, Nigeria, was due to several factors: difficulty in adjusting from the English to Portuguese system of education in Mozambique, Emmanuel's ill health, separation of the family (Emmanuel had to stay and work in Rural Hospital Chicuque, while Florence and the children stayed in Maputo in order for them to attend English school) and, of course, the need for a doctor and nurse at the UMC Rural Health Program, Zing.

Zing, Taraba State, Nigeria, May 2003

We proceeded to Zing in May, having made concrete arrangements for the children's education. They were to return to the Hillcrest School's hostel when the next academic year started in August 2003.

We met with the missionary couple – Dr. Chuck and Pearl Arnett – who were in charge of the Rural Health Program. We were to assist and eventually take over the program from them as their retirement was fast approaching.

We saw the need to improve on patient care and for the Rural Health Program to generate enough income to sustain itself. We therefore embarked on renovating the operating theatre; constructing a new medical and surgical ward; checking on the erratic power supply by obtaining a new 42kva generator for the hospital and another 27kva for the mission compound; and working on how to get qualified nurses and midwives to replace the cheaper-to-pay, but ineffective, community health assistants meant to provide bedside nursing care.

Besides the above and the routine clinical and nursing work, one other project in its inception during our arrival was the construction of the new Zing Eye Centre initiated and supported by Dr. Lowell Gess. Zing Eye Centre would upgrade ophthalmic services, which were supported by the Christian Blind Mission (CBM). Services at the time were provided by Edward, the ophthalmic nurse from Bambur and administered by Ina, previously a German missionary and then married to Dearsley Dabale, son of the late resident UMC bishop, D. P. Dabale. Unfortunately, Edward had to resign soon after the completion of the Eye Centre following misunderstandings, rancor and mistrust in the eye unit administration.

As the construction of the Eye Centre went on, there was need to arrange for a permanent eye doctor.

Dr. Lowell Gess felt the fastest means to get an eye doctor was to ask the mission board to send Dr. Emmanuel Mefor to a short-term course on cataract surgery and for Florence to go for short-term course in ophthalmic theatre nursing at the ECWA Eye Hospital, Kano. This was accepted and implemented by the mission board in 2004.

It is worth mentioning and thanking God for my mentor and teacher Dr. Kiru, (the CBM medical representative in Nigeria), and Dr. Baghy, Dr. Abu and Dr. Akinyemi.

We remember the junior, but invaluable nurses like Mr. Magaji, Mr. Abdullahi, Mr. Joel, Miss Maryam, Safiya, Mr. Thomas Achi (he taught me biometry and use of the then A-scan). There are lots of things one can only learn from these junior ones, as the consultants may not have time to teach those. For example, Mr. Magaji took me on my first incision and subsequent practice under the microscope using a goat head we had purchased from the butchery earlier that day.

During our absence, the hospital was to be managed by an acting administrator, Mr. Alfred Dime, a retired civil servant from one of the schools of agriculture. The then administrator, Mr. Lazarus had gone for one and half-year course in hospital administration as approved by the then health board chaired by the resident bishop D. Dabale and sponsored by the GBGM.

The two major projects going on when Mr. Dime came were the construction of a surgical ward mentioned above by Mr. Dearsley Dabale and supervised by Dr. Mefor, and the finishing of the Eye Centre also by Mr. Dearsley but supervised directly by his wife, Ina.

Mr. Alfred Dime was now directly overseeing the ward construction and participating in the finishing of the Eye Centre. Unfortunately, misunderstandings arose.

We returned to Zing in October 2004 from Kano at the end of the training. Dr. G. Avar was employed and sent for a course in diploma ophthalmology when it was clear that the GBGM will not accept my working with it and at the same time work with the CBM. It was hoped that Dr. Avar would take over the ophthalmic services from me at the end of his D.O. course.

Along with the existing intermittent mass eye camp campaign carried out by a visiting doctor from Mkar Hospital, eye services – including cataract extractions – were commenced in the new Eye Centre. We started performing cataract surgeries. The inauguration and dedication of the Eye Centre officially took place late January 2005 by Bishop Dabale, the UMC resident bishop. Dr. Gess was present and handed over several more ophthalmic and eye surgery instruments, besides the two operating microscopes he already donated. Among the instruments were those that were not of use at the Zing Eye Centre. These were shared with Dr. Kiru. Some also needed repairs in Kano by the ECWA Eye Hospital's technician, Mr. John Harry.

July 2005 found the Mefors confronted with a threatening situation that led to the eventual reassignment to Mutumbara, Zimbabwe. Fortunately, Dr. Gideon Avar was able to continue the eye program following his completion of the D.O. course under the sponsorship of Christian Blind Mission.

August 2006

Florence and I arrived in Zimbabwe early August 2006. It was difficult for our children to move from their school. In conjunction with the GBGM and the Hillcrest School. it was agreed that the children be allowed to continue their schooling where they were as they had already lost two academic years in the process of moving from one country to the other and with the changing of academic systems. The children remained in Jos, Nigeria, at the Hillcrest hostel. Arrangements were made for family members to see them when necessary.

Our arrival and settling down in Harare was facilitated by Mr. Henry Jusu who had arrived in Zimbabwe several weeks earlier to take over from Glen Hirpruich as the AFE for Zimbabwe. I participated in the orientation (or adaptation) course to the Zimbabwe Health System at the Parirenyetwa Hospital for six months and then proceeded to the Mutambara Mission Hospital in January 2007. The socio-economic situation in Zimbabwe had not been stable in recent years. Rampant inflation required the government to strike off several zeros from their currency to make it calculable.

Mutambara Mission Hospital from January 2007

The hospital had been operating at its lowest. The nurse-in-charge had received complicated transferred patients and had sent them on to the provincial hospital about 85 kilometers away. A few months before our arrival, and during my orientation and adaptation course in Harare, the church had engaged a Zimbabwe national doctor, Dr. Tongai Chitsa, to also help out.

On our first day in the ward, there were two adult patients (male and female) who had an exposed leg fracture and an extensively infected wound on the hand (following a snake bite) respectively. The wound, we decided could be grafted if the knife and blade available would work.

For the fracture, the patient was advised on the need for him to be transferred to the provincial hospital because there may not be appropriate instruments for his treatment. He complained of lack of funds to pay for his treatment.

The response from the nurses and the matron was that the provincial hospital usually would demand cash upfront before any treatment would be offered to the patient. "They will end up sending him back to us." Besides, the patient did not have enough money.

Under pressure to do something to help the patient, Emmanuel, (borrowing words from Jesus Christ) replied to the nurses, "You do something to help him." (Matt. 14:16) We searched through the set of available orthopedic instruments left by the previous missionary doctors. Only one complete external fixation set was available after picking improvised parts from here and there. Those were the "five loaves and two fish" the disciples had. (Matt. 14:17)

The surgery was scheduled along with the skin grafting of the other patient. On the day of the surgery, the skin-graft knife was a bit bent, causing difficulty to harvest a uniform skin thickness. Thanks to God, it was not an extensive area to graft, so the graft was done with only moderate difficulty. The graft took and the lady went home after one week.

The external fixation for the exposed fractured bone was a tough one because: 1) Only the manual drill was available, and 2) It broke midway in the process of driving in the last pin through the tibia. For the next thirty minutes, an attempt was made to get it to the right position with minimum success. Believing that though this was not the best, God graciously kept both the set and bone fragments together. Emmanuel finally gave up and fixed up the set to get the bone reduced and splinted. Having tightened the nuts with vehicle #12 spanner (the appropriate spanner for the set could not be located), we hoped that the unstable rods would not slip off. Each time Florence went on ward rounds, she rechecked and retightened the nuts.

It was sad to realize that the x-ray machine was not working well and we couldn't get a bone x-ray. Judging from the shape of the leg, we assumed the displacement was minimal and so went ahead without an x-ray. We hoped we would find the funds for him to have an x-ray in the next town. We also hoped we would be able to get a drill from somewhere to get the pins out.

We continued to struggle with the lack of, and occasionally the existence of, poor instruments in the hospital. The socio-economic problem in Zimbabwe continued to worsen. People joined long queues daily, only to obtain one loaf of bread. The price of bread had risen from Z$1.50 (August 2006 when we arrived in Zimbabwe) to between Z$22,000 to Z$50,000. Other items were equally affected. Sugar had long been off the shelves. People made purchases from private individuals who are mostly cross-border traders to neighboring countries. Beef, fish and chicken had disappeared from grocery stores.

We had to join many Zimbabweans who crossed the border to neighboring countries, like South Africa or Mozambique, to purchase groceries. On return, we were expected to declare all purchases made to the customs at the border and paid duties on them.

Like many other families, we learned to bake our own bread and scones at home either from flour purchased across the border or from locally ground wheat.

The power supply was very unreliable and only made available from about 10:00 p.m. or later to 5:00 or 6:00 a.m. We learned to go to bed early and wake up to do all that could be done with electricity as soon as the power was available. This included baking, cooking, working on the computer, etc. During the day, cooking was done traditionally by using firewood outside in our recently constructed kitchen so we had better shelter while cooking.

Considering our work in the mission hospital, the long hours of power failure affected everything negatively. Our little standby generator was being over worked daily, as it had to run for long hours day and night due to emergencies. Fuel to run the generator was in short supply at the official government price. Following the long hours the generator ran, the fuel supply ran out in no time. Price of fuel at the parallel market was exceedingly exorbitant. But that is what people rely on for fuel supply.

Water supply to the hospital, staff houses and the student hostels in the mission community was almost zero as the pumping machines to the boreholes were all power dependent.

December 2007

The eye unit of the hospital was started by the full support of Dr. Lowell and Ruth Gess, Arvid and Janet Liebe, and other friends. It started – and is still – in one room where we do consultations. In that room is the slit lamp, the keratometer, the A-scan and lens showcase. The general operating theatre also accommodates our locally made wooden operating table and operating microscope for cataract and other eye surgeries.

Construction of the new eye unit began in early 2008 following the gracious support mentioned previously. The building is now being completed.

Florence was much concerned about the welfare of the pregnant mothers in the hospital. Mutambara Mission Hospital is considered the district hospital for Chimanimani district. It is a referral center and the only hospital that can provide elective and emergency Caesarian sections for mothers in the district. There are fuel and transportation problems in the rural areas all over the country. To avoid this problem, mothers approaching full term pregnancy are encouraged – and some are transferred – to come stay in the "waiting mothers' shelter" in the hospital until they deliver.

Most of these mothers appear at the Maternal and Child Health clinic in poor condition. During the "health talk," some complain of lack of funds, having run short of money to purchase the necessary food, soap, sanitary pads and other items for delivery.

Though they are encouraged to come to the "shelter" prepared for the period of stay, they still run short of supplies. And usually there is a lack of funds to return home for supplies. Worst is that their relatives don't check on them.

Since the hospital was unable to assist these mothers, Florence arranged for a breakfast for them of maize porridge mixed with sugar and either peanut butter or milk. Thanks to Janet Liebe who supported Florence with $50, breakfast was provided to the women Monday through Friday. This yielded a good result.

Florence further presented the scenario to friends and supporting churches in the U.S. This left a big impression on them, such that they started and have continued to support the feeding of the mothers through the United Methodist Church HQ (GBGM-UMC) in New York. With the availability of funds, we were able to start feeding them three meals a day. Forty to sixty mothers were and are still being fed daily.

Two years later in 2010, the Health Ministry, with assistance from the Japanese government, wanted to revive and establish the "Mothers' Waiting Homes" nation-wide, having recognized Mutambara's "Mothers' Waiting Home" as a model for the country.

It is pertinent to note that we are working in an environment in which HIV/AIDS and tuberculosis are highly prevalent. About 30 percent of our patients have HIV, AIDS or tuberculosis – or both. We have the support of the Global Fund and other NGOs to provide free treatment to these patients; this includes testing and counseling, laboratory investigations, opportunistic infections and ARV management, home-based care and palliative care outreach, and prevention from mother to child transmission of HIV.

Chapter Forty-one

Letticia Williams

"Oh, give thanks to the Lord for He is good! For His mercy endureth forever."
– Psalm 136:1

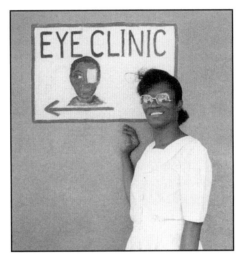

Letticia Williams

The article below does not give the full depth of Lettie's ministry as Director of the Kissy UMC Eye Hospital from its beginning and the twenty-six years that followed. Each working day, she not only assisted in surgery, examined and diagnosed patients, but administratively kept the staff and program running smoothly. She was skilled – but more than that – her spiritual demeanor was felt and experienced by all around her. The people of West Africa were drawn to Christ and to the Church by this close follower of the Lord Jesus Christ. Mrs. Gess and I counted it all joy to have had a dear friend like Lettie for a quarter century. Only in heaven will she realize the thousands who have been blessed by her lifelong ministry of eye care.

I thank God for the empowerment of the Holy Spirit Who directed me to work at the Kissy UMC Eye Clinic, a Christian institution. As an ophthalmic nurse, my witness and ministry to the blind started March 1, 1984. I retired as the administrator on March 31, 2010, after serving for twenty-six years. My sincere gratitude goes to Dr. and Mrs. Lowell Gess who were my mentors.

Dr. and Mrs. Gess started this hospital, which was opened in January 1984. Mrs. Gess gave me zeal, inspired me and accepted me for what I am so I could help give sight to the blind.

In those early days, work was hectic. Dr. and Mrs. Gess and just five staff were seeing 150 to 200 clients each day. Every one of us was involved in multiple aspects of the work, such as registration, filing cards, cleaning, etc. Dr. Gess did the surgeries, doing about six to ten cataract with intraocular lenses each day. What really made our day is that we started with devotions, including the clients, every morning. Prayer was also said for individual clients before surgery was begun. This kept us going and filled us with joy and satisfaction during each day's work. We were all eager to see the joy on the client's face the next day after surgery.

I lived at the far west end of Freetown, while the hospital is at the east end of town. With such a distance, I had to wake early in the morning, ready to do a cross-country drive to work in order not to be late. By the time I arrived at the clinic, over 200 patients would be waiting to see Dr. Gess.

Following some trying and stressful days, all I could do when I got home was to lie on a hot water bottle. My late husband, Henri, supported me in my ministry to the blind who wanted to see the handiwork of God. May his soul rest in peace.

It was and has been my pleasure to work in this Christian institution. Before the war, we had volunteer doctors and their wives, nurses and work teams doing the surgeries, putting up buildings. They also brought medical supplies, instruments, building materials and books for the UMC schools and other items for the churches.

Indeed, I have witnessed in this institution. Can you imagine working with different doctors and individuals every two weeks with different nationalities, cultures and backgrounds? All this I did joyfully. If they could be so devoted, why not me? All this happened due to Dr. and Mrs. Gess' love and devotion for Africa. They wanted the blind to gain back their sight to see nature as it is. Seeing God's work, those with restored vision begin to love Him and continue praising Him.

Working in this Christian institution while witnessing has given me more joy and love to serve humanity. It has made me more humble, mature, patient and sharing – and most of all – has strengthened my Christian faith. I strongly believe that Jesus came to earth, was crucified, buried, raised from the dead, ascended into heaven and is pleading for us until He comes the second time. I cannot wait for His second coming so I can go and have peace, joy and love in heaven.

Having witnessed for twenty-six years and retiring – and after having volunteered there after Henri's death – I know it will be my pleasure to continue witnessing voluntarily. I have joy in my heart for seeing those who I helped – who were blind – seeing and praising God. His praise shall continually be in my mouth.

Thank you, Dr. and Mrs. Gess, for all your help, and the financial and moral support you have given me during the past twenty-six years – and I am still getting from you.

Chapter Forty-two

Esther Megill

"In spite of – or perhaps partially because of – the civil wars and other conflicts in a number of countries in Africa, the Christian churches continue to grow."

Esther Megill

The missionary career of Esther Megill has been varied and exciting. She began as a lab technician then went onto station manager, branching out into Christian education and ultimately serving on the staff of the General Board of Global Ministries. Her passion for Christian education took her to different countries, teaching for seven years at Trinity Theological College in Ghana, with shorter times in Nigeria, Zambia and Kenya – as well as in Mississippi. Her Return To Africa – A Journal *can be considered a historical account of periods of Church growth and her involvement in them. An earlier book,* Sierra Leone Remembered *is fascinating reading. She took Jesus at His word: "…Go and make disciples of all nations…teaching them…."*
–Matthew 28:19-20

Return to Africa

It has been my privilege to serve in Africa for many years. I was first sent by the Evangelical United Brethren Board of Missions, arriving in Sierra Leone in January 1951. I went as the first medical technologist sent by our board, and was soon hard at work setting up a laboratory at Rotifunk Hospital. Gertrude Bloede, R.N., who had just completed her study of midwifery in London, traveled with me. We moved into the house with Dr. Mabel Silver who had served many years and was known and revered throughout Sierra Leone and beyond.

The problems (sickness, an uprising, etc.) and the many good experiences are described in my book, *Sierra Leone Remembered.* Before I left in 1962, I had been involved in extensive work in Christian education, including writing materials and serving as the conference director of youth work (which included children, I soon discovered). As I look back on those days, I think of how through the years Sierra Leone's leadership has developed. Now recovering from a devastating civil war, the Sierra Leone church continues to increase in numbers and is led almost entirely by Sierra Leone leadership. (It was even my privilege to help prepare J. C. Humper, who later became bishop, when he was a student in Trinity College in Ghana.)

There are no U.S. missionaries in Sierra Leone now, but a few Africans from the Sierra Leone and other African conferences are now appointed as missionaries. The same is true in Liberia and some other conferences.

(When I was on the staff at the board, many of our missionaries in Algeria were expelled. One couple – he French, she Algerian – were not able to return because he had been expelled. I asked that they be appointed to work in France with North Africans who had settled there. At first it was insisted that this had "never been done" – to support a missionary in his/her own country. But it was finally approved and now we see it happening everywhere!)

I was area secretary for North and West Africa for four years immediately after union with the Methodist Church to form the United Methodist Church. The problems in interpreting the changes to the churches in Sierra Leone and Nigeria are related in my book, *Return to Africa.*

From 1973 to 1980, I was again in Africa, this time in Ghana, where I taught Christian education (plus a few other courses at times) in what was then Trinity College. There I became part of the lives of many young men (women were ordained by the Presbyterian Church in Ghana only in the last year I was there when there were two women students) who became leaders of the church not only in Ghana, but a number in other places in Africa and a few in the U.S.

While there, I became even more aware of the rapid growth of churches in Africa. Students would return from their "practical" assignments – working with a minister during the "long vac" (vacation) period – and report walking miles to villages where there had been no minister for months. There would be baptisms, communion and weddings while they were there. One student expressed his concern that so many people were joining the church who did not really understand what it meant to be a Christian. There was (and is) such a need for education and training of members of the churches. I saw the need, even when I was in Sierra Leone, for religious education materials for all age groups, and writing and preparing others to write such materials became an important part of my life.

While in Ghana, I was invited by a Mennonite missionary friend to teach some courses at the school they had helped establish for leaders of the "spiritual" or "independent" churches. I came to know some of their leaders. Although I could not agree with all their syncretistic beliefs, I saw how eager they were for more knowledge and training, and was glad to welcome them to our workshops on Christian education. Part of the growth of the churches in Africa is due to these independent churches. They vary a great deal, but all attempt to combine African tradition with Christianity.

In spite of – or perhaps partially because of – the civil wars and other conflicts in a number of countries in Africa, the Christian churches continue to grow. One can only admire the faithfulness of many of their members in spite of hardships. The increase in the number of well educated and trained African leadership is a hopeful sign. There is still need for help, particularly financial, and a place for missionaries who can help fill the need for more training when they are requested by the churches.

I wish that our African churches would become autonomous, although they could remain part of world Methodism. I saw the difference in Ghana of strong churches that had never had the amount of money that our churches had from the mission boards or societies which had started them, and which were growing and sending missionaries of their own. They still have a connection with the European churches that sent the first missionaries, but have developed their own churches and are giving a strong Christian witness. I do know, however, that we need to share of our wealth and other resources to churches struggling in their impoverished countries.

Chapter Forty-three

Rev. Angie Myles

"In our work in the communities, we see the daily outpouring of the Holy Sprit as we enter new villages – even crossing rivers and going through swamps – with the Gospel of Jesus Christ."

Rev. Angie Myles

How the growth of the church in Sub-Saharan Africa is taking place is personified in the witness of the Rev. Angie Myles. She was born and raised on the island of St. Lucia in the West Indies. At the ages of sixteen, she began nurses' training in England. In 1966, she met Joe Myles, a native of Sierra Leone, who was pursuing studies in London. Two years later, they married and in 1970 returned to Sierra Leone nurturing a family of four children.

"The Gospel is Going Like Fire"

In an email to me on August 21, 2010, Rev. Myles included these choice words: "I believe the growth of Christianity has come about as a result of the faithfulness of our God. Life is very hard in Africa…and that has forced us to depend on our God. The way God has saved us through the wars has brought us closer to God. The seeds, which the early missionaries planted, have been watered by the Holy Ghost and are now yielding a bumper harvest. I am happy to be in a remote area teaching the Word of God. There is an urgency to which I am responding."

At the present time, Rev. Myles is country director in Sierra Leone for Children of the Nations, which provides responsible care to orphaned and destitute children. This is done by equipping the nationals and giving the children every possible advantage available to grow in a stable, Christ-centered environment, empowering them to be the leaders of tomorrow. She states: "I had the idea to start creating awareness in the children about how valuable they are as Africans – that they should not feel inferior to other races."

Rev. Myles' early work in Sierra Leone was with the United Methodist Church heading up clinics such as Taiama where she and her family miraculously lived through the bites of a rabid dog. Eventually, she served as the medical coordinator for all of the medical programs, including the Kissy UMC Eye Hospital with which I was affiliated. As an ordained clergywoman, she is a powerful and inspiring preacher.

In a recent email, Angie writes:

"Greetings in His precious name. It was good hearing from you. I pray that Almighty God will keep you safe and give you the desires of your heart, which is to have another book published to the glory of the Lord.

"I am happy to report to you, my spiritual father and mentor, about that time you wrote in the new Thompson Chain Bible which you gave to me to "Preach the Word," II Timothy 4:2. I have been seriously engaged in doing so.

"The Lord posted me to Children of the Nations to care for orphans and destitute children. Our building in Freetown became too small and inadequate for our children who were growing in numbers rapidly. I took over as country director in March 2002 with four children, two boys and two girls. Today, we have 100 children in residential holistic care in Upper Banta seven miles from Serabu in the Moyamba District. Upper Banta commercially is a very rich chiefdom, considering the very large deposit of bauxite. Aggressive bauxite mining is currently being done, yet the people are living in abject poverty. It is the least developed chiefdom. It has a population of approximately 20,000.

"Here in Upper Banta, we have seventeen churches. Two villages have buildings for worship, whilst in others worship takes place on verandas, open spaces and thatched shelters. Each year we see more people being baptized.

"I disagree with those who say that Christianity should not be imposed on other cultures. In fact, I believe that the word 'imposed' is misused. We do no impose Christianity. We teach and introduce Christ to people of different cultures.

"We teach them to obey God. To say that we should leave them where we find them is contrary to the value of development. Why did we accept the latest technology, i.e. internet, Facebook, phones, microwaves, etc. These are just ploys of the enemy. In Hosea 4:6, God laments that his people perish because of lack of knowledge.

"The Word of God says that Jesus is the truth. No one comes to the Father except through Jesus Christ. I believe that all other religions are not the right way to come to the Father. Other religions have both positive and negative aspects. The main point is there is no real satisfaction in any other religion except Christianity.

The Word tells us that Satan is the father of lies. He has been lying from the beginning. He is the source of all their thoughts. II Corinthians 4:4 say the God of this age has blinded the minds of unbelievers so that they cannot see the light of the Gospel of the glory of Christ who is the image of God.

"John 8:44 says you belong to your father, the devil, and you want to carry out your father's desire. He was a murderer from the beginning, not holding to the truth, for there is no truth in him. When he lies, he speaks his native language, for he is a liar and the father of lies.

"We need to pray without ceasing so the Gospel of truth can go through, overcoming every stumbling block by the fire of God. Satan has almost succeeded to blind the eyes of people in the first world, whilst the Holy Spirit has opened the eyes of the Church in Africa to see the glory of the Lord. The Gospel is going like fire. There is a boldness amongst women and men of God, causing them to speak against tribalism, secret societies, polygamy and other ungodly practices on the continent. Alleluia to the God of truth. You shall know the truth and the truth shall set you free. Praise the Lord!

"In Joel 2:28 it says, 'I will pour out my spirit on all people, your sons and daughters will prophesy, your old men will dream dreams and your young men shall see visions.' In our work in the communities, we see the daily outpouring of the Holy Sprit as we enter new villages – even crossing rivers and going through swamps – with the Gospel of Jesus Christ.

"It is a joy on Sundays to see the children and staff moving away from the ministry site towards the interior with the Gospel of Jesus Christ. The Holy Ghost waters the heart and, as the seed enters, it quickly germinates and brings forth fruits of righteousness and holiness. God is alive in Sierra Leone, and we are blessed to be part of a movement geared towards bringing Christ to children who have never heard the gospel. Recently, we had camp for children and youth. Two hundred and sixty-nine children attended children's camp and 180 youth attended youth camp. Ninety-eight percent of them were from Muslim homes. This is so encouraging. We are determined to spread the Gospel and win souls for Christ.

"We need to pray for blind eyes to open so the truth can set people free."

The only response to the above e-mail is: Thank God for effective "witnesses" who serve in little known corners of the world.

Chapter Forty-four

Rev. Doris Caulker

"My Christian experience helps me rule as my Lord teaches –
'To be a servant and not to be served.'"

Ruth Gess and Rev. Doris Caulker

The Rev. Paramount Chief Doris Lenga Gbabiyor Caulker II is a powerful
and persuasive preacher. I still remember her sermon, "Jesus Loves Me This I
Know," based on John 3:16, which she delivered at King Memorial United
Methodist Church several years ago. She is a mighty force for good and, thank
God, is in a position of wide influence. The growth of the church is not in
doubt.

To Be a Servant and Not to be Served

Rev. Paramount Chief Doris Lenga Gbabiyor Caulker II administers the
Kagboro Chiefdom. She comes to this high office well qualified. When asked to
comment on the unusual growth of the Christian Church in Sub-Saharan Africa
and her role as a witness, she writes:

"The growth of the Church in Sierra Leone in recent years has been like yeast
in dough. It works quietly, unseen, but soon one sees the finished product – bread
– which when eaten, satisfies one's hunger.

"Many churches, some in modest forms, have been built in large and remote
towns. Worshipers without transportation walk for miles to fellowship with other
Christians in the Church. Above all, we see the growth of the Church through
the leadership positions its members hold in the nation. Presidents, paramount

chiefs – like me – doctors, nurses, teachers, lawyers, pastors and others have all taken their places in the running of the nation's affairs. The Church has touched the lives of all these people.

"I personally thank God Almighty, for grace through me, which has enabled me to reach to this position as paramount chief of my people in the Kagboro Chiefdom. When I look back at my life and its achievements, I realize that God – through the Church – has prepared me for this position, working as a women's worker in our conference, a teacher, director of Christian education, a pastor, lecturer and even a 'babysitter' for one of Dr. Gess' sons who is now a doctor himself. I have been able to deal with humankind of all ages. These groups and ages are all found in my Chiefdom. My Christian experience helps me rule as my Lord teaches – 'To be a servant and not to be served.' I thank Dr. Gess, and Ruth his partner, for their own contributions to the growth of the Church in this part of God's world – Sierra Leone. I thank God for all, who through the Church, have touched my life."

Chapter Forty-five

Bishop Joseph Humper

"I heard the voice of the Lord saying, 'Whom shall I send, and who will go for us?' Then I said, 'Here am I! Send me.'" – Isaiah 6:8

Bishop Joseph Humper

Bishop Joseph Christian Humper carried on his episcopal duties for the United Methodist Church in Sierra Leone during its 11-year brutal rebel war. His life was spared in a miraculous way. At the end of the war, he chaired the profound and encompassing Truth and Reconciliation Commission (more information on it can be found on the Internet). As a personal friend, Bishop Humper encouraged Ruth and me and the eye care outreach in Sierra Leone.

My Testimony

What a timely and gracious opportunity for me to share my personal experiences with God's people – and more especially, those who planted the "seed" of the Gospel of Jesus Christ in Africa in particular and the global community in general. I use this media to bear testimony to the fact that "With God all things are possible." Coming from a predominantly (99.9%) Muslim village with no more than twenty thatched houses and from an illiterate family, how did this child come to accomplish what is documented in this piece? Perhaps it might be said that whatever God has destined for His servant, it will come to pass no matter the seeming obstacle and near impossible circumstances.

When I was at the age of three years, my mother died after a short illness; her death was followed by my father when I was at the age of six years. My grandmother, Madam Mariama Charley who had lost all her six children – including my mother – took custody of me at our village, which is six miles away from the metropolitan city of Bonthe Sherbro. Fearing that I might be hunted and killed by witches, she took me to my Aunt Adama Kallon who then resided at Bonthe Sherbro. As a child, I followed the religion of my aunt, Islam. I prayed with them and fasted during the month of Ramadan. But this was not to last. Unknowingly, I can now say that God had something else in store for me.

The long journey of my life began when my illiterate aunt sent me to school, then through the Evangelical United Brethren Church, from 1949 to 1960. I was one of the only two of my immediate family members from our village who attended school. During the holidays, I would go to the village and crack palm kernel to sell for my education. It was during those formative years of my existence that Christ discovered me, I would venture to say. Later I was baptized. I joined the Junior and Christian Endeavour Groups, served as a chorister and participated in many other church activities. But all of these did not motivate me or become a factor for my future career. I participated in them because we were required to do so. There was the popular saying: "If you did not go to church on Sunday you would be beaten on Monday."

Encountering Christ

My personal experience of a life changing experience and encounter with Christ occurred in an unexpected manner with a singular event. I spent three years in Standard Six (primary or elementary school) because my grandmother could not afford my secondary education fees. Even for my elementary education, I had to go to our village every holiday to crack palm kernel and go to Bonthe, carrying fermented (foofo) cassava for six miles, to sell in order to pay my school fees. This continued until I completed my primary school education.

After two years in Standard Six, some of my friends left school and got employment with the Sierra Leone Produce Marketing Board as clerks. My grandmother tried to persuade me to leave school to go to work. But I refused, saying that I was not ready to work. I wanted to continue my education but the possibilities were remote because of lack of financial support. The earning power of my grandmother was $5 a year. All seemed lost!

No! I was wrong! God had a plan for me (Jeremiah 29:11). Then it all happened! In the afternoon of August 1961, the Rev. Solomon Horitio Gorvie, senior pastor of Weaver Memorial Evangelical United Brethren Church, visited our class – Senior Primary Two – and announced that those who wanted to attend the Bible Training Institute in Bo would be recommended to do so. Without much thought as to what it all meant, my quest for further education spurred me to go with five other students who had expressed willingness to go. Six of us left on September 10, 1961, for the Bible Training Institute.

My trip to Bo was my first journey outside Bonthe Island. It was exciting, but I had some apprehension as to what my attending the Bible Training Institute would mean for my future. This was an institution established by Dr. Charles W. Leader, a missionary from the United States of America for the training of evangelists and church workers. For me, it ultimately became my secondary school. I graduated "cum laude" in 1963. With my three years of evangelistic education at the Bible Training Institute, a window of opportunity was opened for me to further my education without going to a formal secondary school.

Education

From 1963 to 1966, I became one of the foundation students of Bo Teacher's College, which was started on the campus of the Bible Training Institute. I was appointed the first president of the Students' Union. With a Teacher's Elementary Certificate (TEC), which I obtained in 1966, I embarked on correspondence courses with the University of London and prepared for the West Africa Examinations Council, the result of which earned me a General Certificate of Education in 1972.

In pursuit of further education, I received a Crusade Scholarship and proceeded to Trinity College Legon, Ghana, for theological training from 1973 to 1977. I returned home in 1977 with two certificates, (1) Certificate in Theology (First Class) at Trinity College and (2) Diploma in Theology from University of Legon, Ghana. From 1977 to 1980, I attended Fourah Bay College, University of Sierra Leone, and graduated with a Bachelor of Arts degree (Second Division) reading theology, sociology and philosophy in 1980.

After two years, I proceeded to Union Theological Seminary in New York (1982-1983) graduating with a Masters of Sacred Theology. From 1988 to 1990, I studied at Garrett-Evangelical Theological Seminary for a Doctor of Ministry. In 1998, I received a Doctor of Divinity from Gbanga School of Theology, followed by a Doctor of Humane Letters from the United Methodist University of Liberia in 2003.

All of these achievements would not have been possible without the handiwork of Christ who was equipping me for greater service in the Church, nation and international community. These constituted some life changing and glorious experiences for me. Considering the fact that I never had a formal secondary school education, I can attribute my educational achievement to Christ who was preparing me for greater service in every way possible.

Pursuing a "Servant Ministry"

Contemplating a future career which initially I had no idea of what it might turn out to be, I made a covenant with the Lord in these words: "Lord, if you equip me for the task ahead of me, I shall serve you to the best of my ability until I bid farewell to this world." The Lord did it! But how did a frightened, timid, shy and introverted young man come to the public limelight? Nothing less than God's abiding grace. Articulating Paul's words of Christ, "My grace is sufficient for you…" (II Corinthians 12:9), I committed myself to a "servant ministry."

My first unpaid career was an evangelist from 1961 to 1963, during and after graduation from the Bible Training Institute. While on this mission, God opened windows of opportunity for me to continue to serve him first as a teacher at EUB/UMC Primary School, Kenema. At the same time, I enrolled as a probationer for the ordained ministry in 1967, although my Bible Training Institute education was enough for me to be ordained a clergy. After my theological education, I entered into fulltime dual ministry – teaching and pastoral.

The Lord equipped me and strengthened me to serve in other areas such as a part-time lecturer and director of Theological Studies at the Bible Training Institute (1976-1980), which resulted in training pastors locally for the Church; a part-time lecturer at Fourah Bay College at the Department of Theology, and at the Theological College and Church Training Centre (1980-1982 and 1984-1990). I was also the First Conference Director of Youth Ministries (1978-1986).

I returned home on holidays from Ghana. For the four years I was studying there, I served as student pastor at Koidu Joint Parish (1974); Panguma UMC (1975); Weaver Memorial UM Church, Bonthe Sherbro (1976) and Trinity Church, Moyamba (1977). While studying at Fourah Bay College, I served as associate pastor at Bishop Baughman Memorial UM Church, Brookfields, Freetown (1977-1980).

On completion of my studies, I was stationed as senior pastor at Bishop Baughman Memorial United Methodist Church (1980-1986), taking over from the late Dr. Eustace L. Renner who, incidentally, was my last principal at the Bible Training Institute. As though the Lord was equipping me for greater service, my responsibilities increased with God granting me the energy to carry them out as conference secretary and registrar, Board of Ordained Ministry (1984-1988); council director (1984-1988) and episcopal chaplain to the late Bishop Thomas S. Bangura (1979-1992). All of these were as a result of lack of trained and qualified man-power in the conference. I came on the scene when there were very few trained and qualified pastors.

The molding and equipping of God's servant culminated in assuming other positions and responsibilities in the conference, nation, West Africa Central Conference and international community. I served as the first executive secretary of the West Africa Central Conference (1980-1988).

Bishop Consecration and Ministry

It seemed that while I engaged in all of these activities and responsibilities, God still had something more for me to do for the Church and humanity. On August 14, 1992, I was elected to the Episcopacy and was consecrated bishop on August 16 as the third indigenous bishop of the United Methodist Church, Sierra Leone Annual Conference.

With this elevated position, it was evident that more was in store for me. I assumed office as Episcopal leader for the Sierra Leone area during the eleven-years rebel war which engulfed the country. I worked in and through the period of the rebel war and provided leadership for our people – in the country in particular and international community in general. During the heated period of the rebel war, I stayed with my people, soliciting help from the General Board of Global Ministries for relief services.

God used me in many ways to the point that by the time of my retirement as resident bishop of the Sierra Leone area, the following were accomplished:

- Established a Child Rescue Centre in Bo
- Mercy Hospital in Bo
- Missionary Training Centre at Bible Training Institute campus. (More importantly, I succeeded in securing free hold of the land.)
- Developed Kissy Clinic into a general hospital at Urban Centre
- Dr. Lowell and Ruth Gess built a modern eye hospital with a hostel and canteen at Kissy Urban Centre
- Rehabilitated Rotifunk Hospital, Taiama, and Manjama, Bo clinics
- Rehabilitated Jaiama Clinic
- Increased primary schools from 213 to 264; secondary schools from 18 to 25 and established a second girls' secondary school – United Methodist Girls' Junior Secondary School in Freetown, which was a product of post-conflict development.
- Constructed and rehabilitated many churches in the western area and the provinces
- Increased church membership from 85,000 to 225,000
- Ordained clergy from 75 to 264, most of whom had their pastoral training from Sierra Leone Theological College and Church Training Centre in Freetown

Indeed, the challenges of civil conflict and post-conflict did not deter me from providing the requisite leadership for my people. Instead they refined and reinforced my desire to give all I could for the development of the Church, and my people as a whole in the nation.

At the general church level, I served as one of the directors of the General Board of Higher Education and Ministry (1992-1996) and the General Board of Global Ministries (2000-2008). I also served as one of the executive members of the World Methodist Council (1992-2004).

My responsibilities increased with the demand of the day. In an ecumenical circle, I was first elected vice president of the Council of Churches in Sierra Leone and Inter-Religious Council of Sierra Leone (1996-1999), and later president of the two organizations (1999-2005). Additionally, I was elected honorary president of the World Conference of Religions for Peace at the seventh world assembly of that body in Amman, Jordan, thereby becoming the first Sierra Leonean to be elevated to that position in Africa.

Truth and Reconciliation Commission

I worked with my colleagues in the Council and Inter-Religious Council of Sierra Leone to facilitate the peaceful resolution of the rebel war, which engulfed the country with catastrophic consequences. I led the Council to appeal to President Alhaji Dr. Ahmad Tejan Kabbah to engage Corporal Foday Sankoh, who had already been condemned to death, to come to a peace conference table to end the brutal and barbaric rebel war that was unparalleled in the history of civil conflicts in Africa. The result culminated in the "Lome Peace Agreement," which was signed between the government of Sierra Leone, represented by the president, Alhaji Dr. Ahmad Tejan Kabbah, and the Revolutionary United Front (RUF) leader, Corporal Foday Saybana Sankoh, on July 7, 1999.

The rebel war was considered finally ended on January 18, 2002 when the president declared the war over during the symbolic burning of the instruments of war (guns) at Lungi. The Sierra Leone Truth and Reconciliation Commission was then established. I was appointed chairman of the seven member commission, consisting of four nationals and three internationals, by His Excellency President Alhaji Dr. Ahmad Tejan Kabbah on the recommendation of the selection committee headed by Mr. Oluyeni Adeniji, the executive representative of the Secretary-General of the United Nations.

After eighteen months of intensive work, I presented to the president the four volumes of the TRC Report on October 5, 2004, on behalf of the commission. The report was acclaimed as one of the best comprehensive TRC reports in the world and is a valuable source of reference for conflict resolution. The TRC Report was (is) intended to ensure peace, justice, forgiveness, healing and reconciliation among perpetrators and victims on the one hand, and perpetrators and the nation on the other hand.

Committee on Smooth Transition of Governance

Providence again had it that during the 2007 presidential and parliamentary general elections, the Office of National Security (ONS) invited all civil society organizations in the country to constitute a "Committee on Smooth Transition of Governance." I was appointed to serve as chairman of that committee. The result of that effort was commendable. Our prior admonition to the two main political party leaders – Vice President Solomon E. Berewa of the Sierra Leone People's Party (SLPP) and Mr. Ernest Bai Koroma the opposition leader of the All People's Congress (APC) – to accept the outcome of the results of the general elections contributed to bringing about a smooth transition of governance even though the incumbent governing party (SLPP) leadership lost the elections. Hence, the general elections were acclaimed to be one of the most successful held in a post-conflict country such as Sierra Leone. My leadership was once again affirmed and commended by our people in Sierra Leone.

The Great Commission

Indeed, in my entire journey in the Church and nation – as well as international community – Christ's Commission became vividly clear and applicable to me: "I heard the voice of the Lord saying, 'Whom shall I send, and who will go for us?' Then I said, 'Here am I! Send me.' (Isaiah 6:8). I have never turned down a call to service. So today I can say with certainty that God works out His purpose for those who are attentive to that still small voice and that with God nothing is impossible. For "the will of God cannot send a servant where the grace of God cannot uphold him."

From a humble beginning, I have come to experience the power of God working in me for the salvation of humanity. Today, I can say with humility that my efforts have been rewarded by the recognition I have received with awards and insignia nationally and internationally. These include:

1. Millennium Award for Peacekeeping in Africa by the General Board of Global Ministries on October 19, 1999
2. Millennium Award at the Centenary Celebration of the Sierra Leone Annual Conference
3. Insignia Award – "Commander of the Order of the Rokel" (COR) – by His Excellency, the President, Alhaji Dr. Ahmad Tejan Kabbah, on the occasion of the 40th Independence Anniversary of the Republic of Sierra Leone, April 27, 2000
4. Centenary Award by Albert Academy Old Boys and Girls Association during the centenary celebration of the school on October 8, 2004

5. Insignia Award – "Grand Commander of the Order of the Rokel" (GCOR) – by His Excellency, the President, Alhaji Dr. Ahmad Tejan Kabbah, April 27, 2006

In this personal testimony, I must say that but for the United Methodist Church, I might never have accomplished whatever I have documented here. I can only raise my hands in prayer and gratitude to the thousands of God's people whose contribution towards the Crusade Scholarship Funds, enabling me to equip myself for service to God and humanity. This is my personal testimony. I can convincingly say with John Newtown in his *Amazing Grace*, "Through many dangers, toils and snare, I have already come. 'Tis grace that brought me safe thus far, and grace will lead me home."

Chapter Forty-six

Anna Morford

"God is good – He is always ready to encourage, engage and entertain us – and it is a joy to participate with Him!"

Anna and Virginia Mariama Morford

In her gracious and efficient way, Anna is keeping the Servants of Sierra Leone in touch with each other. She has taken over from Dr. Winifred Bradford who initialed this Google service in 2006. When in doubt, we check with Anna.

In His Service
Sierra Leone, 1965-1971 and 1977-1983; Zimbabwe, 1972-1977

In the spring of 1965, missionary Virginia Pickarts visited the Evangelical United Brethren (EUB) Church in my hometown. That's how I heard that the Harford School for Girls in Moyamba, Sierra Leone, was in need of a business teacher – a subject for which I was about to complete certification.

Along with several others, I joined the staff that September and began an amazing journey into the discovery of a new country, a new culture and a new profession! I went, not as a commissioned missionary, but as a Kingsley teacher, hired by the Sierra Leone government, outfitted and blessed and sent by my local EUB church, to a school known to us through mission stories we had read in church publications.

Harford School, Moyamba

The teaching staff in those days was a mix of missionary, Peace Corps, British VSO (Volunteer Service Overseas) and Kingsley teachers (including both Sierra Leoneans and expatriates). The primary task, of course, was providing structure for the secondary school education of nearly 400 girls who lived on the campus, housed in three large dormitories. Christian witness was added, especially through the extra-curricular activities and the atmosphere of respect and concern for the individual development of each student.

Patterns of school life had been established by missionaries of earlier years – attendance at Sunday and Wednesday church services, vesper services every evening before study hall, morning devotions conducted in the dormitories by the housemothers, and morning devotions conducted by teachers at the school assembly before classes began. Sierra Leonean women of faith – like Elizabeth Hatib, Mary Weaver and Mrs. Challe – led their dormitory groups in hymn singing and devotions early in the morning, which created a very pleasant sound that wafted through the yet-cool pre-dawn air.

Many of the students came from Muslim homes, but there were no complaints about the observance of these Christian traditions. The life of the school pulsed on as any other, with lectures, notes and exams, essays and recitations, the beginning and ending of terms. Young girls grew from playful, carefree and challenging children to young ladies, ready to enter into a career and the responsibilities of an adult world.

Education is afforded a limited number of girls in Sierra Leone; finding graduates in leadership roles as adults is always heart-warming. Many leave secondary school with strongly ingrained Christian habits. In 1965, African leaders like Principal William H. Fitzjohn and his wife, Muriel Alice, and new teachers Doris Caulker Lenga-Kroma, Lois Neale and Mina Bailor, gave the school an African tone and helped all of the young British and American teachers understand and participate in that atmosphere. Their Christian witness was important to all, expatriates and students alike.

Dorcas Kargbo (now Kamanda) was a student in 1965 who had a deep desire to help the people of her small village. She also had a special fondness for Hope and Les Law, an EUB couple from Colorado who had come to Harford School as Kingsley teachers that year. In 2010, Dorcas, Hope and Les witnessed the opening of the Heritage Secondary School in Kabala, and the Nar Sarah Health Clinic nearby – a dream that was forty-five years in the making. It was finally achieved with the help of the United Methodist Rocky Mountain Conference and others who heard the witness of these three!

One year rolled into another and suddenly it was 1971 and time, I thought, to get reacquainted with "life back home." But less than a year later the opportunity to again teach in Africa, this time as a missionary of the General Board of Global

Ministries, was too exciting to pass up! The new assignment wasn't Sierra Leone, but Rhodesia – soon to become independent Zimbabwe.

Nyadiri Teachers Training College

There seemed to be fewer missionaries in Rhodesia – and greater distances made visits from friends infrequent. However, I found myself in a warm and welcoming community of dedicated Christian witnesses in Nyadiri at the preparatory school for elementary teachers. African Christians led most mission institutions. Principal Jim and Janie Makawa, Herbert and Eva Katedza, and others who had studied in the United States through the United Methodist Crusade Scholarship program, led the staff in offering challenging and creative training for students who would soon be tutors to a younger generation.

It was said that Rhodesia (now Zimbabwe) had the highest per capita number of Ph.Ds of any country in Africa. Yet in 1972, Africans still struggled to participate in the economic life of the country. The struggle for independence had already begun.

Mrewa Secondary School

The next year while on the staff at Mrewa Secondary School, I was proud to join Principal Alex Chibanguza and more dedicated teachers to work for the educational achievement of the students that would possibly permit them access to the work world beyond the rural farms where they had grown up.

Life in mission schools was busy and directed, and moved along in a purposeful and peaceful manner. Life in the political realm, however, was at something of a fever pitch. Bishop Muzorewa's involvement continually deepened – always advocating for a peaceful solution – even as the gathering freedom fighters (or guerilla forces, as they were called by the white Rhodesian journalists) were reported nearer and nearer to the centers of white domination. When UM missionaries, Norm and Winnie Thomas, were deported for speaking out against the oppression of Africans (UM missionary, teacher and cartoonist, Morgan Johnson, was censored for a cartoon that appeared in the UM Newspaper Umbowo) – when anger would have overcome all of us – Bishop Muzorewa spoke calmly but sternly, urging restraint and prayers for the offenders.

About this same time, there was a suggestion from the GBGM that it was time for a moratorium on U.S. missionaries, while well-prepared Africans be encouraged to take positions in the mission work currently held by expatriates. Naturally, there was a good deal of confusion in the missionary community over this pronouncement. Again, Bishop Muzorewa calmed the furor with the statement that yes, it may be time for Africans to take that responsibility, but there would always be a need for Christians from all nations to stand with each other and work together for the Kingdom of God.

In the spring of 1977, I returned to the U.S., and that September, was assigned again to Sierra Leone.

"Home" Again

Falling back into the routine of Harford School was quite comfortable, but it didn't last long. The next challenge was two-fold: mothering a two-year-old and attempting to "fill the shoes" of Vivian Olson, who, after more than thirty years of service in various mission jobs in Sierra Leone, was retiring! Hers was a loving gift of a life lived for others!

Because of a close relationship between Virginia Pickarts and a Themne family in Moyamba, their youngest child who had been born in April was "given" to Virginia – following an African tradition – to raise her and to help Virginia in the home. At the time, I shared living quarters with Virginia, and seemed to have the greater interest in tackling the upbringing of a small child. So we embarked together on this new venture.

Vivian Olson was serving as the liaison between the Sierra Leone Conference and the General Board of Global Ministries at the time of her retirement. In early 1979, little Virginia Mariama and I moved to Freetown where I quickly learned that I couldn't manage the care of a small child and do the work at the conference office at the same time. We arranged for cousin Mabinty Conteh to come from Moyamba to help! Suddenly I was "mother" to two girls, ages 2 and 16. This was quite a change of lifestyle, but what a blessing it has been! Mabinty not only cared for little Virginia while I worked, but she helped me to become a more integrated part of the Conteh family.

A major part of the work at the conference office building at 31 Lightfoot-Boston Street was assisting the rapidly growing "Volunteers in Mission" program. Arranging housing, food and supplies for the projects to be undertaken by these short-term missioners kept us busy! The opportunity to meet folks related to many aspects of the church program was as exciting as it was varied! Additionally, providing logistical support for missionaries at up-country stations, and visitors arriving from the U.S. and departing for home, filled the days. So many were the visitors, both from up-country and overseas, that the mission house at King Street, with its idyllic view over Freetown and the bay, rarely had a night without new or old friends in one or both of the guestrooms!

In October 1983, immigration issues around Virginia Mariama's status resulted in a decision to come with her to the United States. Three years of teaching in a rural Oregon school and seven years at the New York offices of the General Board of Global Ministries as assistant treasurer of the World Division preceded our move to Michigan where I have had the privilege of serving as the Detroit Conference treasurer from 1994 to the present.

My degree in business education from Oregon State University has been the passport to a world of experiences that could never have been imagined as I timidly visited with Virginia Pickarts that Sunday night in the little town of Philomath, Oregon. God is good – He is always ready to encourage, engage and entertain us – and it is a joy to participate with Him!

Chapter Forty-seven

Dr. John Karefa-Smart

"His master replied, 'Well done, good and faithful servant! You have been faithful with a few things; I will put you in charge of many things. Come and share your master's happiness!'" — Matthew 25:23

Dr. John Karefa-Smart

In a phone call July 2010, I visited with Dr. John Albert Musselman Karefa-Smart. He told me about *Rainbow Happenings*, a memoir of his life that he had just published. I immediately ordered a copy from Xlibris (Orders@Xlibris.com) and was thrilled with the chronicled life of this educator, minister, physician, public health practitioner/administrator, diplomat, politician and elder statesman. He promised to contribute to *Glorious Witnesses for Africa*. Within two months, he died from pancreatic carcinoma at the age of ninety-five years.

Born in Rotifunk (June 17, 1915-August 26, 2010), Dr. Karefa-Smart was living in the U.S. in Connecticut when his terminal illness was diagnosed. Given a month to live, in late July the Sierra Leone government flew him back to Freetown.

An ethnic Sherbro, John Karefa-Smart was educated at the EUB Primary School in Moyamba District and the Albert Academy in Freetown. He received his B.A. from Fourah Bay College in Freetown in 1936. Four years later in 1940, he received his B.S. from Otterbein College in Westerville, Ohio. From Otterbein, he went to McGill University in Montreal where he received his M.D. and C.M. in 1944 and a diploma in tropical medicine in 1945. His M.P.H. was received in 1948 from Harvard University in Boston.

He became a fellow or professor at many colleges and universities across the world, including Bunumbu Union Teachers Training College in Sierra Leone (1936-1938), University of Ibadan in Nigeria (1949-1952), and several American universities such as Xavier University of Louisiana (1953), Columbia University (1964-1965), Harvard University (1971-1981), Boston University (1972-1977), Wellesley College (1974) and Howard University (1980-1983).

Dr. Karefa-Smart's political career began with his election to Parliament in 1957. From 1957 to 1964, he was a member of Parliament for the Tonkolili District. He also served as Minister of Lands, Mines and Labor; Minister of Defense; and as Foreign Minister (1961-1964). During that time, he also served occasionally as Acting Prime Minister. From 1965 until 1970, he was Assistant Director-General of the World Health Organization in Geneva, Switzerland. In 1996, he returned to Sierra Leone politics as a member of Parliament and presidential candidate. Karefa-Smart lost the 1996 and 2002 presidential elections to former President Ahmad Tejan Kabbah. In his telephone visit with me, Dr. Karefa-Smart accepted these events as the "will of God," although he did concede that the returns did not confirm a victory for the opposition.

I first met Dr. Karefa-Smart on December 1, 1957, when our family was invited to a dinner arranged by his wife, Rena. My family and I were honored to be guests in their home. They were gracious, even though on their way to serve at Rotifunk Hospital in 1948, the missionaries had not received them properly. He was interested in the persons who would be serving at Rotifunk Hospital. Later, he and Sir Milton Margai paid visits to Rotifunk. On one occasion, I offered to step aside and have these two notables complete the herniorrhaphy in which I was engaged. Again in 2001, Dr. Karefa-Smart, with his interest in community health services, visited me at the Kissy UMC Eye Hospital.

A Harvard-educated physician and activist who helped his country become independent, the Rev. John Karefa-Smart did not follow the typical career path of a UM pastor. In the 1940s, he began dialogues with missionaries that laid the foundation for autonomy and the eventual establishment of the Sierra Leone Annual Conference of the UMC.

In 1959, he led the delegation to the Lancaster House Conference in London to discuss Sierra Leone's progress in self-governance that led to the nation's independence on April 27, 1961.

After he passed away Aug. 26 at age 95, Karefa-Smart received not one but two state funerals. Among those attending his Sept. 18 state funeral at the

King Memorial UMC in Freetown were Sierra Leone's President Ernest Bai Koroma, First Lady Sia Koroma and Vice President Samuel Sumana.

Karefa-Smart's body was conveyed to Rotifunk, his home village, immediately after the Freetown service. Mourners had begun pouring into the small community the week before, and that evening more people were outside than inside the filled-to-capacity 400-seat hall where a vigil honored the deceased leader prior to the Sept. 19 memorial service at Martyr's Memorial UMC.[45]

We thank God for Dr. Karefa-Smart's life and the tremendous impact he made on the growth of the Christian Church in Sub-Saharan Africa.

Chapter Forty-eight

Rev. Katherine and James Horn

"That night Paul saw in a vision a man from Macedonia. The man stood and begged, 'Come over to Macedonia and help us.' After Paul had seen the vision, we immediately prepared to leave for Macedonia, understanding that God had called us to tell the Good News to those people." – Acts 16:9-10

Rev. Katherine Horn

The Horns have meant much to the life of the church in West Africa. Kathy co-founded, along with the Rev. Lyndy Zabel, OC Ministries of Minnesota. Her story follows. Jim Horn, her husband, also contributed to the eye program in Sierra Leone. He was able to remedy the disparity in voltage systems. Most of the equipment was American manufactured and used 110 volts. His electrical modifications allowed the use of the 220-volt British system for recharging batteries and providing illumination for the operating microscopes. His expertise was also used to solve other electrical problems.

OC MINISTRIES

OC MINISTRIES is Operation Classroom, Operation Clinic, Operation Church and Operation Connection all rolled into one! It is a mission partnership that began more than two decades ago between United Methodists from Minnesota, Sierra Leone and Liberia. In 1992, the partnership was extended to include Jamaica. (The focus of this recollection is the West African partnership.)

Humble Beginnings

OC MINISTRIES had a humble beginning through the efforts of the Rosemount United Methodist Church in Minnesota, which wanted to increase its knowledge and participation in mission outreach. Rev. Lyndy Zabel and I worked together, as part of the pastoral staff of the church, along with Senior Pastor Rev. Charlie Dundas. In my research about mission projects in Sierra Leone, I learned about the Harford School for Girls in Moyamba. This led to correspondence with the school's principal, Etta Nicol, who wrote to me about the goals and the needs of the school and its students. The Rosemount church was able to respond with several boxes of needed school supplies, which were deeply appreciated.

About this time, I learned that Rev. Smart Senesie and his wife Daisy were going to be visiting churches in Minnesota. I invited them to speak at the Rosemount church. Their presence and message were powerful and inspiring. Rev. Senesie chose Paul's vision of the man of Macedonia (Acts 16:6-10) as the basis for his talk. He effectively shared the results of illiteracy, hunger, sickness and hopelessness through real life stories. He shared the commitment and generosity of pastors and churches in Sierra Leone, as they tried to minister to people's deep need out of their own physical poverty. The key verse (9) was the challenge: "… Come over to Macedonia and help us." Lyndy and I were deeply moved, along with all who were present. From that evening on, we determined to find ways for our congregation to "come over…and help."

Some time after that pivotal evening, I learned that a work team from Indiana was forming to go to the Albert Academy in Freetown through a program called Operation Classroom. Lyndy and I realized that this was the opportunity the congregation needed to take a major step forward in mission involvement. The decision was made that Lyndy and one of our youth, Shannon Stire, would be a part of that team.

Lyndy and I traveled to Indiana to meet with the coordinators of Operation Classroom, Rev. Joe and Carolyn Wagner, to get specifics about the work team project and necessary preparations and to learn about Operation Classroom. It was an amazing and God-inspired visit that filled my mind and heart with ideas of how our Minnesota Conference could create an Operation Classroom, too.

Operation Classroom Minnesota

Lyndy and Shannon had a successful and spirit-stretching experience in Sierra Leone. They returned with pictures and stories that served to further inspire the Rosemount congregation. Among those inspired was Bill Spychalla who readily joined them in promoting the goals of the mission within the Rosemount church and beyond. (To this day Bill Spychalla continues to be a tireless advocate for this mission outreach.)

For my part, I devoted every free moment I had over the next several years to make the dream of a Minnesota Operation Classroom a reality. My husband Jim, who provided countless hours of technical and physical support for the project, joined the effort. His contribution toward the development and production of effective publicity and shipping assistance was a critical factor in our success. The leadership of Operation Classroom in Indiana was also incredibly generous with their time, encouragement, practical advice and help.

First Advance Team: Sierra Leone

After receiving Conference approval to begin Operation Classroom Minnesota, a small core of supporters set about to raise funds to send an advance team to Sierra Leone and Liberia. Our first defined task was to meet with the African bishops and church leaders to determine the particular schools we would work with and the scope of the projects. Since Indiana's work was focused on secondary schools, our Minnesota program would focus on primary schools.

That first advance team included key Conference leaders and was led by Lyndy and myself. The trip took place in September 1989. In Sierra Leone we met with Bishop Bangura and some of his Conference leadership, including Rev. Smart Senesie. Bishop Bangura asked us to begin our work in three locations – Moyamba, Rotifunk and Yonibana. We traveled up country and met with the pastors and school leaders in each setting.

One of the teachers we met in Moyamba, at the Harford School for Girls, was John Yambasu. His good heart and commitment to Christ eventually led him to become a pastor. As a young pastor, he was deeply involved in the Conference Youth Ministry. Today, he serves as Bishop of the Sierra Leone Conference!

In Rotifunk, we visited the cemetery of the Church of the Martyrs, where the earliest missionaries to Sierra Leone are buried. We paid our true respects and were mindful of their faith and sacrifice in the cause of sharing Christ in spite of personal danger. In Yonibana, we met Rev. Hollowell who had been struggling to improve conditions for the children of his parish for a long time. Our coming brought renewed hope for him and his community.

We came away from these visits with a clear understanding of the needs, the full enthusiastic pledge of local guidance and support, and enough information to share the challenge and to inspire participation in Minnesota.

Liberia

We then traveled to Liberia and repeated a similar process. We met with Bishop Kulah and various Conference leaders and missionaries. Bishop Kulah asked us to begin our work in Liberia at Boway, his home village located in a remote area up country about an hour from Ganta. The people of Boway pledged to make all the blocks (made from mud, straw and water) and to have them ready for our work team upon its arrival. They had met the arrival of our group with native singing and dancing. Now they sent us on our way with gifts of thanksgiving, which included fruit and two live chickens!

The two other projects Bishop Kulah identified for us were located at Greenville and Harper City. We visited these sites and gathered information and the grateful support of their church leaders.

A memorable incident occurred while we were in the home of Martha Grisby, a faithful and committed member of the UMC in Greenville. A steady stream of people was seen moving through her back yard. They were filling their buckets from her well. One of the members of our little group commented that it was very kind of her to allow people to draw water from her well. She said, "Oh! We are very happy to have people take from our well. The more water that is drawn, the fresher the well will be." What a wonderful illustration of what happens to our hearts and our lives when we share our faith, hope, love and resources with others. Jesus said, "…Give, and it will be given to you. A good measure, pressed down, shaken together, running over, will be put into your lap; for the measure you give will be the measure you get back." (Luke 6:38) Over and over through the years we have heard persons tell the stories of their experiences on our work teams and end by declaring that they received so much more than they gave.

Meeting the Need

When that first advance team returned to Minnesota, we also were filled with stories to tell, many needs to share, and ideas of ways to help our brothers and sisters in Sierra Leone and Liberia. The shipment of school supplies was a high priority. Jim and I developed channels of publicity, set up a network of collection points in each district and established a central staging area for our shipments.

For the first few years of our program, everything that was shipped was sorted, packed and labeled in our home. It was an exciting and busy time. It was wonderful to witness the generosity of our Minnesota United Methodist congregations! Our shipping efforts grew. We found a shipping coordinator,

Heather Iannacone. With amazing dedication and organization, she has managed each and every shipment for almost two decades. Today, the Lake Harriet UMC serves as the staging area for the shipments.

We also have coordinators in Sierra Leone and Liberia who assist work teams and ensure the safe delivery of the supplies we send. In Sierra Leone, our coordinator, who in fact coordinates all Volunteer In Mission programs, is none other than the son of Rev. Smart Senesie who inspired me to "come over and help." His name is also Smart Senesie! He grew up, a witness to the power of faith and prayer in his parents. He grew up, a witness to the difference Operation Classroom made in his own life and the lives of so many others. Feeling God's call, he left a position with the United Nations to return to Sierra Leone and take up this ministry. Now he is helping to make a difference.

At the heart of Operation Classroom has been the work of and relationships formed through the work team experiences. While I provided leadership for the early organization of Operation Classroom, Lyndy was the one who managed all matters pertaining to the work teams. Over the years, he has led many teams and witnessed many times over the miracle of transformation that takes place in persons lives when Jesus is finally seen in the eyes of persons in great need. "…Just as you did it to one of the least of these who are members of my family, you did it to me." (Matthew 25:40b) Most persons going on work teams end their experience with plans to return. Several have gone on to become team leaders themselves

Liberian Civil War

It was not long after Operation Classroom Minnesota was taking off that fighting erupted in Liberia. It was the beginning of what would be more than a decade of terrible civil war. Eventually, the fighting would spread to Sierra Leone and leave both countries in a state of deep human suffering and political chaos.

While the fighting raged in Liberia, Operation Classroom Minnesota continued its projects in Sierra Leone. We were able to send several teams to help construct school buildings in each of our assigned locations. In some cases, this allowed for twice the number of students to attend school! Through the assistance of Operation Classroom Indiana, we were also able to continue to ship thousands of pounds of school and health supplies and equipment. When the fighting spilled into Sierra Leone, many thousands of displaced persons fled to the safety of Freetown. We worked with church leaders there to assist in creating "transplanted" schools for children and support for teachers. One of those displaced schools was the Harford School for Girls, at that time still under the able and determined direction of Etta Nicol.

During the time we were not able to physically work on schools in Liberia, we managed to send supplies, funds and encouragement along with our prayers.

Hundreds of thousands of people were displaced and became refugees in neighboring countries. Our missionaries, Herbert and Mary Zigbuo, followed refugees into Cote d' Ivoire and were able to be our link that allowed Operation Classroom Minnesota to continue educating children and bringing a small bit of normalcy to their lives and the lives of their desperate parents.

The most frequent request that came to us throughout those years of war was for prayer. There had been lulls in the time of fighting. There had been attempts to establish peace and security. During one of those periods, my husband Jim traveled between Sierra Leone and Liberia to meet with church leaders, assess the situation and determine where our teams would be of most use. At that time, our work needed to be confined to the Freetown area of Sierra Leone and the Monrovia area of Liberia.

Co-Workers

While a participant on an Operation Classroom work team in Jamaica, Linda Koelman, an accountant by profession, felt the call of God on her life. She soon found herself moving in a new direction. That direction was seminary. Linda took up ministry with a passion. An important part of her passion involved Operation Classroom. She traveled to Sierra Leone to conduct accounting seminars that would assist pastors in their administrative work. Before long, she was leading work teams and later agreed to become the Africa Work Team Coordinator, a roll she has ably filled for about a decade.

Lovelle Meester has played an incredibly important roll in the OC MINISTRIES story. Because of health concerns, it was imperative that a nurse travel with each work team we sent to West Africa. Lovelle was a well-trained nurse. But, having been in an accident that affected her vocal chords, she was unable to speak above a whisper. She was therefore unable to work professionally as a nurse. Operation Classroom provided her with an opportunity to provide health education, treatment and care for our work team members as well as for those in the communities we were serving. Her leadership skills were also of great benefit to the program. In fact, she led Operation Classroom Minnesota for several years.

Linda Koelman and Lovelle Meester are among many examples that God continues to use Operation Classroom to make a difference and to change peoples lives.

Peace Restored

Throughout those terrible years of war, it was the power of prayer that sustained the faithful in Sierra Leone and Liberia, and those who had become refugees. Today, peace is restored. Recovery is in process. The aftermath of such terrible fighting, the trauma inflicted by and upon the "child-soldiers," and the destruction of virtually everything was utterly devastating to the people of these two countries.

Throughout the time of war and in its aftermath, the United Methodist Church has stood strong and been the image of Christ's love, compassion and forgiveness. The church and its leaders in Sierra Leone and Liberia have taken the lead in calling people to the path of Christ. He is the Way. He is the truth. He is the life that is eternal. Church leaders continue to help rebuild these two countries and promote the power of forgiveness to achieve reconciliation. The result of their efforts is astounding. The church is growing. In Liberia alone, United Methodist membership stands at 179,000. We have 609 churches and 938 pastors (local and ordained).

Expanding the Mission

The motto of Operation Classroom Minnesota from the beginning was, "Bringing help and hope to children and their families." That effort goes on.

While we started with education ministries in mind, it soon became apparent to us that a broader mission, including physical and spiritual health, was self-evident. In Sierra Leone and Liberia, the Church is the center of faith and life, learning and health. Our churches there had established schools and clinics alongside or just down the road from their church buildings. Very early on, in addition to collecting school supplies, we were also putting health kits together and receiving hymnals, altar paraments and communion ware for shipment. Operation Classroom was asked to give concentrated effort toward helping develop churches and clinics, as well as schools.

In 2000, the name of the program was officially changed to OC MINISTRIES:

- OPERATION CLASSROOM continues to build and supply schools
- OPERATION CLINIC promotes health through education, training of health workers, and building and supplying clinics
- OPERATION CHURCH helps fund the training of lay evangelists, and provides assistance to pastors and supplies for their churches
- OPERATION CONNECTION was recently developed to provide scholarship assistance to students and salary supplements for teachers

A God-inspired Mission Partnership

OC MINISTRIES is a God-inspired mission partnership. For over two decades, this program has sent dozens of work teams into Sierra Leone and Liberia. We have shipped many tons of school, health and church supplies and equipment. We can do this in large part because of the tireless effort of folks like Wayne and Nancy Dunbar. They go from church to church telling the stories of God's miracles taking place in the lives of children through OC MINISTRIES. They offer churches and individuals specific ways they can help. Along with such supplies, we have sent hundreds of thousands of meals made possible by our work with the "Feed My Starving Children" program.

We have funded hope for thousands of children through financial support of schools, students and teachers. The Operation Connection portion of our mission came as the result of the passion of Larry Shelton to remove some of the financial barriers that keep children out of school.

We have assisted our sister Conferences through financial support of pastors and lay evangelists. We have improved the health and lives of persons by digging wells that provide safe water and building and supplying clinics. That work is guided by our present "head nurse," Doris Acton. Funding of health education and clinics is accomplished in great part through our partnership with the Lance and Julie Burma Foundation. Their foundation was created in response to their personal work team experiences through OC MINISTRIES.

Through all these years lives have been changed. Priorities have been re-arranged. Lasting friendships and bonds of love have been formed. It is a circle of love that cannot be broken.

OC MINISTRIES has gratefully received the affirming support of every bishop connected with this mission in Minnesota, Sierra Leone and Liberia. OC MINISTRIES has also gratefully been the recipient of the Minnesota Conference Love Offering on four occasions. Churches and individuals in every district of our Conference have generously provided funds and materials that keep the help and hope moving.

Today, OC MINISTRIES is guided by a committee of wonderful individuals, many of whom you have read in this history. OC MINISTRIES is presently guided by the gifted and committed leadership of Rev. Lyndy Zabel. As co-founder, I continue to offer my support and help, as I am able, and serve on the committee as an at-large member. The organization of this ministry has grown and developed over the years by necessity and opportunity. The mission remains the same, "To minister to the minds, bodies and spirits of children in developing countries." This is God's program. It is our privilege to be a part of it.

Chapter Forty-nine

Rev. Etta Nicol

"As for me, I will always have hope; I will praise you more and more."
— Psalm 71:14

Rev. Etta Nicol

It was an honor for me to shake hands and pray God's blessing on the Rev. Etta Nicol at the Servants of Sierra Leone Reunion, July 30-August 1, 2010, in Cedar Rapids, Iowa. How good it was to thank her for the more than four decades of ministry in the United Methodist Church Sierra Leone. With leadership like this, the growth of the Church goes forward.

Rebuilding Hope

The Rev. Etta Nicol has forty-five years of service in the United Methodist Church Sierra Leone. During the time of Bishop B. A. Carew, she taught at the June Hartranft Memorial UMC Girls' Boarding School in Moyamba, later becoming head teacher (principal). During the administration of Bishop Thomas Bangura, she taught and was later the principal of Harford School. While Bishop Joseph Humper was in the episcopal office, Etta Nicol continued as principal of Harford School. With the financial assistance in the amount of $4,500 from Servants of Sierra Leone, she was able to renovate the dilapidated UMC House at Circular Road and put up a new building at the back in order to relocate Harford School to Freetown while the rebels ravaged in the provinces.

The greatest dividend from the $4,500 grant was the establishment of the United Methodist Girls' Secondary School in 2002 on the same property at 46 Circular Road, Freetown, after Harford School returned to Moyamba. At the present time there are more than 2,000 girls in the school, compelling it to run on two shifts.

After retiring from Harford School, Rev. Nicol was appointed Conference Director, Christian Education with a focus on children's ministry, a ministry to Sunday school and war torn children. Again, Servants of Sierra Leone supported the countrywide medical sensitization program "yu pekin komot na trit" (children get off the streets) by providing educational support so vulnerable children could go to school. The program attracted the attention of the government and Etta was appointed one of eight commissioners for the national War-Affected Children's Commission for four years.

With the assumption of office two years ago, Bishop John K. Yambasu appointed Rev. Etta Nicol as the education secretary over daycare, nursery and primary schools conference-wide, which totals 353 schools. She hires and fires teachers, monitors and evaluates teaching and learning processes, and more. Visiting this number of schools – to make sure that the school environment is ideal and quality primary education is achieved according to Bishop Yambasu's vision 2020 – is challenging. With her assistant aiding her, she has visited all the schools and has held meetings with all head teachers and visited and observed classes in session during the first year in office.

Yet her findings on the visits were appalling: classrooms were overcrowded with most children having to sit on the floor; teaching and learning materials were lacking; school buildings were in poor condition, most being "dangerous" for occupation; some teachers, employed three years ago, still had not received salaries, and more. In this role, Rev. Nicol needs an office, and financial support that includes a vehicle for the work.

Chapter Fifty

Rev. David H. Caulker

"For he will command his angels concerning you
to guard you in all your ways;
they will lift you up in their hands,
so that you will not strike your foot against a stone. . . .
'Because he loves me,' says the LORD, 'I will rescue him;
I will protect him, for he acknowledges my name.
He will call on me, and I will answer him;
I will be with him in trouble,
I will deliver him and honor him.'"
– Psalm 91: 11-12, 14-15

Rev. David H. Caulker

Grandson to the Rev. D. H. Caulker of Kono fame, the Rev. David Caulker is a man of prayer, steeped in Scripture walking with God. Trained originally as a teacher, he has an alert mind, a spirit of humility and a heart with evangelistic passion.

I will never forget a visit I made with Brother Caulker to a fellow clergyman in Connaught Hospital in Freetown, Sierra Leone, who was said to be in extremis.

Reaching into memorized scripture, he shared truths with the Rev. Isaac Ken Green, praying that the Lord would raise him up for further ministry. The miracle occurred and Pastor Green was able to serve the Lord Jesus Christ for additional years in the conference. Subsequently, at the "Convocation of Extended Cabinets" November 9, 2007, at Lake Junaluska, North Carolina, the Rev. Green was in attendance to "learn who we are as United Methodists, the direction we are going and get acquainted with the United Methodist way."[46]

Rev. Caulker was a pillar of strength during the terrible days and months before the February 1998 liberation of Freetown by ECOMOG forces. Although he preached the truth in love, he was not arrested or thrown into jail with the thousands of others who refused to support the junta in their reign of terror. He stated that it was difficult to preach compassion for the captured junta and the rebels who brought death and destruction, but asked if I (Lowell) would try. On July 5, 1998, I faced a large congregation at the King Memorial United Methodist Church and preached on Luke 10:33 where Jesus tells of the Good Samaritan who showed compassion and helped his enemy. As followers of the Lord Jesus Christ, we would be expected to do the same.

The Kissy UMC Eye Hospital had no more ardent supporter than the Rev. David Caulker who participated in all main events. In moments of crisis, he was there. In 1991, Ruth and I did outreach work at Rotifunk and Taiama, which necessitated an overnight stay at Rotifunk. The next evening on arriving back at Kissy, Brother Caulker, Lettie Williams and Rev. Angie Myles (who was chairperson of the medical board) met us. All had somber faces. During the night, thieves had broken into the hospital, making their entrance through our bedroom that providentially we were not occupying because of our stay at Rotifunk. The thieves carried off the medicines and supplies that we had just brought from America. In addition, they took the refrigerator, radio, typewriter, tools and Ruth's new white hat. After taking their loot, gunfire erupted even though the hospital guards had been securely tied. Mysteriously, one of the thieves was killed. He still was clutching the radio that I had purchased days before in Amsterdam while travelling to Sierra Leone.

David Caulker is one of Sierra Leone's spiritual giants. His "Caulker" name reaches back over a century to the very beginnings of our church's ministry in Sierra Leone. He continues to pour out his life for Christ and the Church.

Chapter Fifty-one

Rev. Dr. Crispin Renner

"Pass me not, O gentle Savior, Hear my humble cry;
While on others Thou art calling, Do not pass me by."
– Fanny Crosby, 1868

Rev. Dr. Crispin and Teresa Renner

Receipt of the below biographical information – and that of the 130th
Session Sierra Leone Annual Conference of the United Methodist Church
(1880 to 2010) *– arrived just a few weeks before the material of* Glorious
Witnesses for Africa *was to be sent to the publishers. The three Renners
provided a fitting way, along with Vernon and Mary Phelps, to complete
the contributions from all those who responded to my invitation to share
information about themselves and their participation in the glorious growth
of the Church in Sub-Saharan Africa during the last ninety years.*

The Renner Family

"Renner" is an honored name in United Methodist leadership in Sierra Leone,
Africa. Correspondence with Crispin reveals how deep that commitment to the
United Methodist Church ran.

Rev. Dr. Sylvester Milton Renner

Crispin's father, the Rev. Dr. Sylvester Milton Renner (1895-1980), attended the Albert Academy Secondary School. Following ordination in 1927 in the United Brethren Church, he served in the Moyamba church and King Memorial in Freetown. While in Moyamba, his evangelistic program enabled him to establish thirty preaching centres and to construct ten permanent churches. His past work as assistant carpentry master at Albert Academy was useful in his evangelism.

Rev. Dr. Sylvester Milton Renner brought understanding between the tribal groups of the Protectorate (Provinces) and the Creoles of the Colony (Western Area). As a pastor in Freetown, he established evangelistic programs in which all members of the church participated in sharing the Gospel of Jesus Christ.

The enthusiasm of members of King Memorial Church resulted in the founding and building of Baughman Memorial Church, Brown Memorial Church, Price Memorial Church, Musselman Memorial Church and Campbell Town Church. They established ministries in other areas, such as the central prison, the police barracks and in parts of the slum areas in Kroo Bay.

Rev. Dr. Sylvester Milton Renner was the first African to be nominated to preside as chairman of the Seventy Second Annual Conference of the Evangelical United Brethren Church. He was respected as one of the chief advisors to the governor and all the presidents during his lifetime.

His wife, Martha Rosalind, undergirded his ministry as a truly great prayer warrior. They had four boys: St. Andrew, St. Bernard, St. Crispin and Eustace. It was my privilege to work with Dr. Renner over a period of twenty-three years. He was a natural leader, friendly but firm. He excelled as a "preacher." In his retirement, I bought a tape recorder for him, hoping that he would transcribe some of his powerful sermons. Physical weakness and lack of his typical energy prevented the recording. Passed on to many of his admirers, however, is the inclusion of a hymn like "Pass Me Not Oh Gentle Savior" during his pastoral prayer.

Rev. Dr. Eustace Lloyd Renner

Crispin's brother, the Rev. Dr. Eustace Lloyd Renner (1930 – 2000), followed in his father's footsteps and was ordained in Paynesville, Minnesota, in 1961. He had obtained his Bachelor's degree at Reading University and his Master's degree at Yale University where he also did his theological training. On returning to Sierra Leone, he became the director of the Bible Training Institute at Bo. In Nairobi, Kenya, and later in Lagos, Nigeria, he worked as director in the All-Africa Council of Churches. In Sierra Leone, he served at the Bishop Baughman United Methodist Church and then the United Christian Council. I knew Eustace as an energetic and spirited Christian. Like his father, his prayers were deep and devotional. It was a spiritual experience to pray with him.

Rev. Joseph Kaindai St. Crispin Renner

The Rev. Joseph Kaindai St. Crispin Renner and his wife, Teresa, have been close friends with Ruth and me over the past twenty-six years.

In 1952, when for five years he was the clergyman in charge at the United Methodist Church in Magburaka, we began our mission service in Bambur, Nigeria. His special training in sociology and community development led to his being given important civil service posts as well as allowing him to serve four years as the assistant secretary to His Excellency the President of Sierra Leone. He was the deputy secretary to the Ministry of Social Welfare and Rural Development, permanent secretary to the Ministry of Tourism and Cultural Affairs, permanent secretary to the Ministry of Energy and Power, and ultimately, the secretary to the United Methodist Conference in Sierra Leone from 1984 (when we first became friends) until 1994. From 1994-2001, he was council director of the United Methodist Church.

Along with his many services, he was an associate pastor at King Memorial Church and gave Christian direction to Planned Parenthood programs. Crispin excelled in his organizational ability. Others looked to him for guidance. His firm faith in the power of God to save made him especially successful.

Chapter Fifty-two

Rev. Vernon and Mary Phelps

"Paul and Barnabas appointed elders for them in each church and, with prayer and fasting, committed them to the Lord, in whom they had put their trust." – Acts 14:23

Rev. Vernon and Mary Phelps

Invitations to contribute articles to Glorious Witnesses for Africa *were given to commissioned missionaries who served at least two tours in missionary work. Vernon and Mary Phelps were the exception. I was aware that prior to their arrival in Sierra Leone in the late 1950s, Vernon had made extensive studies relating to culture and Church growth. He was adamant in arranging for African leadership to take place on every scale, which had been the message of Dr. John Karefa-Smart a decade earlier. I asked Vernon if he would make some observations. Fittingly, his contribution is the final submission of the United Methodist co-workers.*

Working in Partnership for the Gospel

I met Mary at York College, a church college of the EUB. Our common interest in each other was enhanced by our common interest in preparing for missionary work in the church. Mary was from a family and a church that were both extraordinarily involved with pastoral and missionary work. My family, too, was extremely devoted to the church.

Both of us graduated from York College, I being the first in my family to go to a full year of college. I had had previous experience teaching in Kansas on an emergency temporary certificate. A representative of the Board of Missions advised us that they preferred that missionaries have seminary preparation so that they fully understood their own faith. In response, I attended United Theological Seminary, graduating in 1955.

I was then ordained in the Kansas Conference of the EUB church. In the meantime, Mary taught in a public school and completed her Master's degree at Miami University of Ohio.

After the Board of Missions appointed us, we were sent to Columbia Teachers' College where I received a Master's degree. We were both then sent by the Mission Board to London University in order to understand the British system of education before being assigned as missionaries to Sierra Leone at the Albert Academy in Freetown.

I had several unique experiences in preparation for service in Sierra Leone. The conference superintendent of the Kansas Conference (my home conference) was Rev. H. H. Thomas, a former missionary in Sierra Leone. I did my senior seminary thesis on the life and missionary philosophy of Rev. A. T. Howard, a former missionary in Sierra Leone and later the UB missionary bishop. While in Sierra Leone, I did a special study on the life of Rev. Ira Albert after whom the Albert Academy was named. In interviews with church leaders in villages in Sierra Leone, these three missionaries –Thomas, Howard and Albert – were the ones most remembered in the history of the mission as being the most influential in the development of the church in Sierra Leone.

While at United Theological Seminary, I asked the missions' professor (who was also my major advisor) to teach a course in social anthropology. While at Columbia Teachers' College, I also chose a course in anthropology and education. These courses especially provided insights into the study of other cultures.

We served in Sierra Leone from 1957 to 1960 assigned to the Albert Academy. I taught Bible classes and was chaplain of the school. With our three children at home, Mary taught part-time as an English teacher and was the director of the church choir.

The period in which we served in Sierra Leone was a turning point in the history of mission work. We were among a very few missionaries at the time who were assigned to work in an institution in which an indigenous person was in charge. It was the beginning of a cooperative approach and relationship of partners.

Dr. Richard Caulker was the principal of the school. There were times when he was called away to other duties and asked me several times to be acting principal in his absence. When he asked, I would encourage him to ask a Sierra Leonean instead, so a member of the staff could have the experience that would prepare him for a future leadership role. The teacher Dr. Caulker asked was Mr. Max Bailor who later became the principal and served for many years.

This story is a good example of working toward developing indigenous leadership that eventually played a major part in the development of the Church in Africa. It also demonstrates the relationship of partners in the witnessing of the Gospel.

1960 was probably the watershed year in which the approach of mission changed from missionary dominance to partnership. This time also coincides with the move to independence of the former colonies in Africa. Obviously, African leadership was key to the development of churches and other institutions in the former colonies.

An Anglican priest and former missionary to Asia, Roland Allen, wrote a book in 1912 called *Missionary Methods, St. Paul's or Ours?* In it, he wrote of the necessity of the partnership approach. He pointed out that Paul would preach (witness) in a city and gather around him a small band of believers. He then would move on, often appointing leaders of the community to continue the ministry. Allen's contention was that this approach was why St. Paul was so influential. He also said that it would be fifty years before the approach of missionaries would change to the approach St. Paul used. That would make it 1960 – and he was so right! When that happened, the Church grew rapidly. Many more examples could be given of how that happened during our time of service.

A Note on the Amistad Story

Soon after I arrived at Albert Academy, I learned of the story of the Mende people who were seized by Portuguese slave traders. I immediately recognized it as a story of outstanding heroism. After doing some research, I presented the story to the students of Albert Academy. (I wanted to first present the story to African students before sending the story back home to churches in the States because it could have been potentially embarrassing.) It turned out I was introducing the story for the first time to the students at the Academy. Some of the boys said, "Oh. Now we know why our school in Banthe was called the 'Amistad Memorial School.'" There were even students from the family of Sengbe Pieh in the school.

Later, we moved to Connecticut and became part of the former Congregational Church (UCC). I am probably the only pastor in the United Methodist Church of Sierra Leone and the UCC in Connecticut who was associated with the churches, that so many years ago, had helped the Amistad captives when they were in prison and could not tell the story of their own cruel and unlawful treatment.

Chapter Fifty-three

Dr. Allen Foster

"We realize how dependent we are on God's sustaining love…and know the peace and joy of God…and grow in our knowledge and trust in Jesus."

Dr. Allen Foster

That Dr. Allen Foster, ophthalmologist, was able to walk away from a plane crash during his missionary service at Mvumi Hospital, Tanzania, in the early 1980s was a blessing not only to himself and his family. It was also a blessing to the Mvumi Hospital patients, the outreach programs to six other Tanzanian hospitals, Christendom in Africa and ultimately around the world. In 1985, he became Christian Blind Mission's medical director, which enlarged his ministry to include India and China, as well as Africa.

Dr. Foster's successes were present from the very start. He graduated with an honors degree in medicine and in surgery from Birmingham University in the United Kingdom. After working in ophthalmology and surgery in Worcester and Birmingham Hospital and specializing in ophthalmology at Addenbrooks Hospital, Cambridge, he joined Christian Blind Mission in 1975. During his ten years at Mvumi Hospital, he also developed a training program for doctors and nurses.

Upon his return to the UK as CBM's medical director, opportunity was given to continue using his teaching skills by becoming consultant to the World Health Organization and World Bank in the development of programs to prevent and treat blindness. He became a senior lecturer in community eye health at the International Centre for Eye Health, London, as well as a senior lecturer in preventive ophthalmology, Institute of Ophthalmology, also in London. He also was an honorary consultant in ophthalmology at Moorfields Eye Hospital,

London. His vital association with these impressive institutions – and his work in Africa – led to his being awarded an OBE (Order of the British Empire) for services to ophthalmology in developing countries.

I considered Dr. Foster an esteemed CBM medical director and friend to the Kissy UMC Eye Hospital, Freetown, Sierra Leone. Realizing the critical need for eye medicines, supplies and equipment in Sierra Leone (which was classified at the bottom of the UN's list for human development in the countries of the world), he provided support for a workable budget. He did not censor a new, but unaccepted, modality of using intraocular lenses following the extraction of cataracts. Under his watch, CBM moved to supply these lenses, which were too expensive for missions to fund.

His vision that this procedure could become the standard for the world is reflected in his present vision for the role of CBM in addressing disabilities – not just from a charity service approach – but to a human rights ministry involving people with visual, hearing, physical, mental and intellectual disabilities. This conviction is based on Jesus' concern for the poor, many of whom had these disabilities. He envisions CBM operating in a healing role in all of their more than 1,000 projects in over 100 countries of the world.

Aware of the need for a highly trained ophthalmologist to serve at Kissy UMC Eye Hospital, Freetown, Sierra Leone, Dr. Foster was instrumental in providing the appointment of skilled ophthalmologist, Dr. John Buchan. Dr. Foster never forgot his beginnings in Tanzania, East Africa, and continues to lead the world's largest and most widespread and influential eye care ministry as president of Christian Blind Mission International. I shall always honor the e-mail he sent in which he said: "We realize how dependent we are on God's sustaining love…and know the peace and joy of God…and grow in our knowledge and trust in Jesus."

Chapter Fifty-four

Dr. Marilyn Scudder

"I thank God for the privilege of serving Him and others...."

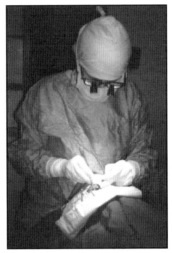

Dr. Marilyn Scudder

Dr. Marilyn Scudder, a dear friend and fellow ophthalmologist, made a great impact on the Sub-Saharan Africa (Tanzania) Christian Church where she was an eye doctor and medical missionary for thirty-five years.

"I Love Jesus . . . With All My Heart"

Born in Amarah, Iraq, of missionary parents, she was the 102nd missionary in her family. For four generations, Scudders had served in the Middle East and India. She moved with her family in 1949 to Kuwait but graduated in 1956 from India's Kodaikanal International School, then Michigan's Hope College in 1960. She secured her M.D. from the University of Michigan in 1965. Besides her residency in ophthalmology, she specialized in retinal diseases at the University of Minnesota, becoming the only retinal eye surgeon in East Africa for many years.

While I was in Sierra Leone – the breadth of the African continent away – she still made visits to Sierra Leone while under appointment to Christian Blind Mission International, which has 1,000 projects in 100 countries. Besides cataract surgery, she was adept at trabeculectomies for glaucoma patients. It was my pleasure to follow a number of these successful surgeries.

I once asked her how it was possible for her to be supported during her active calling as a medical missionary by Christian Blind Mission. I was aware of other applicants who were well qualified and had impressive recommendations who not accepted. Her reply: "They asked me if I loved Jesus. When I replied that I did with all my heart, they ended the interview and I was on my way to Africa."

Dr. Scudder served as a medical missionary for thirty-five years, mostly at Mvuni Hospital and the medical center in Moshi, Tanzania, where she was department head beginning in 1979. With her full training as an ophthalmologist and a fellowship in retinal diseases and their treatment, she was in demand throughout East Africa. She responded by safari vehicle and small plane to as many as thirty mission and government hospitals, tireless in her compassion to provide eye care for needy patients.

On May 28, 2004, Marilyn sent this e-mail: "Some other (the 'other' was feeling better in her treatment for primary amyloidosis) good news! The American Academy of Ophthalmology has given me the great honor of being one of two selected for 2004's Humanitarian Award. It will be presented at the Academy meeting Sunday, October 24, 2004, in New Orleans. It has been and continues to be a very humbling and exciting experience. I thank God for the privilege of serving Him and others in this way (wouldn't trade for anything). Secondly, I thank the Academy for the honor and then my colleagues (they especially mean a lot to me) for nominating and supporting me. Also, I thank my teachers all along the way for their encouragement. Finally, I thank my family, friends and last but not least my patients over the years. May our wonderful Lord and God bless you today and each coming day."

As Marilyn, carrying her portable oxygen cylinder, was presented this award in front of me and thousands of her fellow ophthalmologists, my heart was warmed. I never told Marilyn, until her dying day, that it was I who nominated her. This award was followed by the George Tani Humanitarian Service Award from the Minnesota Academy of Ophthalmology on December 10, 2004. Previously she had been presented with a Distinguished Alumni Award from Hope College on May 7, 1988.

Dr. Scudder's work ethic was demanding. In Sierra Leone, a staff member made the observation that although Dr. Scudder was a tall and attractive lady, "She works like a man."

Ruth and I had the opportunity to entertain Marilyn in our home and were able to visit her at the Shirley Schumaker home in New Brighton during her heroic struggle to overcome primary amyloidosis, which ultimately proved fatal. Previously, we had been able to provide her with an operating microscope that she cherished. In 2001 at Maua, she began working with the Franciscan Capuchin Sisters on the west slopes of Mt. Kilimanjaro near the village of Sanya Juu. Marilyn died May 16, 2005, and is buried on those slopes in the land where she lived her active, productive and transforming life.

Chapter Fifty-five

Dr. Jeanette Troup

"He will cover you with his feathers,
and under his wings you will find refuge;
his faithfulness will be your shield and rampart.
You will not fear the terror of night,
nor the arrow that flies by day,
nor the pestilence that stalks in the darkness,
nor the plague that destroys at midday."
– Psalm 91:4-6

Dr. Jeanette Troup

On January 21, 1970, Jeanette Troup, in the midst of a Lassa fever epidemic in Jos, Nigeria, commented: "We should all bear in mind that nothing can come to a child of God, except that it passes through God's heart of love first. With the Lord, there can be no such thing as spiritual harm."

These words followed a reading of Psalm 91 at a Wednesday night prayer meeting. She said that this psalm gave her strength in the face of crises and provided spiritual nourishment in the face of tragedies which she faced daily in her work.

Jeanette had realized her dream of becoming a medical missionary. Her father was a pastor. Ruth and I had been taken into the care of her parents in Akron, Ohio, where I was doing a surgical residency. They found a house for us to rent during those two years and were our spiritual advisors. We had become dear friends in the Lord with Jeanette and Roger, her medical missionary brother.

216

In her early years at the SIM hospital in Jos, Nigeria, Jeanette medically cared for our children and us during our 1952-1955 tour. Roger and I performed a cholecystectomy for Mrs. Ira McBride, the wife of our mission superintendent, Dr. Ira E. McBride, when gall bladder attacks became unmanageable.

Fourteen years later in January and February 1969, two nurse co-workers under Jeanette's care died with an unidentified hemorrhagic fever. In January 1970, a Nigerian hospital staff member contracted a similar hemorrhagic fever. Again, the illness proved fatal. More than half of the other admitted patients with similar signs and symptoms died. A diagnosis was imperative. Blood and tissue samples were needed to share with Nigerian laboratories as well as those in the U.S.

Having had a residency in pathology as well as in pediatrics, she knew how to do an autopsy and prepare tissue and fluids for analysis. During the procedure, the scalpel slipped and slashed a finger. The wound was irrigated, scrubbed with surgical soap and then flooded with antiseptic. A bandage was applied and Dr. Troup continued her duties.

As a witness to her faith in the Lord Jesus Christ, she was admired to the point of veneration. With regard to death, like other missionaries, she would often affirm "the Lord's will." Every medical option should be employed to preserve life, but according to the will of God, there would be peace in the outcome. This stance was unshakable.

The events of these happening in Jos were ultimately put together in an intimate and heart-wrenching story of Dr. Troup and the search for the cause of Lassa fever. They are presented in *Fever! The Hunt for a New Killer Virus* by John G. Fuller. He covers every minute detail of the saga, being respectful of the driving Christian faith and commitment of each person immersed in these dramatic but tragic events. He especially follows the activity and reactions of Dr. Troup, who kept precise records of each challenging case.

At the time of the accidental cutting of her finger during the autopsy, Dr. Troup asked Dr. Hal White not to share this event with the staff. She continued her backbreaking schedule with a bandaged finger that had "suffered a slight scratch."

But soon, the staff sensed something. Yet, did Dr. Troup have strong forebodings that something was going to happen to her? If she did, she didn't show them. She had gone ahead with the second autopsy, marking and sending a second shipment of specimens to the University of Ibadan.

In the succeeding day, Dr. Troup developed muscle aches and pains accompanied by an ever-increasing temperature. At first, she refused to be admitted to the hospital for care, but ultimately became so weak that she could not handle a glass of water. She placed her care in the hands of Dr. Hal White and left all the decisions to him. "This is the Lord's will," she told him. "I know you will do everything possible."

Dr. Troup's thoughts expressed in the earlier prayer meeting lingered in the minds of many: "What if God does decide to take us home by means of a virus? It is His will. There can be no spiritual harm. In His will, there is peace." It brought a strange combination of both comfort and distress. Did Dr. Troup know then that she was going to die? Or would the Lord now perform a miracle and let her live?

With the real suspicion that Lassa fever was overwhelming Dr. Troup, no thought was given to flying her to New York as had been done for Penny Pinneo before it was known that the virus was exceedingly contagious.

All possible treatment was continued, but her condition continued to deteriorate. Late in the afternoon a week after her illness began, she held out her hand to her favorite Nigerian nursing attendant and said, "You've done everything for me, Comfort. God bless you." Her hand relaxed. One of the truly great witnesses for Christ in Africa was dead. Subsequent findings revealed that her disease, indeed, was the killer virus, Lassa fever.

"Blessed are the dead who die in the Lord. They will rest from their labor, for their deeds will follow them." Revelation 14:13

Chapter Fifty-six

Rev. Billy Graham

*"Neither he who plants nor he who waters is anything, but only God,
who makes things grow.... We are God's fellow workers...."*
– I Corinthians 3: 7-9

Kisumu, Kenya, 1960. Billy Graham with two interpreters. Permission Billy Graham
Evangelistic Association.

Missionary to the World

Billy Graham is included as a witness in this book as I had a *personal* meeting with him early in 1945 at a combined meeting of seven seminaries in the Chicago area. Since I was the president of the student body at Evangelical Theological Seminary in Naperville, Illinois, it was my privilege to represent my school at the meeting. I had appreciated Billy Graham's "Songs in the Night" radio program on WCFL that included popular bass baritone George Beverly Shea while he was a staff announcer on Moody Bible Institute's WMBI.

Billy Graham had asked if he could make a presentation on behalf of Youth for Christ to the inter-seminary group. He was eloquent. I assumed that the vote would be 100 percent for the seminaries to participate. My vote was the only affirming one.

At the close of the meeting, I shared with him my disbelief that there was not full support. I wished him the Lord's blessing in his ministry and assured him I would bring a group of young people from Naperville to attend the Chicagoland Youth For Christ meeting on March 10, 1945. In that service, two of our group went forward to make decisions for Christ. I had the privilege of counseling them and their families in succeeding days.

Eight years after our arrival in Nigeria in 1952, Billy Graham and his team made an extensive preaching tour of Africa, starting in Liberia. By this time, he had acquired world acceptance as a genuine Christian evangelist. He did not stop in Sierra Leone where we were serving at the Rotifunk Hospital.

In his autobiography, "Just as I Am," he tells of the safe landing at Roberts Field, Liberia, in spite of one of the four motors of the airplane belching smoke. He was met by Vice President William R. Tolbert, a noted Baptist leader, and later by Liberia's president William V. S. Tubman, a Methodist. With his team housed in the government's official guest house and the services held in Monrovia's Antonienette Tubman Stadium, there was a warm feeling of government support. The 1,000 inquiries at the crusade greatly encouraged them at the start of their African journey.

It was another story at their next stop, Ghana, where Kwame Nkrumah was less approachable. Mr. Graham was diplomatic, claiming that he was not a politician but rather an ambassador of Jesus Christ who was not a white man but a Middle Easterner darker than himself and lighter than them. He reminded them that when Jesus fell while carrying the His Cross, it was an African, Simon of Cyrene, who was pressed into service to carry it for him. Early on, Jesus' parents had sought refuge in Africa.

In Nigeria, Billy Graham received Muslim hostility and the response to his preaching was muted. In Kaduna, the Muslim headquarters for Nigeria, he had a ninety-minute interview with the sultan who was considered the king of Kaduna. Billy witnessed as best he could only to be told that within ten years the Christians would be pushed into the sea with the Muslims taking over all of Africa. Mr. Graham's reply was that it rested entirely in God's hands. Within six months, an assassin slit the sultan's throat. Between 1960 and 2010, there was a meteoric growth of the Christian Church in Nigeria, with half of the population naming Jesus Christ as Savior and Lord.

Along with visits to various other African countries, they observed the prolific wild animal life, Victoria Falls, Mount Kilimanjaro and Lake Victoria. In Addis Ababa, 10,000 people attended the first meeting – the greatest response in Africa – where nearly one half stayed for counseling afterward. In Cairo, more than 2,000 stayed behind for a period of instruction in what it meant to be a Christian.

Billy Graham knew that God was at work in Africa. He recognized with deep gratitude the faith and sacrifice of those who had been witnessing to the light of the Gospel. He recalled the prophetic words of David Livingstone, the

Scottish missionary to the heart of Africa who said: "Future missionaries will see conversions following every sermon. We prepare the way for them. May they not forget the pioneers who worked in the thick gloom with few rays to cheer except such as flow from faith in God's promise. We work for a glorious future which we are not destined to see." That glorious growth of the Christian Church is the central theme of *Glorious Witnesses for Africa* – witnesses brought about by witnesses.

Mr. Graham met with a group of twenty-five missionaries in Eritrea at a fueling stop on his way home to America. They listened eagerly as the report was made of the African trip, how God was honored with the response of thousands of converts. Several shared their experience of laboring for years with almost nothing to show as tangible results, and yet they had a deep sense that they were called to minister in the "corner" in which they were and were content to know that they were doing the Lord's bidding. Tears flowed as Billy Graham prayed with them in the attitude of I Corinthians 3: "Neither he who plants nor he who waters is anything, but only God, who makes things grow.... We are God's fellow workers...."

In later years, I had the opportunity of viewing Billy Graham crusades with his anointed, persuasive and successful preaching on television, but never again had the privilege of having a face-to-face meeting. In his and his wife, Ruth's, retirement in 2007, I learned that they enjoyed well-done movies produced before the 1960s. I sent them the movie "I'd Climb the Highest Mountain." By way of his secretary, he sent two letters of appreciation. Included were challenging tracts. His sharing of the Gospel will end only with his last breath.

Chapter Fifty-seven

Dr. James and Martha Foulkes

"Whether you turn to the right or to the left, your ears will hear a voice behind you, saying, 'This is the way; walk in it.'" – Isaiah 30:21

Dr. James and Martha Foulkes

James Foulkes, M.D., is a dear friend and fellow medical missionary who served in Zambia for thirty-eight years. After being together in a surgical residency at Akron General Hospital in Ohio in 1956 and 1957, Jim and his bride, Marilynn, answered God's call to medical service in Zambia. Ruth and I – with our family of five (Andrew, our sixth child, would be born in Sierra Leone) – returned to Africa, this time to Sierra Leone.

Jim was born into a United Methodist home of Godly parents. Dr. E. Stanley Jones' message challenged Jim at the age of twelve to kneel at the altar with the commitment to follow Jesus. He excelled as an athlete, setting records in the half-mile event in track. While still "running" in Zambia, Africa, his passion for sports was transferred to hunting and fishing, a very useful interest which helped provide food for patients and missionary families. His life was protected in an unusual way on these forays.

He proved to be a skilled physician and surgeon, saving lives physically and spiritually. His commitment to the Lord Jesus Christ continued after the loss of two children and his wife. A new blessing came into his life and his children with the coming of Martha as his new wife and mother of the home.

Not content to limit his service to needy general surgery patients, Jim and Martha visited us at Kissy UMC Eye Hospital to begin training for eye surgery. He took to this specialty like a duck to water. He became proficient and saw to it that his new passion was transferred to Jairos Fumpa and the volunteer services that followed before he retired in 1997.

Mr. Fumpa had one-year eye course in Malawi and then went back for an additional two years of surgical training. He currently runs the flying clinics to four other hospitals, the local clinics close by that are accessible by land travel, the optical workshop and the bookwork related to donor help. Dr. Foulkes writes: "Jairos is an outstanding church leader and follower of Jesus – almost too good to be true."

Besides being given the Alumni Achievement Award from Ohio State University College of Medicine and Public Health, Jim was honored by the World Medical Mission and received the prestigious Award for Excellence in Medical Missions, conveyed by Franklin Graham.

Jim has written a book, *To Africa With Love: A Bush Doc's Story* (Evangel Publishing House: 1-800-253-9315 or www.evangelpublishing.com). The message on the flyleaf says:

"While James Foulkes' medical school classmates were settling into suburban American practices, Foulkes was treating near-fatal snake bites, hunting big game to feed hospital patients, and seeing God work miracles in the wild and rough African bush.

"In this inspiring and colorful memoir, a modern medical missionary recounts conducting surgery under primitive conditions, becoming lost in the dangerous bush, dealing with witch doctors and being ensnared in a poachers' deadly trap. Through all the adventures, however, the guiding and protective hand of the Lord is evident. From his miraculous escape from a herd of stampeding elephants to winning souls for Christ, the bush doc affirms that God is faithful and good."

In a recent e-mail, Jim wrote:

Mother wanted both of her boys to be missionaries and that desire was quite clear to us when my brother and I were in high school. She certainly did her part, inasmuch that she read many missionary biographies to us. We were pretty well acquainted with the lives of the famous pioneers who were heroes to Mother and became role models for us. Since the eastern representative of Gospel Recordings, Miriam Cree, made her home with us when she wasn't involved in missionary conferences, we had frequent visits from furloughing missionaries who would spend several days in our home at the invitation of Miriam and Mother. So brother Dick and I were well prepared to take up a missionary calling.

However, you don't sign up for a career as a foreign missionary just because you know that it would please your mother. That call must come from the Father and it has to be clear and unequivocal. Both Dick and I separately deepened our relationship with the Lord while we were in the service in World War II. It was a matter of bowing our knees to the Lord and promising "I'll go where you want me to go and do what you want me to do." For Dick, that meant putting his musical career on the altar as a piano graduate of Juilliard Conservatory. Instead, he completed seminary and spent his career as a seminary professor in Costa Rica (which still allowed him the opportunity to concertize regularly in Costa Rica and other capitals of South America). For me, it meant finishing pre-med at Asbury College, attending Ohio State Medical School, having an internship in Columbus and a short surgical residency in Akron.

A very important part of my calling came at the first Urbana Missionary Conference in 1949. A young evangelist, Billy Graham, gave the challenge on Thursday evening and I was ready to sign the pledge card that read: "With God being my helper, I commit myself to a career of foreign missionary service." The great commission became my commission and signing that card was a holy covenant between God and me, not to be broken. (That covenant card was often placed on my mirror as a constant reminder that my life was not my own. It was nine years after signing that pledge before I arrived in Zambia for the first time; how thankful I am for the Lord giving me the grace and the strength to keep my commitment.)

However, when I signed that card, I was an undergraduate at Asbury and I rather assumed that I would just cross the street and attend Asbury Seminary for my further training for the mission field. In my junior year, I was enjoying science courses taught by the brilliant doctors, Hamman and Ray. For the first time in my life, I considered medical school.

One dark night, I spent hours walking down a lonely road pleading with the Lord to show me His will. There was no message written in the sky, but I did feel confident that I should apply to a medical school. Since I would be the only pre-med in my class at Asbury not graduating with honors, my chance of getting into med school in competition with a large number of ex-GIs would take some intervention by God. When I was accepted at Ohio State, I was just as sure that "this is the way, walk ye in it" than if the Lord had sent a herald angel.

Since I was a lifelong Methodist, I had signed up with the foreign board of the Methodist church. The board kindly paid all of my expenses through medical school on the understanding that I would serve as a Methodist foreign missionary for something like twelve years. Since I was a "lifer," that commitment seemed like a sure thing.

However, the wonderful wife that the Lord gave me to serve with me in Zambia had no background with the Methodist church. Our interview with the doctor in charge of Methodist medical missions around the world was not very encouraging to either of us. Since I have always had a very high view of scripture and was a thoroughgoing evangelical, I already had some serious problems with some of the liberal Methodist bishops.

This was upsetting to both of us. In the Lord's kindness, on our honeymoon we visited some good friends who were serving at the InterVarsity training center in Ontario. Also there were Bob and Belva Foster. They were spending several months there after just starting Mukinge Hospital in Zambia. After spending two hours with this wonderful couple, we both knew for sure that this was to be the place to fulfill our calling. In all of the years that followed, we never had the slightest doubt that we were in the center of God's will in serving at Mukinge.

We applied and were accepted to serve with the South African General Mission, the sponsoring mission of Mukinge Hospital. That meant resigning from the Methodist board of missions and paying back every penny that was spent on medical school. An inheritance from one of my father's grateful clients paid back my indebtedness to the Methodist board. It was wonderful to know that we were on the right path, and even though many years of preparation still lay ahead, we were fulfilling the reason we were born. In June of 1958, we finally arrived at Mukinge Hospital where I would spend the next thirty-eight blessed years.

Times of Testing and Sorrow

In the lives of most career missionaries that I know, the Lord allows times of testing. In our family, one of the saddest times was sending our little daughters when they turned six to boarding school 300 miles away; it takes a long, long time to get over the sorrow of that separation. Home schooling wasn't an option at that time and no elementary school was available at Mukinge.

How thankful we were that even with that awful gap our daughters survived without being angry with us or with God for their "abandonment." They learned that their heavenly Father could dry their tears and they developed a close relationship to Him. Their secondary education was completed at Rift Valley Academy in Kenya, a long flight away. Sending away our daughters to boarding schools for all twelve years of their training in Africa was a genuine sacrifice for us and for our children. I'm thankful that boarding schools are almost never required in these days.

Even much sadder was separation by death. We were in Zambia less than a year when our precious little 18-month-old son, David, developed laryngo-tracheal-bronchitis; even with a tracheotomy, he didn't survive. This was devastating to us but the most positive outcome was that the local people felt our pain and cried with us and supported us with their love and the relationship that came out of that shared grief was a bond that bound us to the Kaonde people for our entire career.

In 1977, our dear 16-year-old daughter, Jill, had been deteriorating for a year with a chronic disease that was not diagnosed in the famous hospital in Capetown, even with a two-month admission there. Her final terminal weeks were special to all of us who got to nurse her. Her love for Jesus was precious and sometimes she would break out in a song of her own composition, expressing her love for Him. Several days before she died she had a beatific vision and her spirit entered into the presence of the Lord. The expression on her face was glorious. When she came back down to her bed, with IVs running in both arms and a feeding tube in her nose, she asked "Mommy, why did I have to come back, it was so wonderful there with Jesus." The next day, she returned to the Lord that she loved and served so well.

The day after the funeral, my beloved first wife, Marilynn, revealed that several of her lymph nodes were enlarging. This was a sure sign that she had broken through her chemotherapy and her aggressive cancer of the breast had recurred. We traveled back to Capetown even knowing that this was a death sentence. In the Lord's wisdom, our prayers for divine healing were not answered in extending her life on earth and she entered into eternal bliss three months after Jill died. I was holding her hand when she breathed her last, listening to the *Hallelujah Chorus* on my tape recorder. If my ears had not been so dull, I'm sure that I could have heard the heavenly host welcoming her home. The grief of our family was deep, but we all believed sincerely that God is too good to be unkind and too wise to make a mistake.

Our youngest daughter, Jackie, was only twelve when Marilynn died and she needed a mother and I was a very unsuccessful bachelor. The Lord helped us in our time of need and allowed our family to be blessed with Martha Penner, the outstanding Canadian nurse who had been running our nurses' training school for many years. Martha became quickly a wonderful, loving mother to Jackie and a devoted wife for this lonely widower.

Even before Martha's entry into our family, our second oldest daughter, Gwen, spent a year at home before going to Bible college and she was a big help. Our oldest daughter, Terrie, returned to Asbury College. Her return was premature, since she missed out on the healing we had as a family in Zambia as we sang together and prayed together. We soon found out that praise was a wonderful antidote to grief and we spent time every day with Gwen's gifted guitar playing, leading us to the "Balm of Gilead" as we sang worship songs together.

The Growth of the Church in Zambia

When we arrived at Mukinge Hospital in 1958, there were about forty small churches scattered around in our huge district that were started as fruit of our pioneer, C.S. Foster. There were about thirty churches in the Southern Province at Luampa Mission and possibly twenty-five surrounding Mutanda Mission.

As we celebrated our centennial in August 2010, it was a time to look back and thank God for His faithfulness and also to consider why He was able to multiply our church, the Evangelical Church in Zambia. At present there are 1,300 churches that are scattered all over Zambia. One answer is that the wonderful foundation that was laid by the pioneers was built upon faith, decade by decade. A view that the Bible was the inspired Word of God and was the basis for all doctrine and life was central in our many Bible schools and our seminary throughout the years. Living a holy life was an important emphasis that was a theme of the founder of our mission, Andrew Murray; a godly life was always placed before our church as an essential part of being a disciple.

Another important emphasis was taking very seriously the Lord's demand to "deny yourself, take up your cross and follow me" as a requirement of discipleship. Our faithful bishops have been a wonderful example of self-sacrifice. Our first bishop, Sam Kasonso, was a close friend of Zambia's first president, Kenneth Kaunda, when they were secondary school chums in the capital. When Kaunda became president, he recruited a number of his secondary school friends to accept high offices in his cabinet. He tried for five years to recruit Sam Kasonso, but Sam chose the calling of God rather than a chauffeur-driven Mercedes and two big homes.

Enos Masuhwa was our second bishop. In the ministry of education, he advanced to the high post of being in charge of all adult education for the nation. He followed his calling into the ministry and took early retirement, giving up his car and his high salary to go to seminary and was then voted in as bishop.

He was followed by Paul Makai. As a high achieving young teacher, Paul was selected by the ministry of education to get further training in the UK. Instead, he gave up that golden opportunity and followed the Lord's calling to Bible college and then on to become the bishop. This self-denial of the top leaders of the Evangelical Church in Zambia has set an important example to our church and has certainly been a factor in being blessed of the Lord and the furtherance of the Church.

Chapter Fifty-eight

Dr. Subramaniam (Kiru) and Raji Kirupananthan

"When I prayed, I asked Jesus to forgive me for ignoring Him all those years and invited Him into my life."

Dr. Subramaniam (Kiru) and Raji Kirupananthan

Dr. Kirupananthan headed up ECWA's Eye Hospital in Kano, Nigeria for more than a decade. In a year's time, the hospital would see about 25,000 outpatients, admit another 3,500 and perform surgery on about 4,800. In addition, about 1,200 surgeries were performed during outreach visits. A study conducted in India revealed that about 80 percent of the Christians there had their first exposure to the Christian faith in a medical facility. In light of that fact, a total of approximately 20,000 future Christians were first being reached at Dr. Kiru's hospital.

With witnesses like Dr. and Mrs. Kiru, the Christian Church knew astounding growth in the past ninety years. Dr. Kiru, a Sri Lankan was honored by the Nigerian Ophthalmological Society with an award for exemplary service, contributing to the prevention of blindness and training ophthalmologists in Nigeria. In retirement, Dr. and Mrs. Kir have spent six weeks or more at the Kissy UMC Eye Hospital three times

228

within the last two years. Their administrative, teaching, clinical and surgical skills have upgraded the program in a marvelous way. Their coming to servant hood follows.

Our Conversion

Kiru

My father was a Hindu and my mother a nominal Christian. Up until my father died when I was 14, my brother and I attended church with my mother on Sundays and the temple with my father on Fridays. We moved to our maternal grandparents after we lost our father, and I was educated at the CMS missionary school in Jaffna. Here, at the influence of the Principal Rev. Arulanandan, we received adult baptism (christening), attended confirmation classes and was confirmed by the Anglican bishop, Rt. Rev. Archibold Rollo in 1956.

Until I left for England in 1977, I took part in all church activities, was president of the SCM at school and at the university, and considered myself "a good Christian." In September 1978, my uncle and my cousin from Sri Lanka visited us in England and spoke to us about being a "Christian" and being born again.

This upset both Raji and me. We thought we were Christians by all standards. They explained what was lacking and I was asked to pray. When I prayed, I asked Jesus to forgive me for ignoring Him all those years and invited Him into my life. I broke down and wept. I could sense the warmth in me and from that moment I experienced Joy in my life.

They encouraged me to attend a church. We were led to West Gate Chapel in Bury, St. Edmunds, where under the influence of Pastor Bob Cotton, we were presented Jesus as a living and loving Savior; we received immersion baptism on February 28, 1979.

Raji

Her parents were nominal Christians. Her father, at one time, was a Jehovah's Witness and Christian activities were minimal. She, too, was influenced by the same uncle and cousin during the same period in England and her conversion was also about the same under the guidance of Pastor Bob Cotton. She also received immersion baptism on February 28, 1979.

God is great and we are privileged to meet people like you. We thank our loving Savior for giving us the opportunity to meet you and learn so much from you.

Chapter Fifty-nine

Dr. Gizella Baghy
Opthamologist

*"...But those who hope in the Lord will renew their strength. They will soar
on wings like eagles; they will run and not grow weary, they will walk and
not be faint." – Isaiah 40:31*

Dr. Gizella Baghy

Glorious Witnesses for Africa *is honored to include the testimonies of
witnesses, Dr. Gizella Baghy, an ophthalmologist, and her husband, Dr.
Istvan Patkai, a psychiatrist. In outreach eye surgery, Dr. Baghy ministered
daily to hundreds of people as well as performing in one day as many as twenty
cataract operations with intraocular lens implantation in Africa and the
Philippines. Kissy UMC Eye Hospital in Freetown, Sierra Leone, was blessed
with Dr. Baghy's services for any entire month. Besides her skilled surgery, she
introduced needed adaptations that greatly enhanced the program.*

On Eagles' Wings

I come from an average Catholic family background. My parents went to church on Sundays; we celebrated Christmas, Easter and Pentecost. We had no family Bible, only the catechism. My dear grandma, whom I dearly loved, always prayed for me, especially when I was at the university before exams. She could not understand why I had to study even at night when my sister, who had a course in dentistry, always finished her studies before late hours. She used to tell the neighbors that this Gizella is not as smart as Zsuzsa because she is reading always late at night to prepare for her exams.

I am grateful to the Lord that I grew up in a family where God was present. In those days in socialist Hungary, you were not to mention God in the school or working place. My mother, who was a teacher, used to go to church in another district where nobody knew her. Teachers were forbidden to attend church services and, especially, to teach "wrong doctrine." Looking back, I think it was very wrong to live a life at home and another life with different standards at work. At the same time, there was no other choice, you had to compromise for the survival of the family, you had to have double standards.

We were married in a church in 1971; for that we had to travel upcountry in the afternoon, while the "official" city council wedding was in Budapest in the morning. We wanted our marriage be officiated by Istvan's old friend, priest and advisor, Uncle Joseph. He is still alive and is now ninety years old; he has been helping and counseling us since the day we married.

He has been our great encourager throughout our lifetime journey. I remember Uncle Joseph talked extensively about the submission to my husband, Istvan. It was the first time I heard about submission and I must admit I did not like everything I heard. I had just finished medical school and I felt very much equal to Istvan. I supposed that we were treated in the schools the same way, why had I to follow him everywhere? Much later I understood it very well!

The first shock came to us after Attila, our first-born son died. He only lived five hours. The Lord started to teach us some lessons then. We were a happy, newly married couple. I was just out of the medical school, freshly armed with a basic knowledge of healing; we had no idea that life could end so suddenly, as we were prepared to treat, heal and enjoy. We were left with such a pain from the loss of our first son. We were proud, trusted ourselves and left no room for the Lord. But He was very patient with us.

My dear husband loved travelling and in 1974 he signed a contract with Uganda Kampala Makerere University. He had a deep desire to work for the less privileged. I loved Istvan for his searching spirit. Life became very exciting – we had to learn a new culture, a new language and have new friends from so many countries. In the meantime, Andras and Mihaly were born into our family. We spent four years in Uganda; later, we decided to return to Africa, this time to Maiduguri in Nigeria.

Because both of us worked in Maiduguri and there was no acceptable school nearby, we decided to see the school for our children in Miango. Our children were admitted to Miango Kent Academy SIM Mission School, about 600 km from us. Mr. George Beachem, the principal, was very kind, accepting not only missionary children but also others whose parents (like us) were on government contracts from socialist countries.

Andras and Mihaly were admitted, Mihaly only because his older brother was accepted (Mihaly's English was very poor at that time). Istvan did not like the idea of sending eight-year-old Mihaly to boarding school, but with a heavy heart he finally agreed. For them, it was the best since they didn't have to be separated. Looking back, it was the right decision.

At the beginning, we went every second Friday afternoon to visit them and returned on Sunday afternoon. These were tough, long journeys but later we did this monthly. The Christian dorm parents and teachers loved our children, so we felt they really cared not only for their academic career but also for their spiritual growth. It was wonderful to see them growing in the knowledge of the Lord.

This wonderful school touched us also. We bought our first complete Bible in Miango in 1985. We started reading it regularly together. It was wonderful to dig into the Old Testament and New Testament, to read the Psalms. I loved to pray with our own words and pray as the family was together and also pray before meals. We were introduced to a new world and by the time we came to Kano – we knew Jesus as a personal Savior. The Lord used the school here in Nigeria to make a deep family commitment like Joshua: "…As for me and my family, we will serve the Lord." Then we came to know some of the missionaries.

I always longed to work in a mission hospital, but nobody invited me. While we were still working in Maiduguri and on our usual visit to the children in Miango, we met Prof. Stanley Myers. When we returned to Hungary and settled there, in 1993 I got a letter from him asking me to come and help out in Kano Eye Hospital, saying that if I said "yes" I should contact the CBM in Bensheim, Germany. My heart leaped with joy. I could not believe my eyes that he had thought of me. Out of so many people, how could I be selected and asked? I felt inadequate for this job. In my office in Hungary, I used to do OPD work, prescribing glasses and only doing minor surgeries. It was too much for me, to come to work with such a responsibility in a 170-bed eye hospital!

I put the letter in my drawer and wanted to forget about the offer. It was exciting and the same time frightening. But after a two-week consideration, encouraged by my children and by Istvan, I felt confident. Yes, I will be able to do this job. I wrote to the CBM, telling them that I did not think I was the right person for the job, but if they could not find anybody else I was willing to go.

The reply came quickly: "When would you be available?" I prayed hard then, asking the Lord to help me and equip me for this big job. And the Lord did more than that! He helped me cope with the large number of patients here in Kano and He brought wonderful visitors, ophthalmologists to teach me new techniques in cataract surgery, implant surgery and the sutureless technique.

I am so grateful to Him to have given me a skill that helps give sight – not only physically through Him – but also spiritual sight that they might read the Bible and come to know the saving grace of God. He is using me and my knowledge wonderfully for His Kingdom. To see blind people's faces after surgery the next day, to see them smile when they perceive that they see, it is a smile from Heaven, "Well done good and faithful servant!"

We have been in Kano for eight years. Is it a long time? Yes! Is the town dirty? Yes! Is the work tiresome? Yes! Is it hot sometimes, very hot? Yes! But the Lord asked me to come here and I would not have done differently. I feel closer to the Lord than ever before. I had prayed for Istvan's future with the CBM and less involvement with the Muslim University. The Lord heard my prayer – there were openings with the CBM. Istvan became a global advisor in mental health care this year.

I am thankful to the Lord for His faithfulness, for His loving kindness, care and protection throughout the years.

Let me close with words from Isaiah:

"…But those who hope in the Lord will renew their strength.
They will soar on wings like eagles; they will run and not grow weary,
they will walk and not be faint." – Isaiah 40:31

Chapter Sixty

Dr. Istvan Patkai
Psychiatrist

"His Kingdom (is) boldly present in our lives, with all the wonderful surprises we have had and promised to have in the future."

Dr. Istvan Patkai

Dr. Patkai reached out to numerous people in places around the world while in service with Christian Blind Mission International. With his wife, Dr. Gizella Baghy, their witnessing exemplifies the activity in the Church in the twentieth and early twenty-first centuries.

'Tis Grace Hath Brought Me Safe Thus Far

To relate my testimony, I am both excited and challenged. On one hand, it is straightforward and simple; I must be ready with my reply anywhere and anytime to witness for my Redeemer. On the other hand, it is a "fearfully and wonderfully made" question. May the Lord lead my innermost thinking, wording and writing when I express His presence in my life and my commitment to Him.

My favorite hymn is helpful in renewing the past experiences of faith and unfolding the present and future perspectives:

> *"Through many dangers, toils and snares, I have already come;*
> *'tis grace hath brought me safe thus far, and grace will lead me home."*

My grandparents and parents were believers, and through and with them my Redeemer's saving power reached me. (I happily continue with John Newton, when I remember the first experiences – "It was grace that taught my heart to fear.")

I was born in 1941 when the world was falling apart, when my father was taken into the army, when we were fleeing from our frontline village to the nearby mountains, when my father miraculously escaped from deportation to the Soviet Union. It was a time when I had nightmares – with panic and fear of death – especially when I had a fever. My parents and my dear grandmother gave assurance, relieving me from fears by teaching me this simple prayer, "Oh, Lord, have mercy on me!"

As my fears were relieved by His grace, and my guardian angel protected me from common but potentially severe accidents in the farm, I became first in my class. I was a playful child with many friends in primary and secondary school, and had a tremendous drive to compete and succeed.

Teachers and friends became the mediators of God's faithfulness during the adolescent years when my country was under the expansive power of the Russians, when the oppression was supported by deceptive materialistic, atheistic ideology. God sent me teachers who, with twinkles in their eyes, expressed a different opinion and taught me to survive.

In the summertime and during the public holidays when I was at home, I saw the painful adjustment of my parents to the forced cooperative system, to the "surprise visits" of the secret and official police who enforced the new farming laws. But the parish priest, accepting a considerable risk, took us illegally on bike tours and invited us after Sunday mass for a drink and chat. Those of us who left the village and were schooled in various places continued meeting in summer holidays, especially after the Sunday mass, and we became friends.

I smile when I remember the evenings when my father invited the party secretary (who was, incidentally, my biology teacher in primary school) and the priest to our cellar; they drank and sang Hungarian folk songs together. The official ideology was manipulated for the purpose of survival.

As first in my class, of course I was nominated to be the class captain in the Communist Students' Youth Organization. My excellent academic standard and the class captain position became instruments in my career. I did not remember much communist ideology in the Students' Organization – I was respected by the rest of the class and also by my teachers. I was never forced to witness against Christ but Christ was officially dismissed from the schools in the second part of my primary and during my entire secondary education.

In 1956 when I was fifteen years old, I wrote a poem against the Russians and those Hungarians who served them. But personally – and also, the class as a community – we were too weak to become heroes. Again, survival was a rule. The senior teachers refused to let us leave the hostel and demonstrate against the Russians on the street. They sent us home when it was obvious that the Russian tanks would crush the Hungarian revolt.

Through these loving and thoughtful teachers, my Redeemer was present, likely saving my life from the Russian bullets. I biked home with a friend and saw my father coming to meet us on the road, bringing food and hot drinks (it was a cool day in late October 1956). From the country road, I saw the tanks in the grain fields, but the reunion with my protective father and later with the family brought joy in the tragic time of the Hungarian Revolution.

The manipulation of ideology continued throughout my admission to Budapest Medical School. My father left the cooperative and found a job in a nearby industrial plant. In this way, he became a member of the working class, providing me another "credit" to secure my admission to the university. It took me years – throughout my university training and then specializing in neurology and psychiatry – until I realized that the "survival diplomacy," the loyalty to the ruling power, was not necessarily good for my character. There should be limits in my allegiances to the already soft (after 1956, the Russian rule became soft in Hungary, called "goulash socialism"), but still atheistic ideology of the oppressive foreign power. I was conflicted between the expectations of the state toward being a doctor in a university leadership position and having an uneasy feeling deep in my heart against fully identifying with the official ideology. I agreed with some of the socialist ideas and programs in the system, so much so that I temporarily became a member of the Hungarian Socialist Workers' Party.

Struggling between the opposing powers in my mind, between the drive for a university career associated with a political loyalty/socialist ideology and my sleeping faith, I was hesitant and slow in decision. My Redeemer came and acted in my hesitation, this time through Gizella, whom I met and soon married in February 1971. This beautiful girl diverted me from the university (there was no accommodation for us at Budapest, but there were vacancies for doctors with flats in upcountry hospitals). With two specialties in my bag, a respectful position and a nice flat were offered for us to start our married life. Apart from political components, the university had a strong secular and licentious atmosphere – liberal behavior was almost a rule. Parting from that environment was a relief for my soul. We took a tough lesson from God soon after we married when our first son, Attila, died. Soon after, Andreas and Michael were born and the wounds started to heal.

After much theory at the university, I enjoyed the practical, clinical work but at the same time, I was longing for teaching. When I saw an advertisement in our weekly journal for a job with Makerere University Kampala, I applied for it and was appointed. Kampala made a strong impact on our career – we were already called to serve in Africa, and when we returned after few years, we applied to Nigeria.

My Redeemer granted a special intervention, which saved me from further political involvement. When I was approached and offered a leading position in the party, I refused to accept it, and with the risk of some retaliation, I left the political allegiance. I remember that I made a statement that I do this from my free will because of conscience, not identifying myself with the atheist ideology.

In the meantime, our Redeemer had prepared for us an open and irreversible invitation into His Kingdom. Augustinian priest friends in Maiduguri, great evangelical pastors and teachers in Miango, Kent Academy, Nigeria, where our children were schooled, were instruments in God's hand. We returned again for a short time to Hungary, but in 1994 we came back – I would say we "arrived" – His Kingdom boldly present in our lives, with all the wonderful surprises we have had and promised to have in the future.

Section IV: My Participation

"Therefore God exalted him to the highest place
and gave him the name that is above every name,
that at the name of Jesus every knee should bow,
in heaven and on earth and under the earth,
and every tongue acknowledge that Jesus Christ is Lord,
to the glory of God the Father."

– Philippians 2:9-11

Chapter Sixty-one

Commissioning

*"Then he laid his hands on him and commissioned him, as the LORD
instructed through Moses." – Numbers 23:27*

Ruth and I were kneeling at the altar rail of Calvary Evangelical Church on
November 9, 1952. On our heads were the hands of Bishop E. W. Praetorius, the
Rev. Frank Spong and the Rev. Floyd Bosshardt. We were being commissioned
as medical missionaries of the Evangelical United Brethren Church to Bambur,
Nigeria. Calvary was part of the Evangelical Church that merged with the United
Brethren in Christ Church in 1946 becoming the Evangelical United Brethren
Church. The EUB Church later merged with the Methodist Church in 1968 to
become the United Methodist Church.

I had graduated from the Evangelical Theological Seminary in Naperville,
Illinois, in 1945. Two years were spent in the pastoral ministry in Minnesota.
Following graduation in 1951 from the Washington University School of
Medicine, I completed a rotating internship at the Ancker Hospital in St. Paul,
Minnesota. Several years earlier, Ruth had obtained her registered nurse's degree
from the Winnipeg General Hospital in Manitoba, Canada. We finally had come
to this momentous occasion!

Ruth's Background

Ruth was born in Brookdale, Manitoba, Canada. Her banker father was posted at different locations. While in Regina, Saskatchewan, when Ruth was six years old, the bank staff lost their jobs, including her father. The family moved back to Brookdale where Ruth obtained her primary schooling. Just before she finished high school in Winnipeg, her father suffered a fatal heart attack in 1933. The insurance and savings were meager.

Ruth graduated from a business college at the age of eighteen and was the main support for her mother and two younger sisters for five years at a paper products business; her secretary's salary was just $45 a month. During this time she was converted, yielding her life to the Lordship of Jesus Christ. She felt a strong call to medical missions and dreamed of becoming a nurse. Yet, financial resources were not available. She took courage and asked her boss about a raise in salary. The denial was earth shaking. In shock, she walked out the door and down the street to the principal of the business college where she had received her training. He had in his hand a letter that mentioned a position at a grain exchange. She reported the next day at a salary of $95 a month. In two years she was able to save enough to enter nurses' training.

The three years at Winnipeg General Hospital were demanding but thrilling. She became president of the Christian Nurses' Association. Time was granted to visit her sister in Naperville, Illinois, during her sister's first delivery. Her brother-in-law happened to have been my seminary roommate the year before. I was invited to their home for dinner, which had been prepared by Ruth. I was stunned by her beauty and composure – so much so, I don't even remember what I ate. (Later she informed me that it was pork chops.) Her Christian character was the one for whom I had reserved my love. Within a week, she boarded a train back to Canada, but not out of my life. Letters and visits followed.

Lowell's Background

My beginnings were at Paynesville, Minnesota. I was baptized in the Salem Evangelical Church. Along with home and school, the church was the center of my life – Sunday school, Daily Vacation Bible School, Youth Fellowship and all the social events germane to a German community surrounded by Scandinavian Lutherans to the south and German Roman Catholics to the north.

The church was our social center as well as our place of worship. Lay leader William Sack prayed for me by name. His daughter, Lily, was my early Sunday school teacher. Later, Mr. Rudolph Heitke had a major impact on my life. In spite of our squirming and rowdiness, Mr. Heitke and his prepared lessons got through to me, preparing me for my "conversion" at age ten when, kneeling at the altar rail, I sought and received forgiveness of sins and the assurance of a new life in

Christ Jesus. It was the following year, at age eleven, again kneeling at the altar rail, that I received my "call" to medical missions.

Many years later before he died, I was able to thank Mr. Heitke for his marvelous help in presenting to me the Christian message and the claims of the Lord Jesus Christ on my life. Later, kneeling at the altar at Koronis, my commitment to full time Christian service was sealed.

Love, Honor and Cherish

In 1945, Ruth obtained her registered nurse's degree from the Winnipeg General Hospital. On her visit to St. Cloud, Minnesota, where I was serving the Grace Evangelical Church as well as the Graham Evangelical Church, we knelt at the altar rail. Following prayers, I proposed to Ruth. She accepted my pledge of love and the engagement ring. We prayed again. The ring on her finger was fortunate as it was to ward off a previous suitor a short time later. We were married December 29, 1945. In the ensuing two years, we served churches at St. Cloud-Graham and Mayer, Minnesota, while incorporating some additional pre-medical courses.

Acceptance to the Washington School of Medicine, St. Louis, Missouri, in the summer of 1951 was the opening of the Red Sea. All other applications to medical schools had been denied. An exchange of letters with the dean just weeks before the beginning of the school year "parted the waters." The next four years were to be the most demanding of my life to date. Following the internship at Ancker General Hospital, Ruth and I again knelt at an altar rail, this time in Calvary Evangelical Church for the commissioning service. Twenty-six days later, we were on board the S.S. America on our way to Africa.

Chapter Sixty-two

Arrival in Africa

"I lift up my eyes to the mountains—
where does my help come from?
My help comes from the LORD,
the Maker of heaven and earth."
– Psalm 121:1-2

We arrived in Africa on December 31, 1952. We spent New Year's Eve in Lagos, Nigeria. Our travels had started in Minnesota's freezing weather. The north seas were rough to England, our entire family succumbing to seasickness. Sailing on The Elder-Dempster Line, we enjoyed the balmy, tropical weather along the west coast of Africa. The train ride to Jos, situated on the plateau, was a "missionary" experience. Sudan United Interior missionaries put us up for several days as supplies were secured. Our travel to Bambur was via Pero and Shenge Pass. The beautiful, gleaming structures of the newly built Guinter Memorial Hospital thrilled our hearts. This was to be "home" for the next three years.

Emergency!

The next day, Sunday, found us in church. The preacher was Dr. Harold Elliot who presented the message in Hausa. Other Sundays, evangelist and teacher, Kura Tella, held the rapt attention of the congregation with his easy and descriptive Hausa, which was native to him. On Monday morning, we were introduced to the hospital staff. The beginning tour of the hospital was interrupted by an emergency. The patient was on a litter, which had been carried by four men from an inaccessible area behind a range of hills. At a wedding feast there had been an altercation that had turned ugly. A spear had been thrust into his abdomen.

Along with the patient, I was ushered into the surgical wing – not to examine the equipment, but to immediately use it! Nurse Jean Baldwin administered the anesthesia. Ruth circulated. One of the five Nigerian attendants assisted. We had only met moments before and were not aware of each other's abilities or capabilities.

I was a general practitioner with rotating internship experience, which had included only three months of surgical training. A surgical resident warned me that I might run into bowel problems from strangulated hernia and trauma while in Africa. He had showed me how to do the repair by using orthopedic stockinet. Six months later, my first surgical case involved such a repair.

All thoughts left me. I started to panic. This was tragic – pathetic! I was holding the life of a 21-year-old young man in my hands and I couldn't remember how to proceed. Surely the Lord would come to my assistance. There was no one else available to help. Any helping hands had to be mine. "O Lord – HELP!"

While all of this turmoil was going on in my head, nothing was being done at the table. The silence was awkward and embarrassing. After about a minute, Ruth asked, "Are you alright, dear?" In what seemed appropriate to me, I responded by saying, "Let us pray. Lord, bless this young man with your love and your healing. Show me how to do my part."

At that moment, the manner of procedure became completely clear and the surgery was completed. I worried how this must have looked to the staff. This was my first surgery. They had no idea if I actually were a real doctor. Could they, or could they not, trust me as I was literally coming in on a wing and a prayer?

Mercifully, healing was prompt. The patient, Yusufu, was willing to believe in me with a trust that went beyond the repair of his body. We were made aware of this two years later. An evangelist learned of a Christian gathering in Yusufu's remote area. Yusufu had listened to the hymns, prayers and testimonies of the staff during his time of recuperation. He came to trust God with his life and yielded to the Lordship of Jesus Christ. His spared life made an impact for good on his family and friends. A church fellowship was born.

Following this tense experience, we learned that the hospital was well staffed with nurses who were both indigenous and ex-patriot. However, I often wondered how long it would have taken for my acceptance by staff and community had the first patient I touched died. And now, even six decades later, I have a fond and remarkably clear memory of Yusufu and answered prayer in a time of need.

World – and Mission – Changes

The changes in the world during our life times (born 1917 and 1921) were startling. As late as 1952, the perception still persisted that Sub-Saharan Africa was primitive and savage. The idea was reinforced when we were warned not to do medical clinics in Mumuya Land. Even some of our patients at Bambur came without the benefit of clothing, depending solely on leaves. However, by the end of 1953, we ventured to Zinna (now Zing) and were well received.

In 1955, Walt and Ruth Erbele established a church in Kassa. Especially popular was our dental work. I knew how to give anesthetic blocks for extractions. Having a tooth pulled without pain was news that made its way through the entire drum communicating system. And yet, when our medications gave out, patients still submitted to extractions to free themselves of infected and decaying teeth. My admiration knows no bounds for the stoic character of African people. Over the years we learned not to let their stoicism extend too far and have them be subjected to shock and peril.

While ministering in the remote area of Bambur, we were called upon to do surgeries beyond our training skills. Dr. Carl Heinmiller graciously granted me a two-year residency period of general surgery at Akron General Hospital in Ohio. However, our return to Africa was not to Nigeria but to the Hatfield-Archer Hospital in Rotifunk, Sierra Leone.

Chapter Sixty-three

Sierra Leone

"I, even I, have spoken; yes, I have called him.
I will bring him, and he will succeed in his mission. "
– Isaiah 48:15

School being conducted under a tree.

During my years in Nigeria, the United Methodist Church was vibrant and growing. It was later that trials and tribulations racked the churches and leadership. In Sierra Leone, I was caught up in an eleven-year civil war. It was the Church that maintained some stability, the United Methodist Church being the largest Protestant denomination.

Rotifunk, Sierra Leone, was vastly different from Bambur, Nigeria. Access was by developed roads as well as by train. Hospital work had existed for over half a century. Dr. Mabel Silver was famously known throughout this country of five million people. The program was overwhelming. Within a year, Dr. George Harris was added to the staff.

Great numbers of blind patients challenged the EUB Board of Missions. This time, they asked me if I would consider an eye residency to meet this need. The ophthalmology training was completed in three years at the University of Minnesota. We then developed eye programs at Taiama (1964-1967) and Bo (1972-1975).

247

Thereafter, Ruth and I would return three months of each year to do volunteer eye surgery. The United Methodist Church Sierra Leone Conference desired an eye facility in the capitol, Freetown. The Kissy UMC Eye Hospital was built in 1982 and dedicated in 1984. Besides our three-month coverage each year, a total of forty ophthalmologists participated in the program for periods of one to three months. Eventually, an indigenous, residential eye surgeon, Dr. Ainor Fergusson, served from 1993 until his untimely death from a fatal heart attack in 2007.

In June 2009, Dr. John Buchan, with wife Anne and sons Calum and Joshia, began a four-year commitment to the Kissy program. Dr. Buchan's highly trained skills and deep Christian commitment are bringing a wonderful excellence to the eye ministry even as this book is being written. Kissy UMC Eye Hospital is "The Glory of (West) Africa."

Chapter Sixty-four

The Glorious Growth

"It has always been my ambition to preach the gospel where Christ was not known, so that I would not be building on someone else's foundation. Rather, as it is written: Those who were not told about him (Jesus Christ) will see, and those who have not heard will understand." – Romans 15:20-21

Bishops, indigenous pastors, missionaries, church workers and lay people bring a composite picture to *Glorious Witnesses for Africa*. As a medical missionary, I spent most of my time (from 1952 onward) in surgery and clinics in Nigeria and Sierra Leone. The apostle Paul relished going to peoples and places where the Gospel of Jesus Christ had not been preached. In Romans 15:20-21, he writes: "It has always been my ambition to preach the gospel where Christ was not known, so that I would not be building on someone else's foundation. Rather, as it is written: Those who were not told about him (Jesus Christ) **will see** (emphasis mine), and those who have not heard will understand."

Being an ophthalmologist, I was able to help thousands "to see." Being a missionary, it was my heart's desire that my patients would also gain insight into the love of God as revealed in Jesus Christ. I enjoyed the challenge of going into Mumuya country in the early days following the removal of travel restrictions. I also had the opportunity and privilege of accompanying evangelists to their remote preaching missions, always carrying with me my black bag filled with life-saving medicines. Later in Sierra Leone, I served for a time as the field representative, which took me to far reaching rural churches for dedications and baptisms. Except for some training periods and one short leave of absence, I have lived and served in Africa for over a period of fifty-two years.

The Truth of the Gospel

Early missionaries sowed the seeds of the Christian faith. Understandably, their cultural backgrounds and church politics were reflected in the emerging churches. While their services are not to be denigrated, the "glorious" growth of the Christian Church did not occur until African leadership, with their own cultural forces, came to the fore. Staid-and-true mission leadership was shocked, if "under the Spirit" parishioners danced in the aisles. An African Christian leader was said to have remarked that the Church really did not truly grow until drums were admitted into the service (and it was no longer being headed up by a missionary). The "glorious growth" of the Church was on its way.

During this time, countries were also shedding colonialism. Independence movements were most pronounced in the 1950s and 1960s. The Church was sympathetic to the cause of the African people. The people were appreciative and respectful of the Church in whose schools they had been trained and whose Gospel had freed their spiritual lives and formulated their ideologies. The Church was swept along with this new liberty and grew in great numbers. In this new freedom, early indigenous church and missionary leaders allowed veneration of the graves of those who had given witness.

The truth of the Gospel, as always, was a personal choice. Village catechists and laypeople shared the saving power of the Lord Jesus Christ with their friends and relatives. African music and story telling became prominent expressions in the church ritual. There were Christian meetings in the homes. Christian women were liberated. As in the case of the Zumuntar Mata (Women's Fellowship) in Nigeria, they evangelized. Bands of women visited the homes, experiencing births and deaths, giving each dignity especially with their singing. Arm in arm, they included nonbelievers who were swept into a newfound love and loyalty to Jesus Christ. As many as 28,000 attended some rallies.

The church was not the only meeting place for worship. It was present in the classrooms established by the church. Teachers became "preachers" in front of the blackboards.

Singing, singing and more singing shaped young minds and hearts. Clinics paused for worship prior to attending to the sick. Christians who shared their testimonies staffed hospitals. Christian agriculturalists taught better growing patterns, making cash crops possible. The caring ministry of the church became evident. People were drawn to it. The character of the Christian became obvious.

Trust ensued where integrity had not been engendered. Christian human values became transforming.

Finally, the church became "Africanized," losing its stigma of being imported. Christian faith encompassed African tradition, religion and spiritualism. Self-determination finally had been reached. There was a sharing of leadership between indigenous Christians and missionaries. The relationship was that of co-workers, not dependents; that of brothers and sisters, not parent and child. Sharing the Gospel empowered "witnessing in the name of Jesus." The *"Glorious Witnesses for Africa"* resulted in a glorious and dynamic growth of the Christian Church.

These things I observed as one whom an African pastor referred to as an "African with white skin."

Chapter Sixty-five

Basic Faith

"I am the way, the truth, and the life. No one comes to the Father except through me." – John 14:6

Jesus Christ is Savior and Lord

Down through the years, Ruth and I were often asked about our Christian faith – and only rarely about our registered nurse and medical doctor training. We were asked what we say to people in Africa and whether it is appropriate to expect them to change their beliefs and ways when they have their own culture. My answers contained the following truths.

I came as a Christian, a follower of Jesus Christ, to minister in His name. I felt "called" to provide healing for the sick and sight for the blind. My love for God and my neighbor made my services available to people of all loyalties and faith.

Through Scripture, I shared the truth of the Gospel, which brings hope, strength, and transformation of lives. This Christian truth is not one of many truths about God. It is the revelation brought to us by Jesus Christ, who was not one of many teachers, guides or prophets, but the only-begotten Son of God.

Unfortunately, we are facing today many who may represent the Christian faith who no longer believe that the revelation brought to us by Christ Jesus is THE TRUTH, but a truth. We are called upon to defend the absolute uniqueness of Jesus Christ and the revelation He delivered through His life (words and deeds), sacrificial death and glorious resurrection. I believe the Bible, which affirms that Jesus Christ is THE SAVIOR of the world. Jesus says, "I am the way, the truth and the life. No one comes to the Father except through me." John 14:6

I tell people that I believe it was God's will for me to make known the Gospel of God's love as revealed in Jesus Christ and to bring people to God through Him, whom knowing is life eternal. I wanted to share the Lord Jesus Christ as Savior rather than "some" truth or do some healing that is not redemptive. It was important to me to "Go into all the world and preach the good news to all creation." Mark 16:15

For me, being a missionary is being obedient to Christ's command: "You will be witnesses for me…to the ends of the earth." Acts 1:8 (KJV)

Christ, the Answer for the World

It is my desire to share Christ as the solution to the world's need. I believe it is altogether proper to challenge beliefs and practices ("culture") that recognize evil spirits as inhabiting the world around us which need to be assuaged. I object when cooked rice is scattered into the bush to appease the spirits while undernourished children are standing by. Cleanliness and providing proper foods and protective nets to ward off disease must be practiced instead of placing amulets around a baby's neck.

The immediate appeal of suffering tugs on my heart. Christ had compassion on those in need, and healed all manner of disease in mind and body. I am constrained to follow Him as best I can.

I believe that we build schools, churches and hospitals not only to make Christians out of non-Christians, but because we cannot be Christian without providing them.

I am persuaded that one does not throw away one's life by losing it in service, but rather finds it in the natural expression of the will of God.

We preach not only to bring people to the Lordship of Jesus Christ, but because we cannot help but share with others the overflow of our own abundant faith for victorious living.

We go to needy places in response to Christ's command, "Heal the sick…say, the Kingdom of God is come near you." Luke 10:9 (KJV) As a missionary, I seek to identify with the needs of the people.

We go to foreign fields, not to be Christian by making Christians, but to make Christians by being Christian.

I am convinced that merely the maintenance of life is not important. It is important to remain faithful.

A Life Redeemed

Our hearts are moved by the great need of the neglected poor. We believe we have the solution in Jesus. We cannot deny them the chance for newness of life. "If anyone is in Christ, he is a new creation; old things have passed away; behold, all things have become new." II Corinthians 5:17 (KJV) One powerful example of a life redeemed is the story of Brima.

He was about five years old with a torn shirt and shorts. He would show up on the hospital porch about the time Ruth would come down from the apartment over the surgery to begin the day's work. He was never forward, speaking only in English phrases if spoken to. He was just "there" with a familiarity that prompted greeting. Ruth began to look for him if he wasn't waiting for her each morning. Ultimately, she carried with her some food so she could to slip it to him, presuming he was a hungry boy; his name was Brima.

Brima lived with his grandmother on the hospital compound. His great grandfather, Mango Brown, originally owned the land on which the United Methodist mission was located. About twenty acres had been deeded to the church. It now housed the Brown Memorial United Methodist Church, a UMC primary school, an urban centre, a general hospital with emphasis on maternity and child care, and the Kissy UMC Eye Hospital.

Ruth and I did not respond to requests to provide fees for students wanting to attend school. All of our tithe money went to provide for medicine, supplies and equipment with which to carry out our eye care ministry. However, when Ruth found out that Brima could not attend school because his family did not have the school fees, an exception was made. Brima was available to help with things around the hospital and the apartment as well as run errands. Appropriate apparel was secured.

Even as a small lad, Brima was serious and studious, doing well in school. Ruth continued providing support for his secondary school training and then his computer science work. Ultimately, Brima was hired by Lettie Williams, administrator of Kissy UMC Eye Hospital, to do some computer work for her.

His availability and attention to detail led to his doing correspondence and record keeping. He prepared reports for the Sierra Leone UMC Annual Conference as well as for the Christian Blind Mission, the General Board of Global Ministries and the Central Global Vision Fund. He was trustworthy and always agreeable to take on responsibilities. In my case, he emailed contributions and photos of Sierra Leonean Christian leaders that are contained in *Glorious Witnesses for Africa*.

The time came when the position of business manager at the Kissy UMC Eye Hospital was discontinued. In need of assistance, Dr. John Buchan turned to the one person whom he felt would be honest, trustworthy, and committed to helping with the administration – Brima.

Brima wrote the following email to me on November 15, 2010, as Mrs. Gess had recently passed away on October 25, 2010:

Dear Dr. Gess,
Christian greetings to you and your family. Thank you for your wonderful
email. I am very happy about the central role being given to me by Dr.

Buchan. I am happy to have responsibility to help move the eye hospital forward, by the grace of Almighty God. Everyone on the staff is happy for me, as they knew me when I was a little boy.

All the praise goes to you and the late Mrs. Gess. May her soul rest in perfect peace. She played a great role in my education. Whatever I have achieved, I owe to Mrs. Gess, who allowed me to have the best education. I will continue to pray for her. I believe she is in heaven.

Extend my greetings to your family. With regards, Brima

The Gospel Must Be Shared

As Christian missionaries, we were especially thrilled when, because of the eye ministry, patients who received physical sight also gained insight into the love of God as revealed in Jesus Christ.

We cannot miss such a wonderful opportunity for the fulfillment of their lives as well as our own.

To such a service of love, I am willing to sacrifice friends, comforts and – if need be – life itself.

We face a humanity too precious to neglect.

We know a remedy for the ills of the world too wonderful to withhold.

We have a Savior too glorious to hide.

We experience an adventure too thrilling to miss.

Chapter Sixty-six

God So Loved . . .

"For God so loved the world that He gave His only begotten Son, that whosoever believeth in Him, should not perish, but have everlasting life."
– John 3:16

We have been considering in *Glorious Witnesses for Africa* the growth of the church in Sub-Saharan Africa. In each church and fellowship, the key verse, the key truth, is John 3:16 – the most universally known Bible verse in the world. There are 2.2 billion Christians who have access to this verse. Yet:

- 1.4 billion Muslims have the Koran
- 1 billion Hindus have the Bhagavad Gita
- 400 million Buddhists have the Tipitaka
- 15 million Jews have the Old Testament

The Bible, the Holy Scriptures, contains the means for salvation: "For God so loved the world that He gave His only begotten Son, that whosoever believeth in Him, should not perish, but have everlasting life." John 3:16 (KJV)

"For God sent not His Son into the world to condemn the world, but that the world through Him, might be saved." John 3:17 (KJV)

God in His love provides salvation by giving His Son, Jesus Christ. Belief in Jesus Christ, His life, teachings, and sacrificial death on Calvary's cross and His subsequent resurrection brings everlasting, eternal life.

The Requirements for Eternal Life

This was answered by Jesus in Luke 10:25-29.

A lawyer asked: "Teacher, what must I do to inherit eternal life?"
"What is written in the Law?" he replied. "How do you read it?"
He answered, "'Love the Lord your God with all your heart and with all your soul and with all your strength and with all your mind'; and, 'Love your neighbor as yourself.'"
"You have answered correctly," Jesus replied. "Do this and you will live."
But he wanted to justify himself, so he asked Jesus, "And who is my neighbor?"

Jesus then answered with the parable of the Good Samaritan.

Eternal life – and how it is obtainable – is the greatest news in all the world! The world needs to know of Jesus and accept Him as Lord and Savior.

Love Thy Neighbor . . . As Thyself

To love God is a universally accepted truth.

It is the mandate to love one's neighbor that poses problems. Some religions allow the destruction of infidels, i.e., those who do not believe as they do.

It is understandable that peace will come to this world only when Jesus Christ is Lord, when His teaching of love for God AND for neighbor is practiced. ". . . that at the name of Jesus, every knee shall bow . . . and every tongue confess that Jesus Christ is Lord to the glory of God the Father." Philippians 2:10-11

Redemption

Most religions teach that redemption is possible. The Bible speaks directly to this. It describes our condition:

- **Romans 3:23:** "All have sinned and come (fall) short of the glory of God."
- **Romans 6:23:** "For the wages of sin is death, but the gift of God is eternal life in Christ Jesus our Lord."

It describes God's provision:

- **John 3:16-17:** "For God so loved the world that He gave His only begotten Son, that whosoever believeth in Him, should not perish, but have everlasting (eternal) life. For God sent not His Son into the world to condemn the world; but that the world through Him might be saved."
- **Romans 5:8:** "God commended (demonstrates) His love towards us in that while we were yet sinners, Christ died for us."
- **Romans 5:20:** "Where sin abounded, grace did much more abound."
- **Ephesians 2:8-10:** "By grace you are saved through faith, and that not of yourselves; it is the gift of God, not of works lest anyone should boast." However, this does not mean we are not excused from doing good works, for the verse continues: "For we are His workmanship, created in Christ Jesus for good works."
- **I John 1:8** declares: "If we say that we have no sin, we deceive ourselves, and the truth is not in us." But "If we confess our sins, He is faithful and just to forgive us our sins and to cleanse us from all unrighteousness."
- **John 3:36:** "He who believes on the Son, has everlasting life."
- **II Corinthians 5:17:** "If anyone is in Christ, he is a new creation: old things are passed away; behold, all things have become new."
- **Psalm 37:5:** "Commit your way to the Lord, trust also in Him, and He shall bring it to pass."

That's the Gospel in those few verses! That is the Good News to be shared. For world peace, Jesus' commandments must be taken to every country and climate.

The Call to Missions

Historically, this was the calling of missionaries. Every local congregation encouraged their young men and women to prepare for missionary work. Young people responded – as pastors and evangelists, agriculturalists, teachers, nurses and doctors. In the United Methodist Church, they were supported (even though our original salary in 1952 was only $2,800 for the entire year). Decisions to become missionaries were considered life-long commitments.

In recent years, short-term volunteers have become popular. Now, arrangements for service are made for certain periods in one's life. At first, this was violently opposed by mission boards; then there was a complete turn around as mission boards organized short-term work, especially for volunteers.

Financial Support

Originally, financial support for missionaries was no problem. Churches, schools, and hospitals were financially underwritten. Equipment needed for the project was provided. In Nigeria and in the early years in Sierra Leone, whatever we needed for the hospitals was made available. By the 1980s when the Kissy UMC Eye Hospital was envisioned, it was another story. A grant was given by the General Board of Global Ministries of the United Methodist Church, but $75,000 doesn't build and equip an up-to-date eye hospital.

Challenges were made to U.S. ophthalmologists that involved 10,000 letters sorted and sent by the women's organization of the Alexandria United Methodist Church. Donations arrived and the Kissy Eye Hospital was built. Private donors supplied the equipment. What was meant to be a stopgap measure of providing eye care in Freetown until the government was able to provide it, stretched out over years. There were times when there was no money available for the salary of Dr. Ainor Fergusson, the Sierra Leonean eye doctor. Doctors and individuals shared $500 checks to keep the program going.

Christian Blind Mission International has been impressed with the Kissy UMC Eye Hospital program since it began. CBM has and is generously providing supplies and equipment – including financial assistance for generators and vehicles. CBM is presently helping the General Board of Global Ministries and Central Global Vision Fund by supplying (by underwriting salary and expenses) a highly trained and skilled ophthalmologist from Scotland, Dr. John Buchan and family for a four-year period (2009-2013).

Recently, when I emailed Dr. Buchan informing him that a vitrector was being made available through the Douglas County Golden Brothers' Lion Club, his first words in reply was "Praise the Lord!" This instrument enables the eye surgeon to do the best operation possible, especially on children with cataracts. It will be the only vitrector in a six-country contiguous area of Africa. Sharing the best message, the Gospel, must be accompanied by doing the best surgery possible.

While I spent April and May 2009 at the Kissy Eye Hospital, I made no plans to return in 2010 – the first time in thirty-five years of continuous volunteer work I did not make the journey. In responding to the Master's words to "heal the sick," I have crossed the ocean 182 times.

When I was born in 1921, there was no United Methodist Church in Nigeria. The initial work in Nigeria began two years later in December 1923. After our tour of service in Nigeria was completed in 1955, there were reportedly 900 baptized members. A recent report (2010) states that the present membership now is over 600,000! How remarkable!

What has happened in Nigeria is happening in other Sub-Saharan African countries.

Inquires into this phenomenal growth in contrast to the decline of mainline Christian churches for the last twenty-six years in America prompted Wikipedia to observe that in North America an increasing number of people are becoming more inclined to join theologically conservative denominations.

African United Methodist pastors and people are orthodox. They read the Bible, believe it and act on it. Evangelism has priority over all other programs of education, health, agriculture and social welfare. Their soul-liberating freedom prompts Christian young and old to share their faith. Their enthusiasm is contagious. Non-believers see the radiance of Christians and take a serious look at their belief. With new information and understanding, they join those who name Jesus Christ as Lord and Savior.

In Summary

This brings us back to the opening statements:
- We believe John 3:16.
- We know our condition and the condition of the world.
- We pray for redemption. This involves confessing our sins, making restitution where possible and reaching out in faith to the saving power of the Lord Jesus Christ.
- John 3:36 states: "He that believeth on the Son hath everlasting life."
- The Gospel is the "Good News" that brings:
  - o   Repentance
  - o   Release through forgiveness
  - o   Renewal
  - o   Regeneration

"For God so loved the world, that He gave His only begotten Son, that whosoever believeth in Him should not perish, but have everlasting life." John 3:16 (KJV)

Glory, hallelujah, amen!

Jesus shall reign where'er the sun
Does its successive journeys run;
His kingdom spread from shore to shore,
Till moons shall wax and wane no more.
Blessings abound where'er He reigns,
All prisoners leap and loose their chains;
The weary find eternal rest,
And all who suffer want are blest.

– *Jesus Shall Reign*, United Methodist Hymnal, p. 157

Chapter Sixty-seven

The Future

"All this is for your benefit, so that the grace that is reaching more and more
people may cause thanksgiving to overflow to the glory of God."
– II Corinthians 4:15

Yale University historian, Dr. Lamin Sannch, stated in *Christianity Today* that African Christianity is not just an exotic, curious phenomenon in an obscure part of the world, but African Christianity might be the shape of things to come.

A recent World Council of Churches Report observed, "The statistics from the World Christian Encyclopedia illustrate the emerging trend of dramatic Christian growth on the continent and supposes that in 2025 (fourteen years from now) there will be 633,000,000 Christians in Africa."

African United Methodists are assuming a greater voice, more sharing of power and the ability to adopt (contextualize) some church rules to local needs. Looking ahead to 2020 and beyond, a committee has been set up to study the worldwide nature of the United Methodist Church to consider goals that include: defining the covenant that unites the global church, promoting greater regional connections, exploring how the United Methodist Church's *Book of Discipline* can be adapted for local needs, and examining the U.S. and international roles of general agencies. Recommendations are to be submitted to the 2012 General Conference, the church's top legislative body.

The surveys involved the Democratic Republic of Congo, Liberia, Mozambique and Zimbabwe in August 2010. Church leaders form Cote d'Ivoire shared their views as well, emphasizing an advance, in Bishop Boni's words, into the "deep waters of evangelization and social action with efficient policies that bring forth the **Glory of God** (emphasis mine) to the world."[47]

The growth during the past ninety years of the Christian Church in Sub-Saharan Africa, with special reference to the United Methodist Church, has been "Glorious."

"If my people, who are called by my name, will humble themselves and pray and seek my face and turn from their wicked ways, then will I hear from heaven and will forgive their sin and will heal their land." II Chronicles 7:14

Footnotes

[1]"Christianity in Africa," Wikipedia, http://en.wikipedia.org/wiki/ Christianity_in_Africa.

[2]Tim Stafford, "Historian Ahead of His Time," *Christianity Today Magazine*, February 2007, http://www.christianitytoday.com/ct/2007/february/34.87.html.

[3] *World Council of Churches Report*, http://www.oikoumene.org/en/resources/ documents/general-secretary/speeches/23-08-04-keynote-address-korea.html.

[4] http://www.christianaggression.org/features_statistics.php

[5] Kenneth Osbeck, *Amazing Grace*: 366 Inspiring Hymn Stories for Daily Devotions, Kregel Publications; fifteenth edition (July 1990), p. 314.

[6] Mark A. Noll, *Turning Points, Decisive Moments in the History of Christianity*, Second Edition, Baker Books, Grand Rapids, MI, 2000, p. 290.

[7] Richard Andrew Corby, "The Mende Uprising of 1898 in Sierra Leone as it Related to the United Brethren in Christ Missions," November 1, 1971.

[8] Corby, pp. 32-34.

[9] J. S. Mills, *Mission Work in Sierra Leone*, West Africa, Dayton: Memorial Edition, 1898.

[10] Esther Megill, *Return to Africa: A Journal*, May 2008, pp. 101-102.

[11] "Major Religions Ranked by Size," *Worldwide Missions: The Harvest Fields*, August 9, 2007.

[12] Interview with South Congo Conference Bishop Katembo Kainda, http:// gbgm-umc.org/global_news/full_article.cfm?articleid=4502-Cached-Similar

[13] http://en.wikipedia.org/wiki/Methodism

[14] http://www.northkatangaumc.org/images/THE%20HISTORICAL%20 GROWTH%20OF%20THE%20UMC%20NORTH%20KATANGA.doc.

[15] Georgia Harkness, *The Methodist Church in Social Thought and Action*, Nashville: Abingdon Press, 1964, p. 20.

[16] Wikipedia.

[17]2010 UMR Communications, http://www.umportal.org/articale. asp:id=2260.

[18] Tim Tanton, *Good News*, November/December 2009.

[19] Anastácio Chembeze is an ordained minister in the United Methodist Church. He holds a Bachelor of Divinity (B.D.) and Master of Peace and Governance (M.P.G.) from Africa University, Zimbabwe. He served one congregation in Beira, Mozambique, before working for the African Centre for the Constructive Resolution of Disputes (ACCORD) and the Electoral Institute of Southern Africa (EISA), both based in South Africa. In addition, he has experience working in civil society organizations in Mozambique, Zambia, Angola and South Africa, focusing on conflict, elections, governance and community development organizations. Chembeze has also taught at universities in Mozambique.

[20] http://www.mozambique.mz/dadosbas/eindex.htm

[21] http://www.google.com/publicdata?ds=wbwdi&met=ny_gdp_mktp_kd_zg&idim=country:MOZ&dl=en&hl=en&q=Mozambique+GDP+growth+rate

[22] http://www.google.com/search?q=Mozambique+GDP+per+capita&rls=com.microsoft:*&ie=UTF-8&oe=UTF-8&startIndex=&startPage=1&rlz=1I7SKPB_en

[23] Eduardo Mondlane was educated in the Presbyterian and Episcopal Methodist churches. His formal education was provided by the Methodist Episcopal Church through Cambine Mission before proceeding for higher education abroad. He gained the liberation consciousness through oppression in his village and through interaction with education and Christian experience. With assistance of Methodist missionaries, he went to the U.S. for studies and obtained a Ph.D. from Northwest University before working for the United Nations.

[24] Thomas C. Oden and Leister R. Longden, *The Wesleyan Theological Heritage*, 1991, p. 21.

[25] This story was told by the Rev. Dr. Jamisse Taimo, quoting the Rev. Francisco Fenhiche Machava, a retired minister of the United Methodist Church, South Save Conference.

[26] John Auta Pena, *The Life of Servanthood*, Capwill Printing and Publishing Solutions: Jalingo, Nigeria, 2009, Preface.

[27] Pena, p. 2

[28] Pena, ibid

[29] Pena, p. 3

[30] Pena, p. 29

[31] Pena, p. 30

[32] Pena, pp. 31-32

[33] Pena, p. 16

[34] Esther Megill, *Return to Africa*, 2008, pp. 457-458.

[35] Bishop John Yambasu, speech given at the Academy for Church Growth meeting in Freetown, October 6, 2009.

[36] Gilbert W. Olson, *Church Growth in Sierra Leone*, 1969, p. 205.

[37] J. Steven O'Malley, *"On the Journey Home": The History of Mission of the Evangelical United Brethren Church, 1946–1968*, General Board of Global Ministries: United Methodist Church, 2003, p. 77.

[38] http://new.gbgm-umc.org/umcor/work/health/hospitals/kissy 2010

[39] Mary Beth Coudal, "New Bishop Conveys Hope for East Africa," August 14, 2006, http://gbgm-umc.org/global_news/pr.cfm?articleid=4177&CFID=661591&CFTOKEN-69

[40] Hendrik R. Pieterse, "Bishop Faces Challenges in Zimbabwe," United Methodist News Service,
http://www.bwcumc.org/hopefund/bishop-faces-challenges-zimbabwe.

[41] *Newscope*, September 29, 2010

[42] Elliott Wright, "Thomas Kemper of Germany is New Chief Executive of

United Methodist Mission Agency," January 13, 2010, http://gbgm-umc.org/ global_news/full_article.cfm?articleid=5624. Reprinted with permission of the General Board of Global Ministries.

[43] Dr. Cherian Thomas, "Reviving Methodist Church Hospitals in Africa and Asia," *New World Outlook*, March/April 2001, http://gbgm-umc.org/nwo/01ma/ reviving.html.

[44] Linda Rowe, "I/Eye Care," http://wstumc.org/mission_opportunities.htm.

[45] Newscope, October 6, 2010

[46] http://www.umc.org/site/apps/nl/content3.asp?c=lwL4KnNILtH&b=207 2525&ct=4644277

[47] Isaac Broune, *A UMNS Report*, August 27, 2010.

[48] Google, About.com: Geography.

Bibliography

J. Behney and Paul H. Eller, *The History of the Evangelical and United Brethren Church.* Abingdon Press: Nashville, Tennessee, 1979.

Emmet D. Cox, *The Church of the United Brethren in Christ in Sierra Leone.* William Cary Library: South Pasadena, California, 1970.

Peter Marubitoba Dong, et.al., *The History of the United Methodist Church in Nigeria.* Nashville: Abingdon Press, 2000.

Arthur and Aletha Faust, *From Pero Station.*

John G. Fuller, *Fever! The Hunt for a New Killer Virus.* Clarke, Irwin & Company Ltd.: Toronto and Vancouver, 1974.

Lowell A. Gess, *Mine Eyes Have Seen the Glory,* RLE Press: Alexandria, Minnesota, 2002.

Billy Graham, *Just as I Am.* HarperCollins: Carmel-New York, 1997.

J. S. Mills, *Mission Work in Sierra Leone, West Africa.* United Brethren Publishing House: Dayton, Ohio, 1898.

Mark A. Noll, *Turning Points: Decisive Moments in the History of Christianity.* Baker Book House Company: Grand Rapids, Michigan, 2001.

Olsen, Lois. *Contentment is Great Gain.* Milwaukee: Leone Press, 1996

Gilbert W. Olson, *Church Growth in Sierra Lone.* William E. Eerdman Publishing Co.: Grand Rapids, Michigan, 1969.

J. Steven O'Malley, *On the Journey Home: The History of Mission of the Evangelical United Brethren Church, 1946-1968.* General Board of Global Ministries UMC: New York, New York, 2003.

Kenneth H. Osbeck, *Amazing Grace.* Kregel Publications: Grand Rapids, Michigan, 2002.

Lorraine Esterly Pierce, *Marching Through Immanuel's Ground.* RLE Press: Alexandria, Minnesota, 1999.

WorldNetDaily.com, "Africa's Christian Population on Rise," February 20, 2010.

Appendix

C. V. Rettew / Rotifunk Martyrs

Survivor of the Massacre

C. V. Rettew, one of the schoolboys at Rotifunk during the time of the 1898 missionary massacre, later became a pastor. Several times while visiting with me he would recount the circumstances surrounding the death of the missionaries, whom he referred to as "those beautiful people." Tears would course down his cheeks as he described the death scene – each missionary being surrounded by out-of-control, screaming men who beheaded each of their victims. He lived with great regret that no one had protected the missionaries from this terrible fate. Like all the other students, when the rebels appeared he fled into the bush for protection.

Pastor Rettew and his wife were faithful witnesses of Jesus Christ all the days of their lives. During the time that Ruth and I served in the eye clinic at Taiama, we would often hear the tinkling of a little bell. We would smile to each other, knowing that Mrs. Rettew was on her rounds in the village proclaiming the Good News of salvation, open to all who confess their sins and accept Jesus Christ as Lord and Savior. In a letter from Pastor Rettew in 1961 when he was retired and infirm, he wrote: "Three things are essential for all followers of the Lord Jesus Christ: humility, indiscriminate love for all persons irrespective of color and condition, and a genuine faith in Christ." By running into the bush for protection on that fateful day in 1898, Pastor Rettew was given the privilege of leading hundreds and thousands of people to Jesus Christ as their Lord and their Savior. His destiny was not one of martyrdom but rather of life that he might be instrumental in bringing new life to others during the life that he was given.

Martyrs At Rotifunk

In January 1898, a session of the West African Conference convened at Shenge. Already, rumors of imminent tribal wars were circulating throughout the country. The Howards, Kings and Miss Eaton left for the United States soon after the conference. The other workers returned to their stations. By April, the situation grew worse but the work went on in spite of the rumblings of war.

During the last week of April 1898, Mr. Ward left by rowboat for Freetown to secure cash to pay the workers. Many workers came to Rotifunk to await Mr. Ward's return and attended services in the church. Soon after the service, several Sierra Leoneans came to town half naked and extremely frightened. All the Sierra Leonean women left town Sunday afternoon. Boarding pupils were sent home. In the evening, the war boys attacked the Kwellu barracks and the booming of guns was heard. A watch was kept that night and no one was allowed to sleep. At this crucial time, Dr. Hatfield arrived in a hammock from Taiama prostrate with illness.

On Monday morning, preparations were made for the missionaries to escape by boat, including the Rev. T. F. Hallowell and his family. While waiting for the incoming tide, news came that the war boys had captured Mr. Coker who was a trader and church member. He was brought to Bendasuma and murdered. This crushed all hope of escape by river.

The missionaries quietly made their way into the bush with Dr. Hatfield still in a hammock. The raiders came to town and three policemen escaped. About 1:00 p.m., the mission laborers confided to Rev. Hallowell that they had taken oaths to help in the massacre of the missionaries and unless he did likewise, he too would be killed. He told them he had to consult his boy first with the intent of stalling for time. He went to Rotower and returned early in the morning with his boy. He then went to the missionaries' hiding place to see how they were faring and advised them to go to Freetown. They sent Pa Hallowell with another mission boy to get the records in the mission house. On the road, the missionaries were violently arrested and brought to town by screaming groups of men.

During the three hours of the missionaries' captivity, grizzly events took place. Mr. Cain and Dr. Archer were shot. Miss Ella Schenck fled to the boys' home. When found, she was stabbed to death. Another account was that she was taken to the Frontier Police Barracks where she was raped and murdered. Mrs. Cain reportedly ran into the burning mission house, dying in the flames rather than being subjected to abuse. (The Rev. Walter Schutz, mission superintendent at Rotifunk in the early 1920s, was told that Mrs. Cain was killed in the barracks and did not commit suicide.) Dr. Hatfield, too ill to move, observed the tragic scene, silently standing with folded hands in prayer until the moment of being stripped of her clothing and beheaded.

In Taiama, the McGrews were held captive for several days. On May 8, 1898, they were taken to a small stony island in the Tai River where they were beheaded, their bodies thrown into the river never to be recovered.

Dr. Marietta Hatfield had arrived in Sierra Leone in 1891 and Dr. Mary Archer in 1895. Working with Dr. West, the medical program had expanded with new facilities at Rotifunk. Nurse Ella Schenck was engaged to be married. Her intended was on his way to Rotifunk from Freetown at the time of the tragedy. As his boat entered the mouth of the Bumpeh River from the Atlantic Ocean, he was informed of the Rotifunk massacre in which all the missionaries had been killed. He reversed his course, returned to Freetown, and no further word was known about him.

Rev. Ira N. Cain was a strong and energetic man in possession of firearms. He refused to use them for his defense, explaining that he had come to help and to save – not to kill – the people of Sierra Leone. In recounting this incident, Bishop J. S. Mills, writes:

I have elsewhere said and now repeat that the law of sacrifice is the first law of the kingdom of God. The life of the Master illustrated this fact, for even "the Son of man came not to be ministered unto, but to minister, and to give his life a ransom for many." From the beginning, obedience to this law has been the condition of human progress. The mother gives her life for her child, the patriot dies for his country, and the missionary dies for his King.

When Brother Cain refused to fire on the black mob ready to slay the little party of whites, I have no doubt that when he consulted his noble comrades, they said, "Let us lay down our lives for Africa, even as our Savior did for us." And they were at once enrolled in the great army of martyrs, who counted not their own lives dear unto themselves. The redemption of Africa goes forward by such service. The graves of Christian missionaries and explorers are the steppingstones across Africa. It has pleased God to give our church the honor of furnishing a glorious band, who by this high offering of sacrificial service, has done so much to redeem Africa.

The list is long of other missionaries who for their faith paid the supreme price by laying down their lives in deadly climates with untreatable diseases. Jesus gave His life willingly even though His prayer was, "Father, if you will, take this cup away from me" (Luke 22:42, *Good News for Modern Man*). No missionary ever wants or intends to die, but commitment often places them in harm's way. The fact that these ambassadors for Christ all died in the line of duty did not diminish the response of others to "go into all the world" and fill the ranks of those chosen for the high calling of Christ to preach the Gospel. Because of Chief Thomas Neale Caulker's friendship with missionaries and the government, he was killed along with many hundreds of others.

The likeness of Bai Bureh, 1840-1909, brilliant strategist of the Hut Tax War, appears on the 1000 Leone note. Reportedly he did not plan or condone the murdering of missionaries. Those killed in the Temne country were with the fighting forces. The English missionaries were at his mercy at Ro-Gbere, but they were in no way molested beyond being detained. The Rev. W. J. Humphrey lost his life in his over-solicitude for his people, who were perfectly safe. Bai Bureh killed Mack, Humphrey's murderer. The historian A. B. C. Sibthorpe stated that there were upwards of 200 who were implicated and tried in the protectorate massacres, of whom thirty-three were executed.

When the fighting stopped, Bai Bureh remained illusive for a considerable time. Ultimately, he emerged from the bush, giving himself up with the words "The war done done." The government did not want to punish him as he had fought bravely without killing defenseless people. They did not dare release him for fear that he might start another war, so they deported him to Ghana. In 1905, he was allowed to return to Sierra Leone and ended his days in his own chiefdom. Never again was the British authority challenged.

In unpublished notes, Mr. Henry J. Williams makes enlightened statements about the Hut Tax that caused the rebellion and the impact that it had on the growing Christian church in Sierra Leone. He begins by saying:

It is reasonable to think that a cause as self-giving and considerate as was the Church missionary enterprise, would be received with open arms; that a benevolent government whose purpose was to maintain law and order, provide schools, open roads and promote the common good would be accepted and respected.

But progress and change never come without the shuffling off of old casts and the abandoning of old ways. Man does not make such changes readily. They are usually accompanied by strain, suffering and revolution, and in many instances, death.

Loss to the Mission

Seven lives were destroyed at Rotifunk and Taiama, as well as property, furnishings, churches, schools, dispensaries, industrial buildings and even the boathouse at Shenge. Inexorably, the Church of Jesus Christ moves forward and builds on the blood of martyrs.

"…This is the victory that has overcome the world, even our faith. Who is it that overcomes the world? Only he who believes that Jesus is the Son of God." – I John 5:4b-5

"I have told you these things, so that you might have peace. In this world you will have trouble. But take heart! I have overcome the world." – John 16:33

Personally Known Missionaries

The testimonies of African Christians and missionaries of the United Methodist Church mostly comprise Glorious Witnesses for Africa. It is astounding that I personally knew so many commissioned missionaries in Nigeria and Sierra Leone:

Nigeria:
Rev. Ira McBride and Kathleen Conboy
Rev. Arthur and Aleatha Faust
Rev. Carl Heinmiller
Rev. Karl and Thekla Kuglin
Rev. Wilbur and Juanita Haar
Rev. Armin and Margaret Hoesch
Mr. Woodrow and Wilma Macke
Ms. Crystal Springborn Mercer
Ms. Lois Schmidt
Rev. Duane and Heidy Dennis
Rev. Martin and Ruth Stettler
Dr. Harold and Bea Elliot
Mr. Eugene and Jean Baldwin
Dr. Dean and Jane Olewiler
Rev. Eugene and Helen Westley
Dr. Kenneth and Mrs. Benfer
Ms. Florence Walter
Ms. Emmy Tschannen
Ms. Ruth Witmer (Mrs. Alfred Bollinger)
Ms. Jane Eberle
Ms. Virginia Draeger
Ms. Gertraud Gripentrop
Ms. Joan Hilgenfeld Zoeller
Ms. Doris Horn
Ms. Delphine Jewell
Ms. Ethel Johnson
Ms. Ann Kemper
Ms. Billie Jean Rydberg LaBumbard
Ms. Dorothy McBride Lear
Ms. Phyllis Jean Ludwig
Ms. Dorothy Miner
Ms. Marion Hartenstine Lugo
Ms. Esther Megill
Ms. Lucy Rowe

Ms. Amy Skartved
Ms. Colleen Weekley
Rev. Dean and Lois Gilliland
Dr. David and Laveta Hilton
Dr. Charles and Pearl Arnett
Doctors Jerril and Joyce Mathison
Dr. Ronald and Lu Ann Willey
Rev. James and Nancy Gulley
Rev. Alfred and Marianne Bohr
Mr. Ken and Joan Zoeller
Rev. Alan and Norma Seaman
Rev. Darrel and Ann Spores
Mr. Lon and Billie LaBumbard
Rev. Wolfgang and Gerlinde Bay
Rev. Roger and Sylvia Burtner
Rev. Walter and Ruth Erbele
Pilot James and Bernice Keech
Mr. Michael and Doris Vitzhum
Mr. Stanley and Helen Trebes

Sierra Leone:
Rev. Donald and Joyce Appleman
Miss Waveline Babbitt
Mr. Eugene and Jean Baldwin
Mrs. Joy Thede Beanland
Miss Betty Beveridge
Mr. Lester and Winifred Bradford
Miss Ethel Brooks
Rev. Richard and Mrs. Cabbage
Rev. Frank and Natalie Clossen
Miss Donna M. Colbert
Rev. Romeo Del Rosario
Rev. Walt and Jane Ebert
Rev. Dale and Evelin Eppel
Rev. David and Nancy Forrest
Miss Elaine Gasser
Miss Dorothy Gilbert
Mrs. Esther Grove
Miss Lennie Hache
Mr. Dan and Barb Humphrey
Marcia Johnson
Rev. Henry Jusu

Rev. Ralph Landis
Mr. Les and Hope Law
Miss Lois Lehman
Rev. Ombaku Lomoto
Mr. Jim and Cathy Malcolm
Rev. Frank and Sue Messenger
Mr. Dieter and Andrea Monninger
Miss Anna Morford
Miss Sally Morris
Rev. David and Jean Parker
Rev. Vernon and Mary Phelps
Miss Virginia Pickarts
Rev. Donald and Helen Pletsch
Mrs. Allis Riblet Saint
Rev. James and Cleo Simpson
Dr. Justin and Marge Sleight
Mr. Dean and Ramona Spenser
Dr. David and Alberta Stephenson
Mr. Donald and Lilburne Theuer
Rev. Jack and Dolores Thomas
Rev. Keith and Mary Louise Watkin
Mr. Lee Weaver
Rev. Darrel Weist
Mrs. Betty Esau Wight

Departed:
Dr. George and Norma Harris
Rev. Fred and Margaret Gaston
Rev. Charles and Bertha Leader
Dr. Mabel Silver
Mrs. Ruth Gess
Miss Gertrude Bloede

Dr. Lowell Gess' Curriculum Vitae

Our family photo with our African-educated children. Back row, left to right: Paul, M.Div., Master's in Family Counseling; John, Doctor of Optometry; Andrew, Ph.D. in Communications; Timothy, M.D., Ophthalmologist. Front row, left to right: Mary, Psy.D. in Clinical Psychology; Lowell, B.Div., M.D., Ophthalmologist; Ruth, R.N.; Elizabeth, Master's in Faith-Based Counseling.

Lowell Arthur Gess was born July 13, 1921, in Paynesville, Minnesota. He attended a country school and the Salem Evangelical Church in rural Paynesville. Throughout his early years, he participated in the camping program at Lake Koronis Assembly Grounds, and was active in the Evangelical Youth Fellowship on a state and national level and in the interdenominational Christian Youth Fellowship.

His family moved to St. Paul, Minnesota, where he graduated from Central High School in 1938. He attended North Central College in Naperville, Illinois, for one year, but completed college at Macalester College in St. Paul, Minnesota. At the age of nineteen, he was licensed to preach by the Minnesota Conference of the Evangelical Church and served a rural church. He graduated from Macalester College in 1942 with a B.A. degree. He attended the Evangelical Theological Seminary at Naperville, Illinois, graduating with a B.Div. degree in 1945. Shortly thereafter, he and Ruth Bradley, a registered nurse from Winnipeg, Canada, were united in marriage.

Dr. and Mrs. Gess served the St. Cloud-Graham circuit and the Mayer Church while he completed his pre-medical studies. In 1947, he entered Washington University School of Medicine. He received a Jackson Johnson Scholarship and a scholarship from First EUB Church of Naperville, Illinois. Dr. and Mrs. Gess served a small Federated church in East St. Louis, Illinois, for two years. For the last two years of medical training and internship at Ancker Hospital in St. Paul, the Board of Missions of the Evangelical United Brethren Church placed them under appointment.

In 1952, Dr. and Mrs. Gess and their family were appointed to the Bambur Hospital in Nigeria where they served three years. On their return to the U.S., he entered a surgical residency in Akron, Ohio. The Board of Missions then sent him to Rotifunk, Sierra Leone, to establish a surgical program. During this period, Dr. Gess became aware of the many people who were blind because of cataracts. In 1960, he was accepted into the ophthalmology residency programs at Washington University School of Medicine and the University of Minnesota Department of Ophthalmology. To be near his aging parents, he trained at the University of Minnesota. In 1964, he returned to Sierra Leone and established an eye program at Taiama. In 1967, he went to Bismarck, North Dakota, working for the Quain and Ramstad Clinic as an ophthalmologist. Further postgraduate ophthalmological training was done in 1969 at Harvard.

The General Board of Global Ministries of the United Methodist Church renewed Dr. and Mrs. Gess' missionary appointment in 1972. They were assigned to an eye ministry in Bo, Sierra Leone, for a three-year period. He returned to private practice in Alexandria, Minnesota, and since that time has served the church in Sierra Leone as a volunteer medical missionary. During this period, an eye program was established and the General Board of Global Ministries constructed a new hospital, the Kissy UMC Eye Hospital, to serve the eye needs in Sierra Leone.

Dr. Gess has been actively involved in the latest advances in the ophthalmological field, including intraocular lens implantation. He has designed and copyrighted his own intraocular lens. The program at the Kissy UMC Eye Hospital has made available this advanced surgical technology to the people in West Africa.

He has published the following papers:

1. Onchocerciasis in Sierra Leone, Africa, *The Sierra Leone Medical and Dental Bulletin*, Jan. 1974, Vol. 1 No. 2, pages 57-60.
2. Granulomatous Dacyoadenitis caused by Schistosoma haematobium, *Archives of Ophthalmology*, Feb. 1977, Vol. 95, pages 278-280, Jakobiec, Gess, Zimmerman.
3. Scleral Fixation for Intraocular Lenses, *American Intraocular Implant Society Journal*, Fall 1983, Vol. 9 No. 4, Pages 453-456.
4. Trabeculectomy with Iridencleisis, *British Journal of Ophthalmology*, Vol. 69, No. 12, pages 881-885, Dec. 1985.

Dr. Gess delivered the third article listed above at the annual meeting of the American Intraocular Implant Society in New Orleans in 1983. He delivered the fourth article at the annual meeting of the Welsh Cataract Surgical and Intraocular Lens Congress in Houston in 1980, and an updated version at the International Congress of Ophthalmologists in Cairo, Egypt, in February 1984.

Dr. Gess is an honorary member of the Lions and Rotary Clubs. He received the "Service to Mankind Award" from the Alexandria Sertoma Club in 1979, a Doctor of Humane Letters from Westmar College in 1985, the order of the Rokel for Distinguished Service from the Republic of Sierra Leone in 1991, a Distinguished Citizen Award from Macalester College in 1992, the Outstanding Achievement Award from the Vision Foundation of the University of Minnesota's Department of Ophthalmology in 1992, a Distinguished Humanitarian Service Award from the American Academy of Ophthalmology in 1993, the Alumni Achievement Award from Washington University School of Medicine in 1996, and the Distinguished Alumni Award in 1999 from Garrett Evangelical Theological Seminary, and the 2001 Christian Ophthalmology Society J. Lawton Smith Award.

Dr. Gess is an ordained minister and member of the Minnesota Conference of the United Methodist Church. He serves as an interpreter of the mission outreach of the church. He also serves the people of Sierra Leone as a volunteer ophthalmologist at the Kissy UMC Eye Hospital in Freetown. In recent years, he has done taught and demonstrated surgery for extracapsular cataract extractions with intraocular lens implantation in Sierra Leone, Ghana, Nigeria, Kenya, Zambia, Zimbabwe, Mozambique, Malawi, Bolivia, Honduras, Haiti, Vietnam, China and Mongolia.

Few joys match those that people experience when they are delivered from blindness.

"Inasmuch as you have done it unto one of the least of these my brethren, you have done it unto me." – Matthew 25:40

Populations of the Continents[48]

Where does Africa stand in relation to the continents of the world? **In square miles and population, Africa is second only to Asia.**

Size:
1. Asia – 17,139,445 square miles
2. Africa – 11,677,239 square miles
3. North America – 9,361,791 square miles
4. South America – 6,880,706 square miles
5. Antarctica – 5,500,000 square miles
6. Europe – 3,997,929 square miles
7. Australia – 2,967,909 square miles

Population:
1. Asia – 4,001,623,990 (Over 4 billion)
2. Africa – 934,499,752 (One billion)
3. Europe – 729,871,042
4. North America – 522,807,432
5. South America – 379,918,602
6. Australia – 20,434,176
7. Antarctica – No permanent residents but up to 4,000 researchers and personnel in the summer and 1,000 in the winter.

Index
(Abbreviated)